150 *All-time Favorite Crochet Blocks*

150 *All-time Favorite Crochet Blocks*

MAKE ALL THE BEST BLOCKS IN BEAUTIFUL STITCHES, COLORS & YARNS

Sarah Hazell

ST. MARTIN'S GRIFFIN
NEW YORK

150 ALL-TIME FAVORITE CROCHET BLOCKS

A Quarto Book
Copyright © 2015 Quarto Inc.

Printed in China. For information, address
St. Martin's Press
175 Fifth Avenue, New York
N.Y. 10010

www.stmartins.com

Library of Congress Cataloging-in-Publication Data
Available Upon Request

ISBN: 978-1-250-06878-1
St. Martin's Griffin books may be purchased for
educational, business, or promotional use. For
information on bulk purchases, please contact
Macmillan Corporate and Premium Sales
Department at 1-800-221-7945, extension 5442,
or write specialmarkets@macmillan.com.

First U.S. Edition: September 2015

10 9 8 7 6 5 4 3 2 1

Conceived, designed, and produced by
Quarto Publishing plc
The Old Brewery
6 Blundell Street
London N7 9BH

QUAR.TFCB

Senior Editor: Chelsea Edwards
Senior Art Editor: Emma Clayton
Designer: Tanya Devonshire-Jones
Illustrator: Kuo Kang Chen
Photographers: Nicki Dowey (location)
and Phil Wilkins (studio)
Proofreader: Liz Jones
Pattern Checker: Rachel Atkinson
Design Assistant: Martina Calvio
Indexer: Helen Snaith

Art Director: Caroline Guest
Creative Director: Moira Clinch
Publisher: Paul Carslake

Color separation in Singapore by
Pica Digital Pte Limited

Printed by Hung Hing Off-set Printing Co. Ltd, China

Contents

Sarah's World

There is something very special about being able to take a hook and some odd bits of yarn and transform them into something beautiful and useful! Crochet can take you on many journeys— backwards and forwards as well as up, down and round and round. I particularly like working with blocks, because they are manageable if you are short on time, space, or are traveling. They are incredibly versatile and can be combined in all sorts of ways to make different kinds of projects. They are a great way to experiment with unusual color combinations and textures of yarn. Perhaps one of the most significant things about blocks is their huge appeal. So, whether you are working on a project for yourself or for someone else, your efforts will always be admired and stand the test of time.

About This Book

This book presents a classic collection of 150 crochet blocks, which are sure to become some of your firm favorites. It includes large color-coded charts and row-by-row instructions for every pattern—and a selection of unique crochet projects to put your completed squares to good use.

8-39 CHAPTER 1: ALL-TIME FAVORITE COLLECTION

The All-time Favorite Collection showcases the 150 stunning designs featured in this book. Flick through this colorful visual guide, select your desired design and then turn to the relevant page of instructions to create your chosen block.

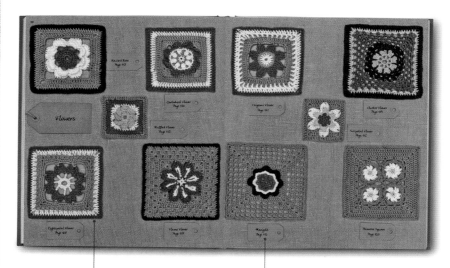

Each design is shown in proportion to the others on the page, which gives you an idea of scale.

Each block is labeled with its name and page number so that you can easily find the pattern.

Photographs show
the complete design

Pattern name

Skill level gives a rough
guide to difficulty

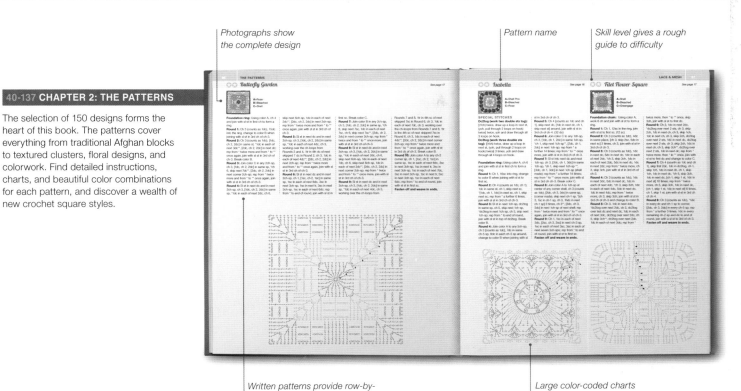

Written patterns provide row-by-
row instructions from start to finish

Large color-coded charts
to keep you on course

40-137 CHAPTER 2: THE PATTERNS

The selection of 150 designs forms the
heart of this book. The patterns cover
everything from traditional Afghan blocks
to textured clusters, floral designs, and
colorwork. Find detailed instructions,
charts, and beautiful color combinations
for each pattern, and discover a wealth of
new crochet square styles.

Project title

Tools, materials,
and measurements

138-145 CHAPTER 3: THE PROJECTS

This chapter features five gorgeous
projects to put your crochet squares and
skills to use. Instructions explain how to
join your blocks together, and each project
provides advice on additional tools,
materials, and expert finishing techniques
to create something unique for yourself or
to give as a gift.

How to work
the crochet

Guidance on
finishing techniques

Large photographs illustrate
the finished project

1

All-time Favorite Collection

This collection displays all 150 blocks in beautiful, stitch-themed groups. Flip through for inspiration, then turn to the relevant page in the Patterns chapter to make the block.

Four-patch
Granny
Page 44

Alternative
Granny
Page 46

Rectangle
Granny
Page 43

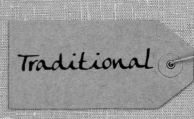

Traditional

Plain Granny
Page 42

Granny in
the Middle
Page 42

Nine-patch
Granny
Page 47

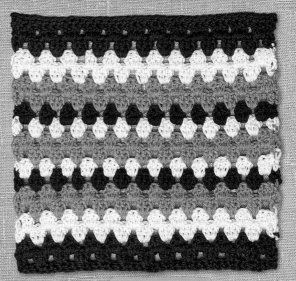

Granny
Stripes
Page 43

Mitered
Granny
Page 45

Flower Granny
Page 45

Raised Flower
Granny
Page 47

Celtic Cable
Page 53

Bobble Stripes
Page 51

Textures

Textured Stripes
Page 48

Big Bloom
Page 59

Diagonal
Raised Double
Page 54

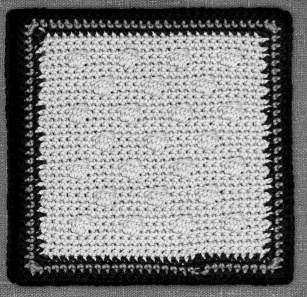

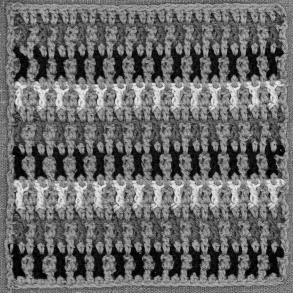

Pineapple
Cluster
Page 55

Tricolor Trinity
Page 56

Alternating
Bobbles
Page 50

Aligned
Railing Block
Page 57

Winter Blueberry
Patch
Page 52

Lemon Peel
Page 49

Two-color
Raised Ripple
Page 56

Bobbles on the
Diagonal
Page 52

Striped Knot
Page 49

Honeycomb
Page 55

Candy Stripe
Bobbles
Page 50

Classic Cable
Page 58

Basket Weave
Page 54

Fine Texture
Page 48

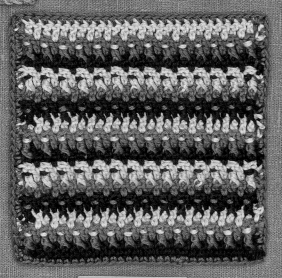

Interwoven Block
Page 57

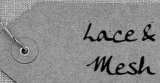

Lace & Mesh

Spiraling
Lace
Page 72

Openwork
Page 60

Queen Anne's
Lace
Page 63

Isabella
Page 67

Lacy Wheel
Page 61

Old Vienna
Page 62

Butterfly
Garden
Page 66

Picot Rose
Page 69

Filet Flower
Square
Page 67

Victorian
Lace
Page 62

Daisy Chain
Square
Page 71

Filet Mesh
Center
Page 73

Popcorn Square
Page 69

Pineapple Lace
Page 65

Belgian Lace
Page 60

Eyelet Lace
in the Round
Page 64

Sunshine Lace
Page 70

Fleur
Page 68

Double Filet
Mesh
Page 73

Popcorns & Lace
Page 68

Shape Changers

Spinner
Page 74

Circle in a
Hexagon
Page 84

Cluster Circle
Page 76

Starflower
Circle
Page 77

Framed Circle
Page 78

Double
Diamonds
Page 85

Starburst
in a Square
Page 75

Flower in a Web
Page 79

Fretwork Circle
Page 76

Star in a Square
Page 80

Squaring
the Circle
Page 75

Diamonds
Page 83

Octagon Framed
Flower
Page 82

Edwardian
Fancy
Page 81

Hexagon in a
Square
Page 84

Diamond in a
Square
Page 80

Mitered Curve
Page 83

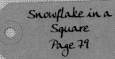

Octagon Tile
Page 82

Snowflake in a
Square
Page 79

Circle in a
Square
Page 74

Italian Cross
Page 89

St. Petersburg
Page 97

Crosses

Embossed Cross
Page 91

Sunray Cross
Page 87

Wisteria
Page 95

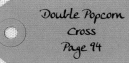

Double Popcorn
Cross
Page 94

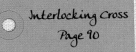

Gothic Square
Page 92

Interlocking Cross
Page 90

Seville
Page 88

Lacy Cross
Page 86

Catherine Wheel
Page 92

Compass Cross
Page 94

Looped Cross
Page 90

Popcorn Cross
Page 87

Double Cross
Page 93

Danish
Diamond
Page 96

Criss Cross
Page 86

Crossroads
Page 91

Anemone
Page 88

Tricolor Square
Page 97

Hourglass
Page 103

Random Patches
Page 99

Colorwork

Florentine Tile
Page 105

Seminole
Page 100

Intarsia Steps
Page 98

Dip Stitch Cross
Page 107

Trio
Page 103

Spiky Square
Page 107

Jaquard Stripes
Page 101

Half and Half
Page 102

Tuscan Tile
Page 106

Rose of Sharon
Page 106

Flying Carpet
Page 104

Quartet
Page 98

Darts
Page 102

Interlocking
Stripes
Page 100

Zig Zag
Page 99

Stacking Squares
Page 105

Bold Block
Page 104

Jaquard Checks
Page 101

Raised Rose
Page 113

Cartwheel Flower
Page 110

Flowers

Ruffled Flower
Page 113

Eight-petal Flower
Page 108

Flame Flower
Page 117

Origami Flower
Page 111

Cluster Flower
Page 114

Six-petal Flower
Page 112

Marigold
Page 116

Primrose Square
Page 120

Poppy
Page 115

Poinsettia
Page 123

Chrysanthemum
Page 119

Filet Flower
Page 121

Lacy Daisy
Page 115

Raised Petal
Flower
Page 112

Framed Flower
Page 109

Rosetta
Page 122

American
Beauty
Page 118

Waterlily
Page 121

Special Techniques

Shell and Bar
Border
Page 134

Arched Border
Page 135

Picot Border
Page 134

Fan Border
Page 135

Shell Border
Page 133

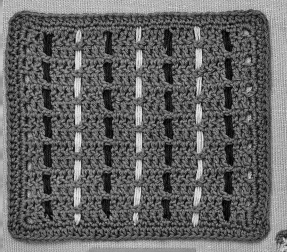

Vertical woven
Block
Page 126

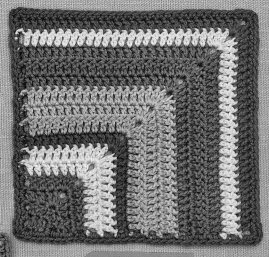

Mitered
Increase
Page 124

Two-sided
Granny
Page 132

Mitered
Decrease
Page 125

Horizontal
Woven Block
Page 131

Harlequin
Page 131

Loop Stitch
Columns
Page 130

Chain Loops
Flower
Page 130

Beaded Single
Crochet
Page 129

Sequined Single
Crochet
Page 129

Cross-stitched
Border
Page 137

Log Cabin Granny
Page 126

Log Cabin
Page 128

Corner Log
Cabin
Page 127

Cluster Border
Page 136

2

The patterns

Organized by theme, this chapter contains patterns and charts for all of the 150 blocks featured in this book.

⭐ *Plain Granny*   *See page 10*

A=Lavender

Foundation ring: Using color A, ch 6 and join with sl st in first ch to form a ring.

Round 1: Ch 3, (counts as 1dc), 2dc in ring, ch 3, *3dc in ring, ch 3; rep from * twice more, join with sl st in 3rd ch of first ch-3.

Round 2: Sl st in each of next 2dc, sl st in ch-3 corner sp, ch 3, [2dc, ch 3, 3dc] in same sp to make corner, *ch 1, [3dc, ch 3, 3dc] in next ch-3 sp; rep from * twice more, ch 1, join with sl st in 3rd ch of first ch-3.

Round 3: Sl st in each of next 2dc, sl st in ch-3 corner sp, ch 3, [2dc, ch 3, 3dc] in same sp to make corner, *ch 1, 3dc in ch-sp, ch 1, [3dc, ch 3, 3dc] in next ch-3 sp; rep from * twice more, ch 1, 3dc in ch-sp, ch 1, join with sl st in 3rd ch of first ch-3.

Round 4: Sl st in each of next 2dc, sl st in ch-3 corner sp, ch 3, [2dc, ch 3, 3dc] in same sp to make corner, *[ch 1, 3dc in each ch-sp] along the side of the square, ch 1, [3dc, ch 3, 3dc] in next ch-3 sp; rep from * twice more, [ch 1, 3dc in each ch-sp] along the side of the square, ch 1, join with sl st in 3rd ch of first ch-3.

Rounds 5–9: As Round 4.
Fasten off and weave in ends.

⭐ *Granny in the Middle*   *See page 10*

A=Blackcurrant
B=Persimmon
C=Ecru
D=Greengage
E=Lavender

Foundation ring: Using color A, work 6 ch and join with sl st in first ch to form a ring.

Round 1: Ch 3, (counts as 1dc), 2dc in ring, ch 3, *3dc in ring, ch 3; rep from * twice more, join with sl st in 3rd ch of first ch-3. Break color A.

Round 2: Join color B to any ch-3 corner sp with a sl st, ch 3, [2dc, ch 3, 3dc] in same sp to make corner, *ch 1, [3dc, ch 3, 3dc] in next ch-3 sp; rep from * twice more, ch 1, join with sl st in 3rd ch of first ch-3. Break color B.

Round 3: Join color C to any ch-3 corner sp with a sl st, ch 3, [2dc, ch 3, 3dc] in same sp to make corner, *ch 1, 3dc in ch-sp, ch 1, [3dc, ch 3, 3dc] in next ch-3 sp; rep from * twice more, ch 1, 3dc in ch-sp, ch 1, join with sl st in 3rd ch of first ch-3. Break color C.

Round 4: Join color D to any ch-3 corner sp with a sl st, ch 3, [2dc, ch 3, 3dc] in same sp to make corner, *[ch 1, 3dc in each ch-sp] along the side of the square, ch 1, [3dc, ch 3, 3dc] in next ch-3 sp; rep from * twice more, [ch 1, 3dc in each ch-sp] along the side of the square, ch 1, join with sl st in 3rd ch of first ch-3. Break color D.

Round 5: Join color E and work as Round 4. Break color E.

Round 6: Join color A with a sl st to any dc of previous round. Ch 1, 1sc in every dc and ch-sp of previous round, working 5sc in each ch-3 corner sp, join with sl st in first ch.

Round 7: Ch 1, 1sc in every sc of previous round, working 3sc in center st of the 5sc corner groups, join with sl st in first ch, changing to color B at last yoh.

Round 8: Ch 2, 1hdc in every sc of previous round, working 3hdc in center st of the 3sc corner groups, join with sl st in 2nd ch of first ch-2, changing to color C at last yoh.

Round 9: Ch 2, 1hdc in every hdc of previous round, working 3hdc in center st of the 3hdc corner groups, join with sl st in 2nd ch of first ch-2, changing to color D at last yoh.

Round 10: Ch 1, 1sc in every hdc of previous round, working 3sc in center st of the 3hdc corner groups, join with sl st in first ch.

Fasten off and weave in ends.

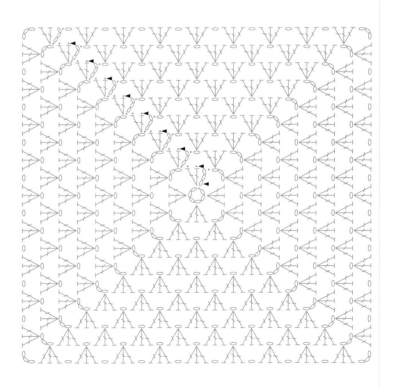

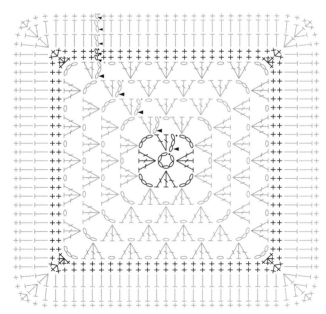

⭐ Rectangle Granny

See page 10

A=Lavender
B=Ecru
C=Persimmon
D=Blackcurrant
E=Greengage

Foundation ring: Using color A, work 12 ch.

Round 1: [2dc, ch 2, 3dc, ch 2, 3dc] in 4th ch from hook, ch 2, skip next 2ch, 1dc in each of next 3ch, ch 2, skip next 2ch, [3dc, ch 2, 3dc, ch 2 3dc] all in last ch, ch 2, skip next 2 ch on opposite side of foundation ch, 1dc in each of next 3ch, ch 2, skip next 2ch, join with sl st in 3rd of ch-3. Break color A.

Round 2: Join color B to the last ch-2 sp made, ch 3 (counts as 1dc), 2dc in same sp, ch 2, *[3dc, ch 2, 3dc, ch 2] in next 2 ch-2 sps (2 corners made), [3dc in next ch-2 sp, ch 2] twice; rep from * once again, join with sl st in 3rd of ch-3. Break color B.

Round 3: Join color C to the first ch-2 sp of last round, ch 3 (counts as 1dc), 2dc in same sp, ch 2, *[3dc, ch 2, 3dc] in next ch-2 sp (corner), ch 2, 3dc in next ch-2 sp, ch 2, [3dc, ch 2, 3dc] in next ch-2 sp (corner), [ch 2, 3dc] in each of next 3 ch-2sps, ch 2; rep from * once more, omitting last [3dc, ch 2], join with sl st in 3rd of ch-3. Break color C.

Round 4: Join color D to the first ch-2 sp of last round, ch 3 (counts as 1dc), 2dc in same sp, *ch 2, [3dc, ch 2, 3dc] in next ch-2 sp (corner), [ch 2, 3dc] in every ch-2 sp] along the short side of the rectangle, ch 2, [3dc, ch 2, 3dc] in next ch-2 sp (corner), [ch 2, 3dc] in every ch-2 sp along the long side of the rectangle, ch 2; rep from * once more, omitting last [3dc, ch 2], join with sl st in 3rd of ch-3. Break color D.

Round 5: As Round 4 in color E. Break color E.

Round 6: As Round 4 in color A.

Fasten off and weave in ends.

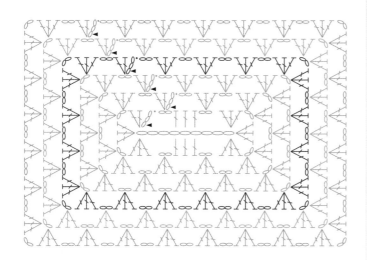

⭐ Granny Stripes

See page 11

A=Blackcurrant
B=Ecru
C=Persimmon

Foundation chain: Using color A, work 38 ch.

Foundation row (RS): 1sc in 2nd ch from hook, 1sc in each ch to end, turn. (37 sc)

Row 1: Ch 3 (counts as 1dc), 1dc in same place, [skip 2sc, 3dc in next sc] to last 3sc, skip 2sc, 2dc in last sc, turn.

Row 2: Ch 3 (counts as 1dc), [3dc in next sp between dc groups] to end of row, 1dc in 3rd ch of ch-3 from previous row, turn. Break color A.

Row 3: Join color B. Ch 3 (counts as 1dc), 1dc in same place, [3dc in next sp between dc groups] to end of row, 2dc in 3rd ch of ch-3 from previous row, turn.

Row 4: Ch 3 (counts as 1dc), [3dc in next sp between dc groups] to end of row, 1dc in 3rd ch of ch-3, turn. Break color B.

Rows 5–6: Using color C, work as Rows 3-4.

Row 7: Using color A, work as Row 3.

Row 8: Using color B, work as Row 4.

Rows 9–10: Using color C, work as Rows 3-4.

Row 11: Using color B, work as Row 3.

Row 12: Using color A, work as Row 4.

Rows 13–14: Using color C, work as Rows 3-4.

Rows 15–16: Using color B, work as Rows 3-4.

Rows 17–18: Using color A, work as Rows 3-4.

Row 19: Ch 1, 1sc in every dc to end of row.

Fasten off and weave in ends.

✪✪ *Four-patch Granny*

See page 10

A=Greengage
B=Ecru
C=Lavender

FIRST MOTIF

Foundation ring: Using color A, work 6 ch and join with sl st in first ch to form a ring.

Round 1: Ch 3 (counts as 1dc), 2dc in ring, ch 3, *3dc in ring, ch 3; rep from * twice more, join with sl st in 3rd ch of first ch-3. Break color A.

Round 2: Join color B to any ch-3 corner sp with a sl st, ch 3, [2dc, ch 3, 3dc] in same sp to make corner, *ch 1, [3dc, ch 3, 3dc] in next ch-3 sp; rep from * twice more, ch 1, join with sl st in 3rd ch of first ch-3. Break color B.

Round 3: Join color C to any ch-3 corner sp with a sl st, ch 3, [2dc, ch 3, 3dc] in same sp to make corner, *ch 1, 3dc in ch-sp, ch 1, [3dc, ch 3, 3dc] in next ch-3 sp; rep from * twice more, ch 1, 3dc in ch-sp, ch 1, join with sl st in 3rd ch of first ch-3. Break color C.

Round 4: Join color B to any ch-3 corner sp with a sl st, ch 3, [2dc, ch 3, 3dc] in same sp to make corner, *[ch 1, 3dc in each ch-sp] along the side of the square, ch 1, [3dc, ch 3, 3dc] in next ch-3 sp; rep from * twice more, [ch 1, 3dc in each ch-sp] along the side of the square, ch 1, join with sl st in 3rd ch of first ch-3.
Fasten off.

Make one more motif as above and two motifs reversing the position of colors A and C.

SECOND MOTIF

Foundation ring: Using color C, work 6 ch and join with sl st to form a ring.

Round 1: Ch 3 (counts as 1dc), 2dc in ring, ch 3, *3dc in ring, ch 3; rep from * twice more, join with sl st in 3rd ch of first ch-3. Break color C.

Round 2: Join color B to any ch-3 corner sp with a sl st, ch 3, [2dc, ch 3, 3dc] in same sp to make corner, *ch 1, [3dc, ch 3, 3dc] in next ch-3 sp; rep from * twice more, ch 1, join with sl st in 3rd ch of first ch-3. Break yarn B.

Round 3: Join color A to any ch-3 corner sp with a sl st, ch 3, [2dc, ch 3, 3dc] in same sp to make corner, *ch1, 3dc in ch-sp, ch 1, [3dc, ch 3, 3dc] in next ch-3 sp; rep from * twice more, ch 1, 3dc in ch-sp, ch 1, join with sl st in 3rd ch of first ch-3. Break color A.

Round 4: Join color B to any ch-3 corner sp with a sl st, ch 3, [2dc, ch 3, 3dc] in same sp to make corner, [ch 1, 3dc in each ch-sp] along side of the square, ch 1, 3dc, in next ch-3 sp, sl st in any ch-3 corner sp of first motif,

3dc in same ch-3 corner sp as previous cluster, [join through next ch-1 sp of first motif with sl st, 3dc in next ch-1 sp of current motif] twice, join through next ch-1 sp of first motif with sl st, 3dc, in next ch-3 sp, sl st in next ch-3 corner sp of first motif, 3dc in same ch-3 corner sp as previous cluster, *[ch1, 3dc in each ch-sp] along side of the square**, ch 1, [3dc, ch 3, 3dc] in next ch-3 sp; rep from * once more, [ch 1, 3dc in each ch-sp] along side of the square, ch 1, join with sl st in 3rd ch of first ch-3.
Fasten off.

THIRD MOTIF

Work Rounds 1–3 of first motif.

Round 4: Join color B to any ch-3 corner sp with a sl st, ch 3, [2dc, ch 3, 3dc] in same sp to make corner, [ch 1, 3dc in each ch-sp], along side of the square, ch 1, 3dc in next ch-3 sp, sl st in bottom LH corner of ch-3 corner sp of second motif, 3dc in same ch-3

corner sp as previous cluster, [join through next ch-1 sp of second motif with a sl st, 3dc in next ch-1 sp of current motif] twice, join through next ch-1 sp of second motif with a sl st, 3dc, in next ch-3 sp, sl st in next ch-3 corner sp of second motif, 3dc in same ch-3 corner sp as previous cluster, *[ch1, 3dc in each ch-sp] along side of the square**, ch 1, [3dc, ch 3, 3dc] in next ch-3 sp; rep from * once more, [ch1, 3dc in each ch-sp] along side of the square, ch1, join with sl st in 3rd ch of first ch-3. Fasten off.

FOURTH MOTIF

Work Rounds 1–3 of second motif.

Round 4: Join color B to any ch-3 corner sp with a sl st, ch 3, [2dc, ch 3, 3dc] in same sp to make corner, [ch 1, 3dc in each ch-sp] along side of the square, ch 1, 3dc in next ch-3 sp, sl st in bottom LH corner of ch-3 corner sp of first motif, 3dc in same ch-3 corner sp as previous cluster, [join through

next ch-1 sp of first motif with a sl st, 3dc in next ch-1 sp of current motif] twice, join through next ch-1 sp of first motif with a sl st, 3dc in next ch-3 sp, sl st in next ch-3 corner sp of third motif, 3dc in same ch-3 corner sp as previous cluster, [join through next ch-1 sp of third motif with a sl st, 3dc in next ch-1 sp of current motif] twice, join through next ch-1 sp of third motif with a sl st, 3dc, in next ch-3 sp, sl st in next ch-3 corner sp of third motif, 3dc in same ch-3 corner sp as previous cluster, [ch1, 3dc in each ch-sp] along side of the square**, ch 1, [3dc, ch 3, 3dc] in next ch-3 sp, ch 1, 3dc in each ch-sp] along side of the square, ch 1, join with sl st in 3rd ch of first ch-3. Fasten off.

Border: Join color A to any dc. Ch 1, 1sc in same place, 1sc in every dc and ch-1 sp and 3sc in each ch-3 corner sp to end of round. Join with sl st in first sc.

Fasten off and weave in ends.

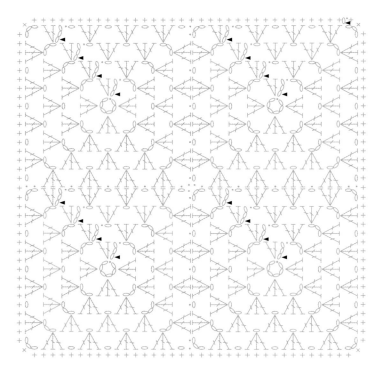

⭐ Mitered Granny

See page 11

A=Persimmon
B=Ecru
C=Lavender
D=Greengage

Foundation ring: Using color A, work 6 ch and join with sl st in first ch to form a ring.

Round 1: Ch 3 (counts as 1dc), 2dc in ring, ch 3, *3dc in ring, ch 3; rep from * twice more, join with sl st in 3rd ch of ch-3.

Round 2: Sl st in each of next 2dc, sl st in ch-3 corner sp, ch 3, [2dc, ch 3, 3dc] in same sp to make corner, *ch 1, [3dc, ch 3, 3dc] in next ch-3 sp; rep from * twice more, ch 1, join with sl st in 3rd of ch-3. Break color A.

Row 3: Join color B to any ch-3 corner sp with a sl st, ch 3, 2dc in same place, *[ch 1, 3dc in each ch-sp] along the side of the square**, ch 1, [3dc, ch 3, 3dc] in next ch-3 sp; rep from * to **, ch 1, 3dc in 2nd ch of ch-3 corner sp, turn.

Row 4: Ch 3 (counts as 1dc), *[ch 1, 3dc in each ch-sp] along the side of the square**, ch 1, [3dc, ch 3, 3dc] in ch-3 corner sp; rep from * to **, ch 1, 1dc in 3rd ch of ch-3 from previous row. Break color B.

Row 5: Using color C, ch 3 (counts as 1dc), 2dc in same place, *[ch 1, 3dc in each ch-sp] along the side of the

square**, ch 1, [3dc, ch 3, 3dc] in next ch-3 sp; rep from * to **, ch 1, 3dc in 3rd ch of ch-3 from previous row, turn.

Row 6: Ch 3 (counts as 1dc), *[ch 1, 3dc in each ch-sp] along the side of the square**, ch 1, [3dc, ch 3, 3dc] in next ch-3 sp; rep from * to **, ch 1, 1dc in 3rd ch of ch-3 from previous row, turn. Break color C.

Rows 7–8: Using color B, work as rows 5-6. Break color B.

Rows 9–10: Using color D, work as rows 5-6. Break color D.

Rows 11–12: Using color B, work as rows 5-6. Break color B.

Round 13: Using color A, ch 3 (counts as 1dc), 2dc in same place, *[ch 1, 3dc in each ch-sp] along the side of the square**, ch 1, [3dc, ch 3, 3dc] in next ch-3 sp; rep from * twice more then from * to ** once, ch 3, join with sl st in 3rd ch of ch-3.

Round 14: Ch 2 (counts as 1hdc), 1hdc in each dc and ch-1 sp and [1hdc, 1dc, 1hdc] in every ch-3 sp to end of round, join with sl st in 2nd ch of ch-2.

Fasten off and weave in ends.

⭐⭐ Flower Granny

See page 11

A=Persimmon
B=Blackcurrant
C=Greengage
D=Lavender
E=Ecru

SPECIAL STITCHES

Beg cl: Work two dc sts to the last "yoh, pull through," yoh once again and draw through all three loops on the hook.

Cl: Work three dc sts to the last "yoh, pull through," yoh once again and draw through all four loops on the hook.

Foundation ring: Using color A, work 6 ch and join with sl st in first ch to form a ring.

Round 1: Ch 3 (counts as 1dc), beg cl in ring, ch 3, [cl in ring, ch 3] seven times, join with a sl st in top of beg cl. Break color C.

Round 2: Join color B to any ch-3 sp, ch 3 (counts as 1dc), [beg cl, ch 3, cl] in same ch-3 sp, ch 1, *[cl, ch 3, cl] in next ch-3 sp, ch 1; rep from * a further six times, join with sl st in top of beg cl. Break color B.

Round 3: Join color C to any ch-3 corner sp, ch 3, [2dc, ch 3, 3dc] in same sp to make corner, *ch 1, 3dc in ch-sp, ch 1, [3dc, ch 3, 3dc] in next ch-3 sp; rep from * twice more, ch 1,

join with sl st in 3rd ch of ch-3.

Round 4: Sl st in each of next 2dc, sl st in ch-3 corner sp, ch 3, [2dc, ch 3, 3dc] in same sp to make corner, *[ch 1, 3dc in each ch-sp] along the side of the square, ch 1, [3dc, ch 3, 3dc] in next ch-3 sp; rep from * twice more, ch 1, join with sl st in 3rd ch of ch-3.

Round 5: Join color D to any ch-3 corner sp with a sl st, ch 3, [2dc, ch 3, 3dc] in same sp to make corner, *[ch 1, 3dc in each ch-sp] along the side of the square, ch 1, [3dc, ch 3, 3dc] in next ch-3 sp; rep from * twice more, ch 1, join with sl st in 3rd ch of ch-3.

Round 6: As Round 4. Break color D.

Round 7: Using color C, work as Round 5. Break color C.

Round 8: Using color A, work as Round 5. Break color A.

Round 9: Join color B to any dc, ch 1, 1sc in same place, 1sc in every dc and ch-1 sp of previous round, working [1sc, 1hdc, 1sc] in every ch-3 corner, join with sl st to first sc.

Fasten off and weave in ends.

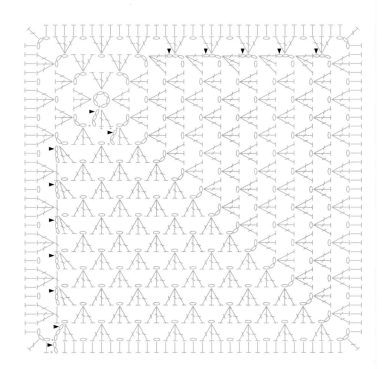

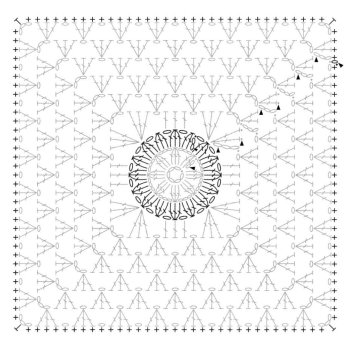

★ Alternative Granny

See page 10

A=Greengage
B=Blackcurrant
C=Ecru
D=Lavender
E=Persimmon

Foundation ring: Using color A, work 4 ch and join with sl st in first ch to form a ring.

Round 1: Ch 3 (counts as 1dc), 2dc in ring, ch2, *3dc in ring, ch2; rep from * twice more, join with sl st in 3rd ch of ch-3. Break color A.

Round 2: Join color B to any ch-2 corner sp with sl st, ch 1, [1sc, ch 3, 1dc] in same sp, *ch 3, [1dc, ch 3, 1dc] in next ch-2 sp; rep from * twice more, ch 3, join with sl st to first dc. Break color B.

Round 3: Join color C to any ch-3 corner sp with sl st, ch 3, [2dc, ch 3, 3dc] in same sp, ch 1, *[3dc, ch 3, 3dc] in next ch-3 sp, ch 1, 3dc in next ch-3 sp, ch 1; rep from * twice more, join with sl st in 3rd ch of ch-3. Break color C.

Round 4: Join color B to any ch-3 corner sp with sl st, ch 1, [1dc, ch 3, 1dc] in same sp, ch 3, [1dc in next ch-1 sp, ch 3] twice more, *[1dc, ch 3, 1dc] in next ch-3 corner sp, ch 3, [1dc in next ch-1 sp, ch 3] twice; rep from * twice more, join with sl st in first dc. Break color B.

Round 5: Join color D to any ch-3 corner sp with sl st, ch 3, [2dc, ch 3, 3dc] in same sp, ch 1, [3dc in next ch-3 sp, ch 1] 3 times, *[3dc, ch 3, 3dc] in next ch-3 sp, ch 1, [3dc in next ch-3 sp, ch 1] three times; rep from * twice more, join with sl st in 3rd ch of ch-3. Break color D.

Round 6: Join color B to any ch-3 corner sp with sl st, ch 1, [1dc, ch 3, 1dc] in same sp, ch 3, [1dc in next ch-1 sp, ch 3] four times, *[1dc, ch 3, 1dc] in next ch-3 corner sp, ch 3, [1dc in next ch-1 sp, ch 3] four times; rep from * twice more, join with sl st in first dc. Break color B.

Round 7: Join color E to any ch-3 corner sp with sl st, ch 3, [2dc, ch 3, 3dc] in same sp, ch 1, [3dc in next ch-3 sp, ch 1] five times, *[3dc, ch 3, 3dc] in next ch-3 sp, ch 1, [3dc in next ch-3 sp, ch 1] five times; rep from * twice more, join with sl st in 3rd ch of ch-3. Break color E.

Round 8: Join color B to any ch-3 corner sp with sl st, ch 1, [1dc, ch 3, 1dc] in same sp, ch 3, [1dc in next ch-1 sp, ch 3] six times, *[1dc, ch 3, 1dc] in next ch-3 corner sp, ch 3, [1dc in next ch-1 sp, ch 3] six times; rep from * twice more, join with sl st in first dc. Break color B.

Round 9: Join color C to any ch-3 corner sp with sl st, ch 3, [2dc, ch 3, 3dc] in same sp, ch 1, [3dc in next ch-3 sp, ch 1] seven times, *[3dc, ch 3, 3dc] in next ch-3 sp, ch 1, [3dc in next ch-3 sp, ch 1] seven times; rep from * twice more, join with sl st in 3rd ch of ch-3. Break color C.

Round 10: Join color A to any dc with sl st, ch 1, 1dc in same place, 1dc in every dc and ch-1 sp from previous round, working 3dc in every ch-3 corner sp, join with sl st in 3rd ch of ch-3.

Fasten off and weave in ends.

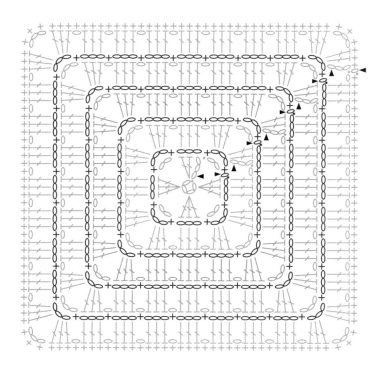

⬢⬢ *Raised Flower Granny*
See page 11

A=Ecru
B=Greengage
C=Blackcurrant

SPECIAL STITCHES

pc (popcorn): Work 5dc in designated st, remove hook from last loop, and insert hook from front to back in top of first dc, pick up the dropped loop and pull this through the loop on the hook to complete the popcorn.

Foundation ring: Using color A, work 6 ch and join with sl st in first ch to form a ring.
Round 1: Ch 3 (counts as 1dc), 15dc in ring, join with sl st in 3rd ch of ch-3. (16 dc)
Round 2: Ch 3 (counts as 1dc), 1dc in same place, 2dc in each dc to end of round, join with sl st in 3rd ch of ch-3. (32 dc)
Round 3: Ch 3 (counts as 1dc), 1pc in next dc, [1dc in next dc, 1pc in next dc] 15 times, join with sl st in 3rd ch of ch-3. (16 pc, 16 dc)
Round 4: Ch 1, 1sc in first dc (3rd ch of ch-3 from previous row), *ch 2, skip next pc, 1sc in next dc; rep from * a further 14 times, ch 2, join with sl st in first sc. (16 ch-2 sp)
Round 5: Sl st in next ch-2 sp, ch 3 (counts as 1dc), 2dc in ch-2 sp, *[ch 1, 3dc] in next ch-2 sp; rep from * a

further 14 times, ch 1, 1sc in 3rd ch of ch-3, (instead of last ch-1 sp). (16 ch-1 sps.) Break color A.
Round 6: Join color B to any ch-1 sp with sl st, ch 3, [2dc, ch 3, 3dc] in same sp to make corner, *[ch 1, 3dc in each ch-sp] three times, ch 1, [3dc, ch 3, 3dc] in next ch-1 sp; rep from * twice more, [ch 1, 3dc in each ch-sp] three times, ch 1, join with sl st in 3rd ch of ch-3. Break color B.
Round 7: Sl st in each of next 2dc, sl st in ch-3 corner sp, ch 3, [2dc, ch 3, 3dc] in same sp to make corner, *[ch 1, 3dc] in each ch-sp along the side of the square, ch 1, [3dc, ch 3, 3dc] in next ch-3 sp; rep from * twice more, [ch 1, 3dc] in each ch-sp along the side of the square, ch 1, join with sl st in 3rd ch of ch-3. Break color B.
Round 8: Using color A, work as Round 7. Break color A.
Round 9: Using color B, work as Round 7. Break color B.
Round 10: Join color C to any dc, ch 1, 1sc in same place, 1sc in each dc and ch from previous round, working 3sc in every ch-3 corner sp, join with sl st in 3rd ch of ch-3.
Fasten off and weave in ends.

⬢⬢ *Nine-patch Granny*
See page 11

A=Persimmon
B=Ecru
C=Lavender
D=Greengage
E=Blackcurrant

Foundation ring: Using color A, work 6 ch and join with sl st in first ch to form a ring.
Round 1: Ch 3 (counts as 1dc), 2dc in ring, ch 3, *3dc in ring, ch 3; rep from * twice more, join with sl st in 3rd ch of ch-3. Break color A.
Round 2: Join color B to any ch-3 corner sp with a sl st, ch 3, [2dc, ch 3, 3dc] in same sp to make corner, *ch 1, [3dc, ch 3, 3dc] in next ch-3 sp; rep from * twice more, ch 1, join with sl st in 3rd ch of ch-3. Break color B. Work 3rd, 7th, and 9th motifs in color A, the 2nd and 8th motifs in C, and the 4th and 6th motifs in 5th motif in D

for Round 1 and one with color E for Round 1. Use the photograph as a guide to join as you go on Round 2 as described for Four-patch Granny.
Border
Round 1: Join D to any dc with sl st, ch 3 (counts as 1dc), 1dc in every dc and ch sp and [1dc, 1tr, 1dc] in every ch-3 corner sp from previous round, join with sl st in 3rd ch of ch-3. Break color D.
Round 2: Using E, work 1dc in every dc from previous round and 3dc in each corner tr, join with sl st in 3rd ch of ch-3.
Fasten off and weave in ends.

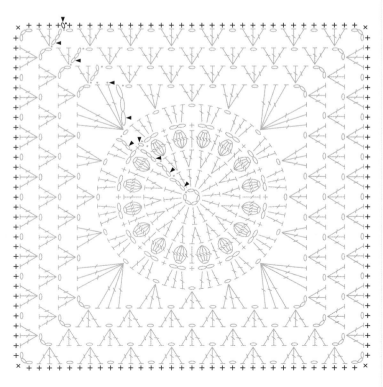

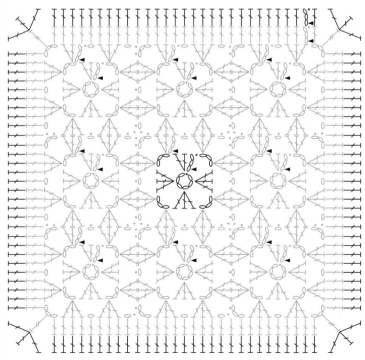

⭐ Fine Texture

See page 15

A=Persimmon
B=Toffee

Foundation chain: Using color A, work 32 ch.
Foundation row (RS): 1sc in 2nd ch from hook, 1sc in every ch to end, turn. (31 sc)
Row 1: Ch 1, 1sc in first sc, *ch 1, skip next sc, 1sc in next sc; rep from * to end, turn.
Row 2: Ch 1, 1sc in first sc, *1dc in next ch-1 sp, 1sc in next sc; rep from * to end, turn.
Row 3: Ch 1, 1sc in first sc, *ch 1, skip next sc, 1sc in next sc; rep from * to end, turn.

Rep Rows 2 and 3 a further 11 times ending with Row 3.
Next row: Ch1, 1sc in every st to the end of the row. Fasten off.
Border
Round 1: Join color B to any ch along Foundation edge. 1ch, 1sc in same place, 1sc in every ch, to corner, *[1sc, 1hdc, 1sc] in corner, work 22sc evenly along row-end edge, [1sc, 1hdc, 1sc] in corner**, 1sc in each of next 29ch; rep from * to ** once more, 1sc in every ch to end of round, join with sl st in first sc.
Fasten off and weave in ends.

⭐ Textured Stripes

See page 12

A=Toffee
B=Persimmon
C= Bleached

Foundation chain: Using color A, work 29 ch.
Foundation row (WS): [1sc, 1ch, 1sc] in 2nd ch from hook, *skip 1ch, [1sc, 1ch, 1sc] in next ch; rep from * to last ch, 1sc in last sc, turn.
Row 1: Ch1, *[1sc, 1ch, 1sc] in first sc of each group of sts from previous row; rep from * to last st, 1sc in last st changing to color B on last pull though, turn. Do not break A.
Row 2: Ch1, *[1sc, 1ch, 1sc] in first sc of each group of sts from previous row; rep from * to last st, 1sc in last st changing to color C on last pull though, turn. Do not break B.
Row 3: Ch1, *[1sc, 1ch, 1sc] in first sc of each group of sts from previous row; rep from * to last st, 1sc in last st changing to color A on last pull though, turn. Do not break C.
Rep Rows 1–3 a further 8 times then Row 1 only once more. Fasten off.
Border
Round 1: Join color B to any ch along Foundation edge. Ch1, 1sc in same place, 1sc in every ch, to corner, *[1sc, 1hdc, 1sc] in corner, work 26sc evenly along row-end edge, [1sc, 1hdc, 1sc] in corner**, 1sc in each of next 26dc; rep from * to ** once more, 1sc in every ch to end of round, join with sl st to first sc.
Fasten off and weave in ends.

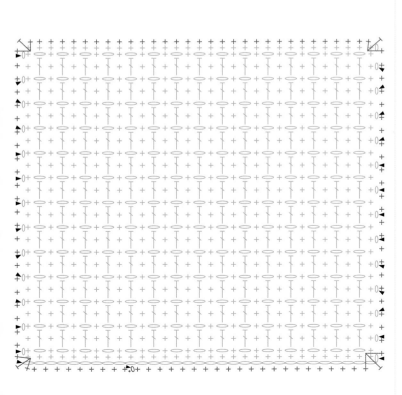

Striped Knot

See page 14

A=Bleached
B=Persimmon
C=Toffee

Foundation row: Using C, make 29ch.

Row 1: 1sc in 2nd ch from hook, 1sc in every ch to end, turn. Break color C. (28 sc)

Row 2: Join A, ch 1, 1sc in next sc, *1dc in next sc, 1sc in next sc; rep from * to last st, 1sc in last sc, turn. Break color A.

Row 3: Using B, ch 1, 1sc in every st to end of row, turn. Break color B.

Row 4: Using C, ch 1, 1sc in next 2sc, *1dc in next sc, 1sc in next sc; rep from * to last 2 sts, 1sc in each of last 2sc, turn. Break color C.

Row 5: Using A, ch 1, 1sc in every st to end of row, turn.

Keeping the stripe sequence as set,

rep Rows 2–5, a further 5 times, ending with Row 5 in color B. Fasten off.

Border: Join color A with sl st to any sc on Foundation row edge.

Round 1: Ch 1, 1sc in every st and row end and 3sc in each corner to end of round, join with sl st to first sc. Break color A.

Round 2: Using B, ch 1, 1sc in every sc of previous round and, 3sc in center st of 3sc at each corner to end of round, join with sl st to first sc. Break color B.

Round 3: Using C, ch 1, 1sc in every sc of previous round and, 3sc in center st of 3sc at each corner, to end of round, join with sl st to first sc.

Fasten off and weave in ends.

Lemon Peel

See page 14

A=Toffee
B=Ecru
C=Persimmon

Foundation chain: Using color A, work 31 ch.

Foundation row (RS): 1sc in 3rd ch from hook, *1dc in next ch, 1sc in next ch; rep from * to end, turn.

Row 1: Ch 1, 1sc in first dc, 1dc in next sc, *1sc in next dc, 1dc in next sc; rep from * to end.

Rep Row 1 a further 23 times.
Fasten off.

Border

Round 1: Join color B to any ch along Foundation edge. Ch1, 1sc in same

place, 1sc in every ch, to corner, *[1sc, 1hdc, 1sc] in corner, work 24sc evenly along row-end edge, [1sc, 1hdc, 1sc] in corner**, 1sc in each of next 29 sts; rep from * to **, 1sc in every ch to end of round, changing to color C when joining with sl st to first sc.

Round 2: Ch 1, 1sc in blo of every sc and [1sc, 1hdc, 1sc] in every hdc from previous round, join with sl st to first sc.

Fasten off and weave in ends.

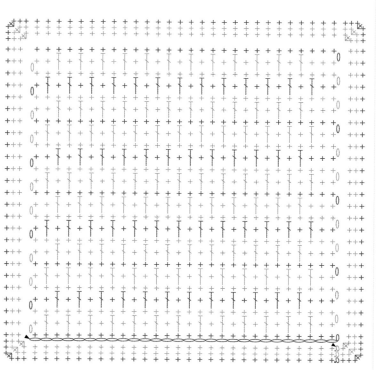

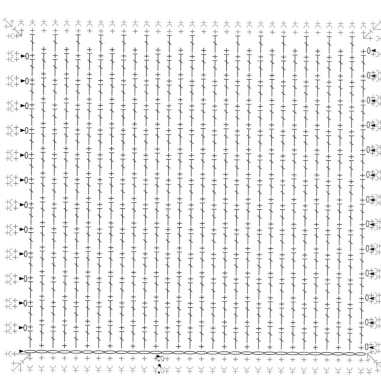

Alternating Bobbles   See page 13

A=Oyster
B=Nightshade
C=Persimmon

SPECIAL STITCHES

MB (Make bobble): Work four treble stitches together: Working into the same stitch, [yarn over hook, draw up a loop, yarn over hook, pull through two loops on the hook] four times, yarn over hook and pull through all five loops on hook.

Foundation chain: Using color A, work 28ch.
Row 1 (WS): 1sc in 2nd ch from hook, 1sc in every ch to end of row, turn. (27 sc)
Rows 2–4: Ch1, 1sc in every sc to end of row, turn.
Row 5: Ch1, 1sc in each of next 4sc, [MB, 1sc in each of next 5sc] 3 times, MB, 1sc in each of next 4sc, turn.
Rows 6–8: As Rows 2–4.
Row 9: Ch1, 1sc in each of next 7sc, [MB, 1sc in each of next 5sc] twice, MB, 1sc in each of next 7sc, turn.

Rep Rows 2–9 twice more, then Rows 2–8 only once more.
Fasten off.
Border
Round 1: Join color B to any ch along Foundation edge. Ch1, 1sc in same place, 1sc in every ch, to corner, *[1sc, 1hdc, 1sc] in corner, work 25sc evenly along row-end edge, [1sc, 1hdc, 1sc] in corner**, 1sc in each of next 27ch; rep from * to **, 1sc in every ch to end of round, changing to color C when joining with sl st in first sc.
Round 2: Ch1, 1sc in every sc and [1sc 1hdc, 1sc] in every corner hdc to end of round, changing to color B when joining with sl st in first sc.
Round 3: Ch2 (counts as 1hdc), 1hdc in every sc and [1hdc, 1dc, 1hdc] in every corner hdc, to end of round, join with sl st to first sc.
Fasten off and weave in ends.

 Candy Stripe Bobbles   See page 15

A=Nightshade
B=Sky
C=Oyster
D=Bleached
E=Toffee

SPECIAL STITCHES

MB (Make bobble): Work four treble stitches together: Working into the same stitch, [yarn over hook, draw up a loop, yarn over hook, pull through two loops on the hook] four times, yarn over hook and pull through all five loops on hook.

Foundation chain: Using color A, work 28ch.
Foundation row (WS): 1sc in 2nd ch from hook, 1sc in every ch to end, turn. (27 sc)
Row 1: Ch1, 1sc in every sc to end of row, turn.
Row 2: Ch1, 1sc in each of next 10sc, [MB, 1sc in each of next 2sc] twice, MB, 1sc in each of next 10sc, turn.
Rep last 2 rows according to the following sequence:
Using color B, work Row 1, 3 times.
Using color C, work Row 2, then Row 1 twice.
Using color D, work Row 1, Row 2, Row 1.
Using color B, work Row 1 twice and then Row 2.
Using color C, work Row 1, 3 times.
Using color B, work Row 2 and then Row 1 twice.
Using color D, work Row 1, Row 2, Row 1.
Using color C, work Row 1 twice and then Row 2.
Using color B, work Row 1, 3 times.
Using color A, work Row 2 and then Row 1 twice.
Fasten off.
Border
Round 1: Join color E to any ch along Foundation edge. Ch2 (counts as 1hdc), 1hdc in every ch, to corner, *[1hdc, 1dc, 1hdc] in corner, work 24hdc evenly along row-end edge, [1hdc, 1dc, 1hdc] in corner**, 1hdc in each of next 25sc; rep from * to **, 1sc in every ch to end of round, changing to color A when joining with sl st in 2nd ch of ch-2.
Round 2: Ch1, 1sc in every hdc and [1sc, 1hdc, 1sc] in every corner dc, to end of round, join with sl st in first sc.
Fasten off and weave in ends.

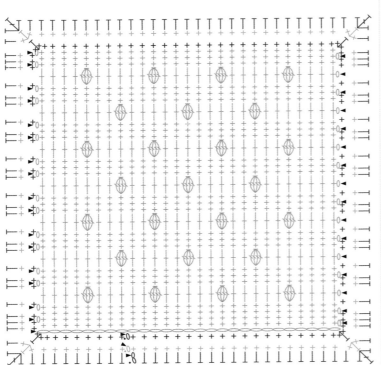

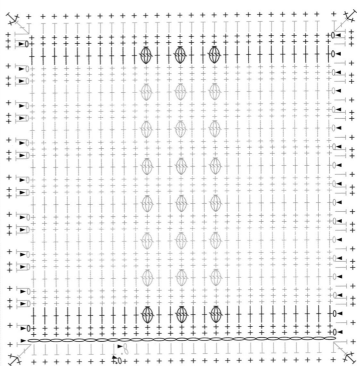

Bobble Stripes

See page 13

A=Oyster
B=Nightshade
C=Sky
D=Bleached
E=Persimmon
F=Toffee

SPECIAL STITCHES

MB (Make bobble): Work four treble stitches together: Working into the same stitch, [yarn over hook, draw up a loop, yarn over hook, pull through two loops on the hook] four times, yarn over hook and pull through all five loops on hook.

Foundation chain: Using color A, make 28ch.
Row 1 (WS): 1sc in 2nd ch from hook, 1sc in every ch to end of row, turn. (27 sc)
Row 2: Ch 1, 1sc in every sc to end

of row, turn.
Rows 3–4: As Row 2, changing to color B when working last sc, turn.
Row 5: Ch 1, 1sc in next sc, [MB, 1sc in each of next 5sc] 4 times, MB, 1sc in next sc changing to color A when working last pull through, turn.
Rows 6–10: As Row 2, changing to color C when working last sc of Row 10, turn.
Row 11: As Row 5, changing to color A when working last sc, turn.
Rows 12–16: As Row 2, changing to color D when working last sc of Row 16, turn.

Row 17: As Row 5, changing to color A when working last sc, turn.
Rows 18–22: As Row 2, changing to color E when working last sc of Row 22, turn.
Row 23: As Row 5, changing to color A when working last sc, turn.
Rows 24–28: As Row 2, changing to color F when working last sc of Row 28, turn.
Row 29: As Row 5, changing to color A when working last sc, turn.
Rows 30–33: As Row 2.
Fasten off.

Border

Round 1: Join color D to any ch along Foundation edge. Ch 2 (counts as 1hdc), 1hdc in every ch to corner, *[1hdc, 1dc, 1hdc] in corner, work 27hdc evenly along row-end edge, [1hdc, 1dc, 1hdc] in corner**, 1hdc in each of next 25sc; rep from * to **, 1hdc in every ch to end of round, changing to color B when joining with sl st in 2nd ch of ch-2.
Round 2: Ch 1, 1sc in every hdc and [1sc, 1hdc, 1sc] in every corner dc to end of round, join with sl st in first sc.
Fasten off and weave in ends.

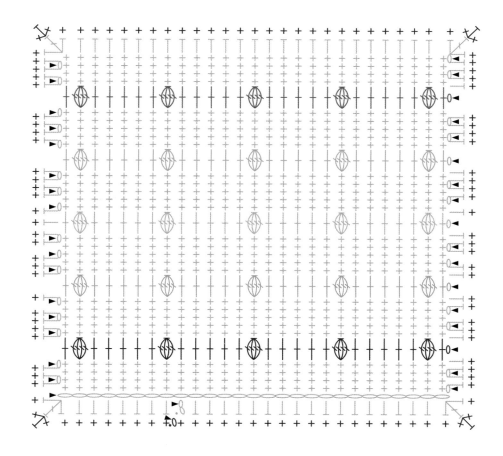

⊛⊛ Winter Blueberry Patch
See page 13

A=Sky
B=Ecru
C=Persimmon
D=Oyster

SPECIAL STITCHES

MB (Make bobble): Work four treble stitches together: Working into the same stitch, [(yarn over hook) twice, draw up a loop, yarn over hook, pull through two loops on the hook] four times, yarn over hook and pull through all five loops on the hook.

Foundation chain: Using color A, make 12ch.
Row 1 (RS): 1sc in 2nd ch from hook, 1sc in every ch to end of row, turn. (11 sc)
Row 2: Ch 3 (counts as 1dc), 1dc in next st, MB in next st, 1dc in next 2 sts] 3 times, turn.
Row 3: Ch 1, 1sc in every st to end of row, turn.
Rows 4–7: Rep Rows 2–3 twice more.
Commence working in the round as follows:
Round 1: Join color B to corner st, ch1, 1sc in same st, *[1sc in base of sc, 2sc around post of dc] 3 times, 1sc in base of sc**, 2sc in first foundation ch, 1sc in next 9 foundation ch, 2sc in last foundation ch; rep from * to ** once more, 1sc in next 10 sts, changing to color C when joining with sl st in first sc made. Break B. (44 sts)
Round 2: Ch 1, *[1sc, 1hdc, 1sc] in same st, 1sc in next 10 sts; rep from *

a further 3 times, changing to color D when joining with sl st in first sc made. Break C. (52 sts)
Round 3: Ch 1, 1sc in same st, *[1sc, 1hdc, 1sc] in hdc of corner**, 1sc in each st to next hdc; rep from * twice more then from * to ** once again, 1sc in each st to end of round, changing to color B when joining with sl st in first sc made. Break D. (60 sts)
Round 4: As Round 3 in B.
Round 5: As Round 3 in D.
Round 6: As Round 3 in A.
Round 7: As Round 3 in C, changing to color D when joining with sl st in first sc made.
Round 8: Ch 3, (counts as 1dc), 1dc in every st from previous round, working 3dc in every corner hdc to end of round, changing to color B, when joining with sl st in 3rd ch of ch-3.
Round 9: Ch 3, (counts as 1dc), 1dc in every st from previous round, working 3dc into center dc of each 3dc corner cluster to end of round, changing to color A, when joining with sl st in 3rd ch of ch-3.
Round 10: Ch 3, (counts as 1dc), 1dc in every st from previous round, working 3dc in center dc of each 3dc corner cluster to end of round, join with sl st in 3rd ch of ch-3.

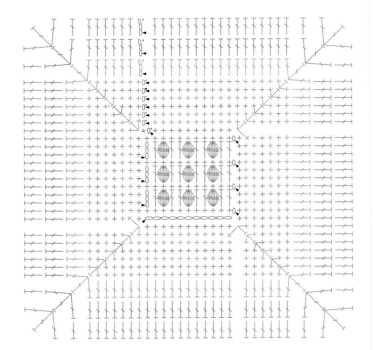

⊛⊛ Bobbles on the Diagonal
See page 14

A=Oyster
B=Nightshade
C=Persimmon
D=Sky

SPECIAL STITCHES

MB (Make bobble): Work five treble sts tog: [(yoh) twice, draw up a loop in next st, (yoh, pull through two loops on hook) twice] 5 times, yoh and pull through all six loops on hook.

sc3tog: Work 3sc over 3 sts to last yoh, yoh and pull through all 4 loops on hook. (2 sts decreased)

Foundation row: Using color A, make 2ch.
Row 1: 3sc in 2nd ch from hook, turn. (3 sts)
Row 2: Ch 1, 2sc in first st, 1sc in each st to last st, 2sc in last st, turn. (5 sts)
Rows 3-4: As Row 2. (9 sts)
Row 5: Ch 1, 1sc in every sc, turn.
Rows 6-8: As Row 2. (15 sts)
Row 9: As Row 2, change to color B in last sc of row, turn.
Row 10: Ch 1, 2sc in first st, [MB, 1sc in each of next 3 sts] 3 times, MB, 2sc in last sc, turn. Break color B. (17 sts)
Rows 11: Join color A and rep Row 2. (19 sts)
Row 12: As Row 2. (21 sts)
Row 13: As Row 5.
Rows 14-15: As Row 2. Fasten off color A. (25 sts)
Row 16: Join color C, ch 1, 2sc in first st, 1sc in next st, [MB, 1sc in each of next 3 sts] 5 times, MB, 1sc in next st, 2sc in last sc, turn. (27 sts)
Row 17: As Row 2. (29 sts)
Row 18: Ch 1, skip 1 st, 1sc in each of next 3 sts, [MB, 1sc in each of next 3 sts] 5 times, MB, 1sc in each of next 2 sts, skip 1 st, 1sc in last st, turn. Fasten off color C. (27 sts)
Row 19: Join color A, ch 1, skip 1 st,

1sc in each st to last 2 sts, skip 1 st, 1sc in last st, turn. (25 sts)
Row 20: As Row 19. (23 sts)
Row 21: As Row 5. (23 sts)
Rows 22-24: As Row 19. (17 sts)
Row 25: As Row 5. Fasten off color A (17 sts)
Row 26: Join color D, ch 1, skip 1 st, 1sc in next st, [MB, 1sc in each of next 3 sts] 3 times, MB, 1sc in last sc, turn. Fasten off color D. (15 sts)
Rows 27: Join color A and rep Row 19. (13 sts)
Row 28: As Row 19. (11 sts)
Row 29: As Row 5. (11 sts)
Rows 30-33: As Row 19. (3 sts)
Row 34: Sc3tog. (1 st)
Fasten off.
Border
Round 1: Join color C to any ch along in any row-end or corner. Ch 1, 1sc in same place, 1sc in every row-end to corner, *[1sc, 1hdc, 1sc] in corner, work 17sc evenly along row-end edge, [1sc, 1hdc, 1sc] in corner**, 1sc in each of next 17 row-ends; rep from * to **, 1sc in every ch to end of round, changing to color A when joining with sl st in first sc.
Round 2: Ch 1, 1sc in every sc and [1sc 1hdc, 1sc] in every corner hdc to end of round, changing to color B when joining with sl st in first sc.
Round 3: Ch 1, 1sc in every sc and [1sc, 1hdc, 1sc] in every corner hdc to end of round, changing to color D when joining with sl st in first sc.
Round 4: Ch 2 (counts as 1hdc), 1hdc in every sc and [1hdc 1dc, 1hdc] in every corner hdc, to end of round, join with sl st to first sc.
Fasten off and weave in ends.

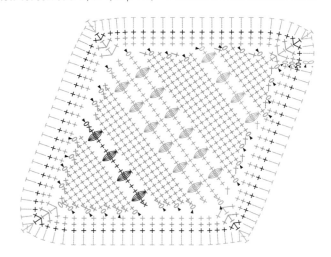

⭐⭐⭐ *Celtic Cable*

See page 12

A=Persimmon
B=Oyster

SPECIAL STITCHES

FPdc (Front Post double): Yoh, insert hook from front to back around post of designated st, yoh and pull up a loop, (yoh and pull through 2 loops on hook) twice. Skip the sc behind the FPdc.

Foundation chain: Using color A, make 26 ch.
Row 1: 1sc in 2nd ch from hook, 1sc in every ch to end of row, turn. (25 sts)
Row 2 and all WS rows: Ch 1 (does not count as st), 1sc in every sc to end of row, turn.
Row 3: Ch 1, 1sc in each of first 7 sts, work FPdc around sc one row below next sc, [1sc in next sc, work FPdc around sc one row below next sc] 5 times, 1sc in each of last 7sc, turn.
Row 5: Ch 1, 1sc in each of first 8 sts, work FPdc around next FPdc, 1sc in next sc, work FPdc around next FPdc, skip next FPdc, work FPdc around next FPdc, 1sc in next sc, working behind FPdc just made, work FPdc around the skipped FPdc, work FPdc around next FPdc, 1sc in next sc,

work FPdc around next FPdc, 1sc in each of last 8 sc, turn.
Row 7: Ch 1, 1sc in each of first 9 sts, work FPdc around next FPdc, skip next FPdc, work FPdc around next FPdc, working in front of FPdc just made, work FPdc around the skipped FPdc, 1sc in next sc, skip next FPdc, work FPdc around next FPdc, working in front of FPdc just made, work FPdc around the skipped FPdc, work FPdc around next FPdc, 1sc in each of last 9 sc, turn.
Row 9: Ch 1, 1sc in each of next 9sc, *skip next FPdc, work FPdc around next FPdc, working behind FPdc just made, work FPdc around the skipped FPdc; rep from * twice more, 1sc in each of last 9 sc, turn.
Row 11: Ch 1, 1sc in each of next 8sc, work FPdc around next FPdc, 1sc in next sc, *skip next FPdc, work FPdc around next FPdc, working in front of FPdc just made, work FPdc around the skipped FPdc, 1sc in next sc; rep from * once more, work FPdc around next FPdc, 1sc in each of last 8 sc, turn.

Row 13: Ch 1, 1sc in each of next 7sc, [work FPdc around next FPdc, 1sc in next sc] twice, skip next FPdc, work FPdc around next FPdc, 1sc in next sc, working behind FPdc just made, work FPdc around the skipped FPdc, [1sc in next sc, work FPdc around next FPdc] twice, 1sc in each of last 7sc, turn.
Rows 15, 17, 19: Ch 1, 1sc in each of first 7sc, work FPdc around next FPdc, [1sc in next sc, 1FPdc around next FPdc] 5 times, 1sc in each of last 7sc, turn.
Row 20: Ch 1, 1sc in every sc to end of row, turn.
Rep Rows 5–15.
Next row: Ch 1, 1sc in every sc to end of row. Do not turn.
Side edges
First edge
Row 1: Working down the first set of row-ends, ch 2 (counts as 1hdc), work 23hdc evenly along row edge, turn. (24 hdc)
Row 2: Ch 2 (counts as 1hdc), 1hdc in every hdc to end of row. Fasten off.

Join color A to second side edge and work as for First edge.
Border
Join color B to any ch along Foundation edge.
Round 1: Ch 1, 1sc in same place, 1sc in every ch to first row end edge, 2sc in this row end, [1sc, 1hdc, 1sc] in second row end, *1sc in every hdc to next row end edge, [1sc, 1hdc, 1sc] in first row end, 2sc in next row end, *1sc in every sc to next row end edge, 2sc in next row end, [1sc, 1hdc, 1sc] in second row end; rep from * to * once more, 1sc in every ch along Foundation edge to end of round, join with sl st in first sc.
Round 2: Ch 1, 1sc in every sc and 3sc in every middle sc of corner 3sc to end of round, change to color A when joining with sl st in first sc.
Round 3: Ch 1, 1sc in every sc and 3sc in every middle sc of corner 3sc to end of round, join with sl st in first sc.
Round 4: As Round 3.
Fasten off and weave in ends.

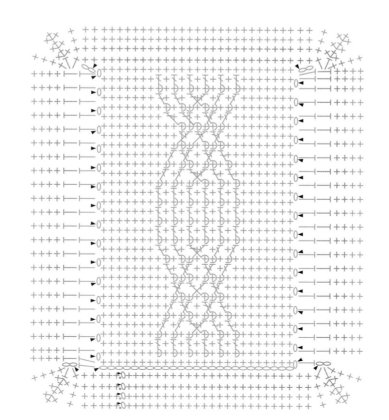

⊕ ⊕ Basket Weave
See page 15

A=Sky

SPECIAL STITCHES

FRdc (Front Raised double crochet): Yarn over hook, insert hook from front to back around the post of designated stitch, yarn over hook, pull up a loop, [yarn over hook, pull through two loops on the hook] twice more.

BRdc (Back Raised double crochet): Yarn over hook, insert hook from back to front around the post of designated stitch, yarn over hook, pull up a loop, [yarn over hook, pull through two loops on the hook] twice more.

Foundation chain: Using color A, make 37ch.
Row 1: 1dc in 4th ch from hook, 1dc in every ch to end of row, turn. (34 dc)
Row 2: Ch2, skip first dc, *1FRdc around each of next 3dc, 1BRdc around each of next 3dc; rep from * to last 3 sts, 1FRdc in each of last 3dc,

1dc in 3rd ch of ch-3, turn.
Row 3: Ch2, skip first dc, *1BRdc around each of next 3 FRdc, 1FRdc around each of next 3 BRdc; rep from * to last 3 sts, 1BRdc in each of last 3 FRdc, 1dc in 2nd ch of ch-2, turn.
Row 4: Ch2, skip first dc, *1BRdc around each of next 3 BRdc, 1FRdc around each of next 3 FRdc; rep from * to last 3 sts, 1BRdc in each of last 3 BRdc, 1dc in 2nd ch of ch-2, turn.
Row 5: Ch2, skip first dc, *1FRdc around each of next 3 BRdc, 1BRdc around each of next 3 FRdc; rep from * to last 3 sts, 1FRdc in each of last 3 BRdc, 1dc in 2nd ch of ch-2, turn.
Row 6: Ch2, skip first dc, *1FRdc around each of next 3 FRdc, 1BRdc around each of next 3 BRdc; rep from * to last 3 sts, 1FRdc in each of last 3 FRdc, 1dc in 2nd ch of ch-2, turn.
Rep Rows 3-6, a further 4 times, then Rows 3-4 only once more.
Fasten off and weave in ends.

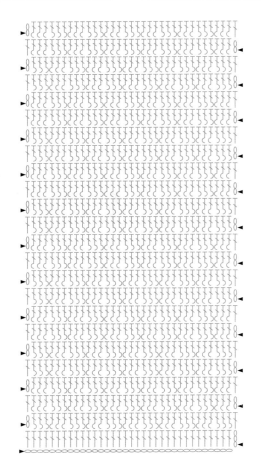

⊕ ⊕ Diagonal Raised Treble
See page 12

A=Sky

SPECIAL STITCHES

FRdc (Front Raised double crochet): Yarn over hook, insert hook from front to back around the post of designated stitch, yarn over hook, pull up a loop, [yarn over hook, pull through two loops on the hook] twice more.

BRdc (Back Raised double crochet): Yarn over hook, insert hook from back to front around the post of designated stitch, yarn over hook, pull up a loop, [yarn over hook, pull through two loops on the hook] twice more.

Foundation chain: Using color A, make 40ch.
Row 1: 1dc in 4th ch from hook, 1dc in every ch to end of row, turn.
Row 2: Ch2, skip first dc, *1FRdc around each of next 2dc, 1BRdc around each of next 2dc; rep from * to end of row, 1dc in 3rd ch of ch-3, turn.

Row 3: Ch2, skip first dc, *1FRdc around first BRdc, *1BRdc around each of next 2 sts, 1FRdc around each of next 2 sts; rep from * to last 3 sts, 1BRdc around each of next 2 sts, 1FRdc around last st, 1dc in 2nd ch of ch-2, turn.
Row 4: Ch2, skip first dc, *1BRdc around each of next 2 sts, 1FRdc around each of next 2 sts; rep from * to end of row, 1dc in 2nd ch of ch-2, turn.
Row 5: Ch2, skip first dc, 1BRdc around first FRdc, *1FRdc around each of next 2 sts, 1BRdc around each of next 2 sts; rep from * to last 3 sts, 1FRdc around each of next 2 sts, 1BRdc in last BRdc, 1dc in 2nd ch of ch-2, turn.
Row 6: As Row 2 to end of row, 1dc in 2nd ch of ch-2, turn.
Rep Rows 3-6 a further 4 times.
Fasten off and weave in ends.

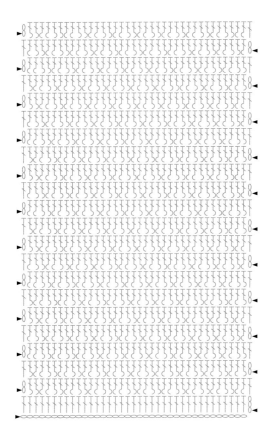

Pineapple Cluster

See page 13

A=Persimmon

 ## Honeycomb

See page 14

A=Persimmon

SPECIAL STITCHES

PS (Pineapple stitch): [Yarn round hook, insert hook in designated stitch or space, draw a loop through] 4 times in same place, yarn round hook, draw loop through first 8 loops on hook, yarn round hook, draw through two remaining loops.

Foundation chain: Using color A, work 34ch.
Row 1: 1PS in 4th ch from hook, ch1, *miss 1ch, 1PS in next ch, ch 1; rep from * to last 2 ch, miss 1 ch, 1dc in last ch, turn.
Row 2: *Miss 1ch, 1PS in next ch, ch 1; rep from * to last 2ch, miss 1ch, 1tr in last ch, turn.
Row 3: Ch 3, miss first dc, 1PS in first ch-sp, *ch1, miss 1 PS, 1PS in next ch-sp; rep from * to last PS, ch 1, miss last PS, 1tr in the 3rd ch of ch-3, turn.
Rep Row 3 a further 13 times.
Fasten off and weave in ends.

Foundation ring: Using color A, work 26ch.
Row 1: 1sc in 2nd ch from hook, 1sc in every ch to end, turn.
Row 2: Ch 1, 1sc in each of first 2dc, *tr5tog in next sc, 1dc in each of next 2sc; rep from * to last dc, tr5tog in last sc, turn.
Row 3: Ch 1, *1sc in top of first cl, 1sc in each of next 2sc; rep from * to end of row, turn.
Row 4: Ch 1, tr5tog in next sc, *1dc in each of next 2sc, tr5tog in next sc; rep from * to last 2sc, 1sc in each of last 2sc, turn.
Row 5: Ch 1, 1sc in each of first 2sc, *1sc in top of first cl, 1sc in each of next 2sc; rep from * to last cl, 1sc into top of the last cl, turn.
Rep rows 2–5 a further 7 times.
Fasten off and weave in ends.

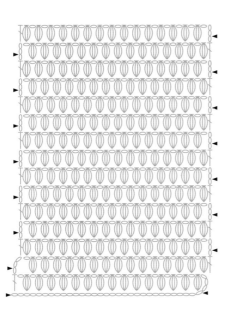

Tricolor Trinity

See page 13

A=Nightshade
B=Toffee
C=Oyster

SPECIAL STITCHES

Cl (Cluster): Work three double crochet stitches together: Insert hook and draw up a loop in each of the 3 designated sts, yarn round hook and draw through all 4 loops on hook.

Foundation chain: Using color A, work 30ch.
Row 1: 1sc in 2nd ch from hook, sc3tog inserting hook in same ch as first sc and then in next 2ch, *ch1, sc3tog inserting hook in same ch as 3rd leg of previous cluster and then in next 2ch; rep from * to last ch, changing to color B when working 1sc in same ch as 3rd leg of previous cluster, turn.
Row 2: Ch1, 1sc in first st, sc3tog inserting hook in same place as first sc, then in top of next cl and then in next ch-sp, *ch1, sc3tog inserting hook in same place as 3rd leg of previous cl, then in top of next cl and then in next ch-sp; rep from * to end working 3rd leg of last cluster in last sc, changing to color C when working 1sc in same place, turn.

Row 3: Rep Row 2 changing to next color at end of row as given in the sequence below.
Continue to rep Row 2 using the following color stripe sequence: [A, B, C] 6 times.
Fasten off.
Border
Round 1: Join color B to any ch along Foundation edge. Ch1, 1sc in same place, 1sc in every ch to corner, *[1sc, 1hdc, 1sc] in corner, work 20sc evenly along row-end edge, [1sc, 1hdc, 1sc] in corner**, 1sc in each of next 25cl and ch-sp; rep from * to **, 1sc in every ch to end of round, changing to color C when joining with sl st in first sc. (98sc, 4hdc)
Round 2: Ch 2 (counts as 1hdc), 1hdc in every sc and [1hdc, 1dc, 1hdc] in every corner hdc to end of round, changing to color A when joining with sl st in 2nd ch of ch-2.
Round 3: Ch 3 (counts as 1dc), 1dc in every hdc and 3dc in every corner dc to end of round, join with sl st in 3rd ch of ch-3.
Fasten off and weave in ends.

Two-color Raised Ripple

See page 14

A=Toffee
B=Oyster

SPECIAL STITCHES

FRdc (Front Raised double crochet): Yarn over hook, insert hook from front to back around the post of designated stitch, yarn over hook, pull up a loop, [yarn over hook, pull through two loops on the hook] twice more.
BRdc (Back Raised double crochet): Yarn over hook, insert hook from back to front around the post of designated stitch, yarn over hook, pull up a loop, [yarn over hook, pull through two loops on the hook] twice more.

Foundation chain: Using color A, work 31ch.
Row 1: 1dc in 4th ch from hook, 1dc in every ch to the end of the row, turn.
Row 2: Ch 1, skip first st, 1sc in every dc to end of row, 1sc in 3rd ch of ch-3, turn.
Row 3: Ch 3, skip first sc, *skip next sc and work 1FRdc around dc in row

below skipped sc, 1dc in next sc; rep from * to end of row, changing to color B when working 1dc in ch-1, turn.
Row 4: As Row 2.
Row 5: Ch 3, skip first sc, *1dc in next sc, 1 FRdc around the dc in the row below the skipped sc; rep from * to last dc, change to color A when working 1 FRdc around the dc in the row below ch-1, turn.
Rep Rows 2-5 a further 5 times.
Fasten off.
Row-end edge: With RS of work facing, join yarn A to top LH corner of block. Ch 1, 1dc in same place, work 32dc evenly along edge. Fasten off.
Rep for other edge, joining yarn at bottom RH corner and working 31dc evenly along edge. Do not break yarn.
Top edge: 3dc in corner, 1dc in every ch along last row of block, 2dc in corner, join with sl st to first dc. Fasten off.
Fasten off and weave in ends.

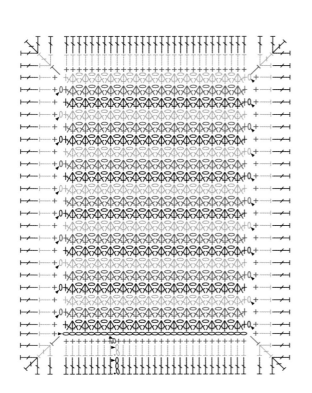

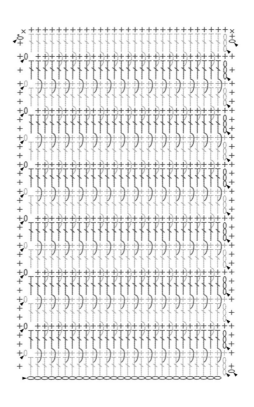

Interwoven Block

See page 15

A=Nightshade
B=Toffee
C=Oyster

Aligned Railing Block

See page 13

A=Persimmon
B=Nightshade
C=Toffee
D=Oyster
Additional Notions: Stitch holder or safety pin

SPECIAL STITCHES

FRtr (Front Raised treble crochet):
Yarn over hook, insert hook from front to back around the post of designated stitch, yarn over hook, pull up a loop, [yarn over hook, pull through two loops on the hook] twice more.

Foundation chain: Using color A, work 31ch.
Row 1 (RS): 1dc in 4th ch from hook, 1dc in every ch to end of row, changing to color B at end of last dc, turn. (28 dc)
Row 2: Ch 3 (counts as 1dc), skip first st, *1FRtr around next st, 1dc in next st; rep from * changing to color C when working last dc in 3rd ch of ch-3, turn.

Row 3: Rep Row 2 changing to next color at end of row as given in the sequence below.
Continue to rep Row 2 using the following color stripe sequence: [A, B, C] 4 times.
Fasten off.
Border
Round 1: Join color B to any ch along Foundation edge. Ch 1, 1sc in same place, 1sc in every ch, to corner, *[1sc, 1hdc, 1sc] in corner, work 26sc evenly along row-end edge, [1sc, 1hdc, 1sc] in corner**, 1sc in each of next 27 sts; rep from * to **, 1sc in every ch to end of round, join with sl st in first sc.
Fasten off and weave in ends.

SPECIAL STITCHES

FRtr (Front Raised treble crochet):
Yarn over hook, insert hook from front to back around the post of designated stitch, yarn over hook, pull up a loop, [yarn over hook, pull through two loops on the hook] twice more.

Foundation chain: Using color A, work 31ch.
Row 1: 1dc in 4th ch from hook, 1dc in every ch to end of row, turn. (28 ch)
Row 2: Ch 3 (counts as 1dc), skip next st, 1dc in every dc to end of row, 1dc in 3rd ch of ch-3.
Row 3: Place working loop on a stitch holder and draw a loop of color B through top of last completed background stitch, ch 1, work 1FRtr around stem of 2nd st in second to last row, *ch 1, skip 1 st, 1FRtr around

stem of next st in second to last row; rep from * ending with sl st in 3rd ch of ch-3 at beg of last background row. Fasten off, but do not turn the work.
Row 4: Replace hook in working loop of color A, ch 3, work 1dc inserting hook through top of raised st and background st at the same time, *work 1dc inserting hook under contrast color ch and top of next st in color A at the same time, work 1dc inserting hook under top of next raised st and next st in color A as before; rep from * to end, 1dc in 3rd ch of ch-3, turn.
Row 5: Ch3 (counts as 1dc), skip next st, 1dc in every dc to end of row, 1dc in 3rd ch of ch-3.
Rep Rows 3-5 a further 7 times using the following color stripe sequence for Row 3: [C, D, B] twice.
Fasten off and weave in ends.

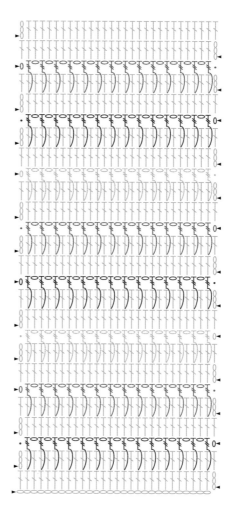

Classic Cable

See page 15

A=Oyster

SPECIAL STITCHES

FPtr (front post treble): [Yoh] twice, insert hook from front to back around the post of designated stitch, yoh, pull up a loop, then [yoh, pull through two loops on the hook] three times.

BPtr (Back post treble): [Yoh] twice, insert hook from back to front around the post of designated stitch, yoh, pull up a loop, then [yoh, pull through two loops on the hook] three times.

Foundation chain: Using color A, make 30ch.

Row 1: 1sc in 2nd ch from hook, 1sc in every ch to end of row, turn.

Row 2: Ch 2, 1hdc in every sc to end of row, turn.

Row 3: Ch 2, 1hdc in each of next 3hdc, *[1FPtr in next st, 1hdc in next st] twice, 1FPtr in each of next 4 sts, 1hdc in next st; rep from * once, [1FPtr in next st, 1hdc in next st] twice, 1hdc in each of last 3hdc, turn.

Row 4: Ch 2, 1hdc in each of next 3hdc, *[1BPtr in next st, 1hdc in next st] twice, 1BPtr in each of next 4 sts, 1hdc in next st; rep from * once, 1BPtr in next st, 1hdc in next st] twice, 1hdc in each of last 3hdc, turn.

Row 5: Ch 2, 1hdc in each of next 3hdc, [1FPtr in next st, 1hdc in next st] twice, *skip next 2 sts, 1FPtr in each of next 2 sts, working in front of the 2 sts just worked, 1FPtr in each of the 2 sts just skipped, 1hdc in next st; rep from * once, 1FPtr in next st, 1hdc in next st] twice, 1hdc in each of last 3hdc, turn.

Row 6: As Row 4.
Row 7: As Row 3.
Row 8: As Row 4.
Row 9: As Row 5.
Row 10: As Row 4.
Row 11: As Row 3.
Row 12: As Row 4.
Row 13: As Row 5.
Row 14: As Row 4.
Row 15: As Row 3.
Row 16: As Row 4.
Row 17: As Row 5.

Row 18: Ch 2, 1hdc in every st to end of row, turn.

Row 19: Ch 1, 1sc in every hdc to end of row, do not turn or fasten off.

**Row-end edge 1: Ch 2, 1hdc in every row end edge to end of row. (18 hdc)

Row-end edge 2: Ch 2, 1hdc in every hdc to end of row. Fasten off.** Join yarn with a sl st to bottom right hand corner.

Repeat from ** to **.

Border

Round 1: Ch 1, 1sc in every st around working [1sc, ch 1, 1sc] in each corner to end of round, join with sl st in first sc.

Fasten off and weave in ends.

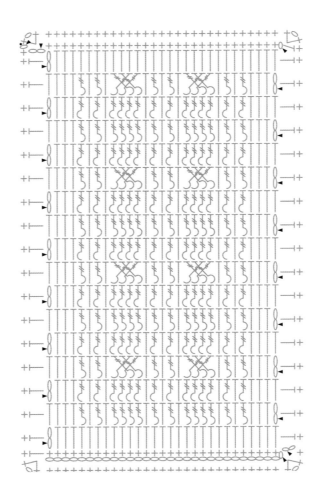

Big Bloom

See page 12

A=Persimmon
B=Bleached
C=Oyster
D=Blackcurrant

Foundation ring: Using A, make a Magic Ring (see page 153).

Round 1: Ch 2 (counts as 1hdc), 11hdc in the ring, join with sl st in flo of 2nd ch of ch-2. (12 hdc)

Round 2: *Ch 7, sl st in flo of next hdc; rep from * a further 10 times, ch 7, join with sl st in blo of 2nd ch of ch-2 from Round 1. (12 ch sp)

Round 3: Ch 2 (counts as 1hdc), 1hdc in blo in same place, 2hdc in blo of every st to end of round, join with sl st in blo of 2nd ch of ch-2 from Round 2. Break color A. (24 sts)

Round 4: Using B, *ch 7, sl st in flo of next hdc; rep from * a further 22 times, ch7, join with sl st in blo of 2nd ch of ch-2 from Round 3. (24 ch sps)

Round 5: Ch2 (counts as 1hdc), *2hdc in blo of next st, 1hdc in blo of next st; rep from * a further 11 times, 2hdc in blo of next st, join with sl st through back loop of 2nd ch of ch-2 from Round 4. Break color B. (36 sts)

Round 6: Using C, *ch 7, sl st in flo of next hdc; rep from * a further 34 times, ch7, join with sl st in blo of 2nd ch of ch-2 from Round 5. Break color C. (36 ch sp)

Round 7: Join D in blo, ch 1 and 1sc in blo of same space *1sc in blo of next st, 1hdc in blo of next st, 1dc in blo of next 2 sts, [1dc, 1tr, 1dc] in next st, 1dc in blo of next 2 sts, 1hdc in blo of next st**, 1sc in blo of next st; rep from * twice more, then from * to ** once more, join with sl st to first sc. (44 sts)

Round 8: Ch 3 (counts as 1dc), *1dc in each st across to corner tr, [1dc, 1tr, 1dc] in tr; rep from * a further 3 times, 1dc in each st to end of round, join with sl st to 3rd ch of ch-3. (52 sts)

Round 9: Work as Round 8. Break color D. (60 sts)

Round 10: Using C, ch 1, 1sc in same place, *1sc in each st across to corner tr, [1sc, 1hdc, 1sc] in tr; rep from * a further 3 times, 1sc in each st to end of round, join with sl st to first sc. Break color C. (68 sts)

Round 11: Using A, ch 1, 1sc in same place, *1sc in each st across to corner hdc, [1sc, 1hdc, 1sc] in hdc; rep from * a further 3 times, 1sc in each st to end of round, join with sl st to first sc. Break color A. (76 sts)

Round 12: Using C, work as Round 11. Break color C. (84 sts)

Round 13: Using D, ch 3 (counts as 1dc), *1dc in each st across to corner hdc, [1dc, 1tr, 1dc] in hdc; rep from * a further 3 times, 1dc in each st to end of round, join with sl st to 3rd ch of ch-3. Break color D. (92 sts)

Round 14: Using C, ch 3 (counts as 1dc), *1dc in each st across to corner hdc, [1dc, 1tr, 1dc] in hdc; rep from * a further 3 times, 1dc in each st to end of round, join with sl st to 3rd ch of ch-3. Break color C. (100 sts)

Round 15: Using D, ch 2 (counts as 1hdc), *1hdc in each st across to corner tr, [1hdc, 1dc, 1hdc] in tr; rep from * a further 3 times, 1hdc in each st to end of round, join with sl st to 2nd of ch-2. (108 sts).

Fasten off and weave in ends.

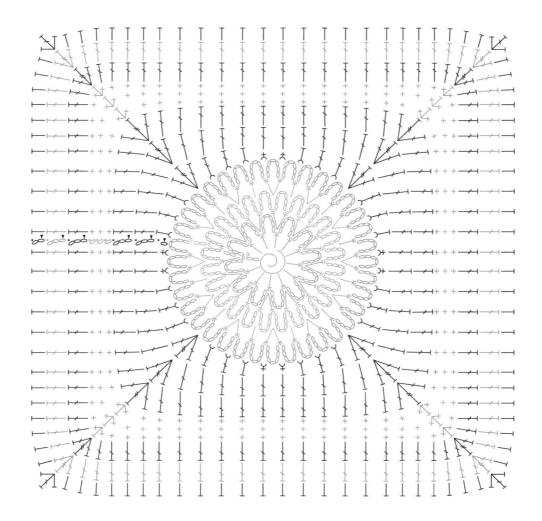

⭐ *Openwork*

See page 16

A=Shell
B=Bleached
C=Rose

Foundation chain: Using color A, work 36 ch.

Row 1 (RS): 1sc in 2nd ch from hook, 1sc in every ch to end, turn. (34 sc)

Row 2: Ch 4 (counts as 1dc and 1ch), skip 1sc, 1dc in next sc, *ch 1, skip next sc, 1dc in next sc; rep from * to end, turn. (17 ch-1 sp)

Row 3: Ch 1, 2sc in every ch-1 sp to end, 2sc in ch-1 sp created by turning ch, turn. (33 sc)

Row 4: Ch 1, 1sc in every sc to end of row, turn.

Rep Rows 2-4 a further 6 times.
Fasten off.

Border

Round 1: Join color B to any sc along previous row, ch 1, 1sc in same place, 1sc in every sc and row end, working 3sc in each corner, join with sl st to first sc. Break color B.

Round 2: Join color C to any sc along previous row, ch 2, 1hdc in every sc to end of round, working [1hdc, 1dc, 1hdc] in 2nd sc of each 3sc corner group, join with sl st to 2nd of ch-2.

Fasten off and weave in ends.

⭐⭐ *Belgian Lace*

See page 18

A=Lavender

SPECIAL STITCHES

Beg cl (Beginning cluster): Work 3 dc sts tog to the last "yrh, pull through," yrh once again and draw through all four loops on the hook.

Cl (cluster): Work 4 dc sts tog to the last "yrh, pull through," yrh once again and draw through all five loops on the hook.

Foundation ring: Using color A, work 8 ch and join with sl st to form a ring.

Round 1: Ch 3 (counts as 1dc), 6dc in ring, [ch 7, 7dc in ring] 3 times, ch 4, 1dc in 3rd ch of ch-3. (4 ch-7 sp)

Round 2: Ch 10 (counts as 1dc and ch 7), skip next 3dc, *1sc in next dc, ch 7, skip next 3dc**, 7dc in next ch-7 sp, ch 7, skip next 3dc; rep from * twice more and from * to ** once again, 6dc in next ch-7 sp, join with sl st in 3rd ch of ch-10. (8 ch-7 sp)

Round 3: Sl st to center of next ch-7 sp, beg cl in same sp, *ch 3, cl in next ch-7 sp, ch 11, skip next 3dc, 1dc in next dc, ch 11**, 1 cl in next ch-7 sp; rep from * twice more and from * to ** once again, join with sl st in 3rd ch of ch-3.

Round 4: Sl st in next ch-3 sp, beg cl in same sp, *ch 8, 7dc in each of next two 11-ch sps, ch 8**, 1cl in next ch-3 sp; rep from * twice more and from * to ** once again, join with sl st to top of beg cl.

Round 5: Ch 4 (counts as 1tr), 2tr in first cluster (half corner made), *4dc in next ch-8 sp, skip 1dc, 1dc in next 12dc, skip 1dc, 4dc in next ch-8 sp**, [3tr, ch 4, 3tr] in top of next cl (corner made); rep from * twice more and from * to ** once again, 3dc in top of beg cl from previous round, ch 4, join with sl st to 4th ch of beg ch-4.

Fasten off and weave in ends.

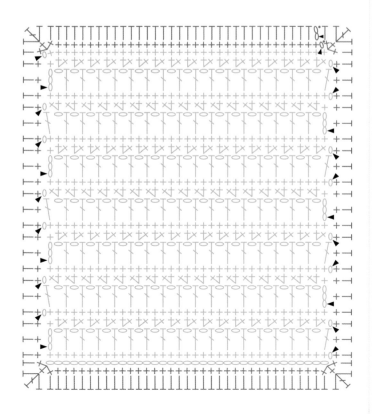

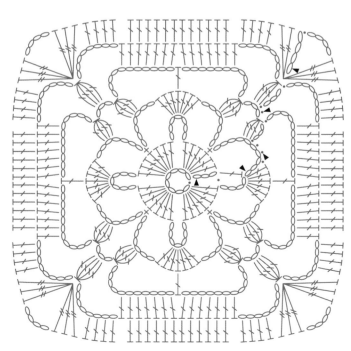

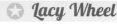 **Lacy Wheel**

See page 16

A=Dawn Gray
B=Nightshade
C=Lavender

Foundation ring: Using color A, work 8 ch and join with sl st in first ch to form a ring.

Round 1: Ch 6 (counts as 1dc and 3ch), [1dc in ring, ch 3] seven times, join with sl st in 3rd ch of ch-6. (8 spaced dc)

Round 2: Sl st in next ch-3 sp, ch 3 (counts as 1dc), 3dc in same sp, [ch 2, 4dc in next ch-3 sp] 7 times, ch 2, join with sl st in 3rd ch of ch-3. Break color A.

Round 3: Join color B to any ch-2 sp, ch 3 (counts as 1dc), 5dc in same sp, *ch 1, 6dc in next ch-2 sp, ch 3**, 6dc in next ch-2 sp; rep from * twice more and from * to ** once again, join with sl st in 3rd ch of ch-3. Break color B.

Round 4: Join color C to any ch-3 sp, ch 1, 1sc in same sp, *ch 3, 1sc between 3rd and 4th dc of next 6dc group, ch 3, [2dc, ch 3, 2dc] in next ch-3 sp, ch 3, 1sc between 3rd and 4th dc of next 6dc group, ch 3**, 1sc in next ch-3sp; rep from * twice and from * to ** once again, join with sl st in first sc. Break color C.

Round 5: Join color B to any ch-3 corner sp, ch 3 (counts as 1dc), [1dc, ch 3, 2dc] in same sp, *[ch 3, 1sc in next ch-3 sp] four times, ch 3**, [2dc, ch 3, 2dc] in next ch-3 corner sp; rep from * twice more, and from * to ** once again, join with sl st in 3rd ch of ch-3. Break color B.

Round 6: Join color A to any ch-3 corner sp, ch 3 (counts as 1dc), [2dc, ch 3, 3dc] in same sp, *[ch 3, 1sc in next ch-3 sp] five times, ch 3**, [3dc, ch 3, 3dc] in next ch-3 corner sp; rep from * twice more, and from * to ** once again, join with sl st in 3rd ch of ch-3.

Round 7: Sl st in next 2dc and in next ch-3 corner sp, ch 3 (counts as 1dc), [2dc, ch 3, 3dc] in same sp, *[ch 3, 1sc in next ch-3 sp] six times, ch 3**, [3dc, ch 3, 3dc] in next ch-3 corner sp; rep from * twice more, and from * to ** once again, join with sl st in 3rd ch of ch-3. Break color A.

Round 8: Join color C to any ch-3 corner sp, ch 3 (counts as 1dc), [2dc, ch 3, 3dc] in same sp, *[ch 3, 1sc in next ch-3 sp] seven times, ch 3**, [3dc, ch 3, 3dc] in next ch-3 corner sp; rep from * twice more, and from * to ** once again, join with sl st in 3rd ch of ch-3.

Round 9: Sl st in next 2dc and in next ch-3 corner sp, ch 2 (counts as 1hdc), [1dc, 1hdc] in same sp, *1hdc in each of next 3dc, 3hdc in every ch-3 sp to corner, [1hdc, 1dc, 1hdc] in next ch-3 corner sp; rep from * twice more, 1hdc in each of next 3dc, 3hdc in every ch-3 sp to corner, 1hdc in each of next 3dc, join with sl st in 2nd ch of ch-2.

Fasten off and weave in ends.

 **Victorian Lace**   See page 17

A=Shell

SPECIAL STITCHES

tr2tog: Work two dc sts to the last "yoh, pull through," yoh once again and draw through all three loops on the hook.

Beg cl (Beginning cluster): Work two dc sts to the last "yoh, pull through," yoh once again and draw through all three loops on the hook.

Cl (Cluster): Work three dc sts to the last "yoh, pull through," yoh once again and draw through all four loops on the hook.

Foundation ring: Work 10 ch and join with sl st in first ch to form a ring.

Round 1: Ch 4 (counts as 1tr), 1tr in ring, ch 2, [tr2tog in ring, ch 2] 11 times, join with sl st in 4th ch of ch-4.

Round 2: Sl st in next dc and in next ch-2 sp, ch 3 (counts as 1dc), beg cl in same sp, ch 3, [cl in next ch-2 sp, ch 2] 11 times, join with sl st to top of beg cl.

Round 3: Ch 5, (counts as 1hdc and ch 3), [cl in next ch-3 sp, ch 2, cl, ch 4, cl, ch 2, cl] in next ch-3 sp, ch 3, *skip next ch-3 sp, 1hdc in top of next cl, ch 3, skip next ch-3 sp, [cl, ch 2, cl, ch 4, cl, ch 2, cl] in next ch-3 sp, ch 3; rep from * twice, join with sl st in 2nd ch of ch-5.

Round 4: Sl st in next ch-3 sp, ch 4, (counts as 1dc and ch 1), 1dc in same sp, *ch 1, 1dc in top of next cl, ch 1,

1dc in next ch-2 sp, ch 1, [cl, ch 2, cl, ch 4, cl, ch 2, cl] in next ch-4 sp, ch 1, 1dc in next ch-2 sp, ch 1, 1dc in top of next cl, ch 1, 1dc in next ch-3 sp, ch 1**, 1dc in next hdc, ch 1, 1dc in next ch-2 sp; rep from * twice and from * to ** once again, join with sl st in 3rd ch of ch-4.

Round 5: Ch 4 (counts as 1dc and ch 1), [1dc in next dc, ch 1] three times, *1dc in top of next cl, ch 1, 1dc in next ch-2 sp, ch 1, [cl, ch 2, cl, ch 4, cl, ch 2, cl] in next ch-4 sp, ch 1, 1dc in next ch-2 sp, ch 1, 1dc in top of next cl, ch 1**, [1dc in next dc, ch 1] seven times; rep from * twice more and from * to ** once again, [1dc in next dc, ch 1] three times, join with sl st in 3rd ch of ch-4.

Round 6: Ch 4 (counts as 1dc and ch 1), [1dc in next dc, ch 1] five times, *1dc in top of next cl, ch 1, 1dc in next ch-2 sp, ch 1, 5dc in next ch-4 sp, ch 1, 1dc in next ch-2 sp, ch 1, 1dc in top of next cl, ch 1**, [1dc in next dc, ch 1] 11 times; rep from * twice and from * to ** once again, [1dc in next dc, ch 1] five times, join with sl st in 3rd ch of ch-4.

Round 7: Ch 2 (counts as 1hdc), 1hdc in every dc and ch-1 sp, working [1hdc, 1dc, 1hdc] in 3rd dc of 5dc corner group, join with sl st to 2nd ch of ch-2.

Fasten off and weave in ends.

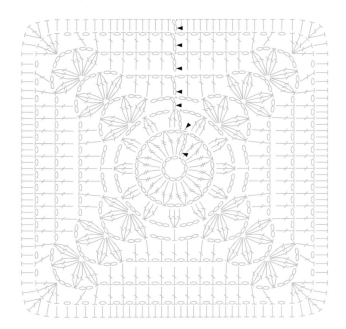

 Old Vienna   See page 17

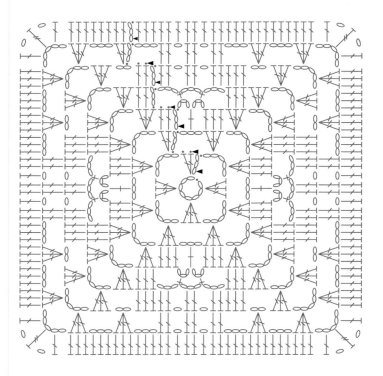

A=Rose

Foundation ring: Work 8 ch and join with sl st in first ch to form a ring.

Round 1: Ch 3 (counts as 1dc), 2dc in ring, ch 5, *3dc in ring, ch 5; rep from * a further 3 times, join with sl st in 3rd ch of ch-3.

Round 2: Sl st in next 2dc and in next ch-5 sp, ch 3, (counts as 1dc), [2dc, ch 5, 3dc] in same sp, *ch 3, [3dc, ch 5, 3dc] in next ch-5 sp; rep from * twice, ch 3, join with sl st in 3rd ch of ch-3.

Round 3: Ch 3, (counts as 1dc), 1dc in each of next 2dc, *[3dc, ch 5, 3dc] in next ch-5 sp, 1dc in each of next 3dc, ch 3, 1dc in next ch-3 sp ch 3**, 1dc in each of next 3dc; rep from * twice more and from * to ** once again, join with sl st in 3rd ch of ch-3.

Round 4: Sl st in next 3dc, ch 3, (counts as 1dc), 1dc in each of next 2dc, *[3dc, ch 5, 3dc] in next ch-5 sp, 1dc in each of next 3dc, ch 3, [1sc in next ch-3 sp, ch 3] twice**, skip next 3dc, 1dc in each of next 3dc; rep from * twice more and from * to ** once again, join with sl st in 3rd ch of ch-3.

Round 5: Ch 3, (counts as 1dc), 1dc in each of next 2dc, ch 2, skip 3dc, *[3dc, ch 5, 3dc] in next ch-5 sp, ch2,

skip next 3dc, 1dc in each of next 3dc, [2dc in next ch-3 sp, ch 1] twice, 2dc in next ch-3 sp**, 1dc in each of next 3dc, ch 2; rep from * twice more and from * to ** once again, join with sl st in 3rd ch of ch-3.

Round 6: Sl st in next 2dc and next ch-2 sp, ch 3, (counts as 1dc), 2dc in same ch-2 sp ch 2, skip next 3dc, *[3dc, ch 5, 3dc] in next ch-5 sp ch 2, skip next 3dc, 3dc in next ch-2 sp, ch 3, skip next 3dc, [1dc in next 2dc, ch 1] twice, 1dc in next 2dc, ch 3, skip next 3dc**, 3dc in next ch-2 sp, ch 2; rep from * twice more and from * to ** once again, join with sl st in 3rd ch of ch-3.

Round 7: Ch 3 (counts as 1dc), 1dc in next 2dc, 2dc in next ch-2 sp, *1dc in each of next 3dc, [1dc, ch 1,1 tr, ch 1, 1dc] in ch-5 corner sp, 1dc in each of next 3dc, 2dc in next ch-2 sp, 1dc in each of next 3dc, 3dc in next ch-3 sp, [1dc in next 2dc, 1dc in next ch-1sp] twice, 1dc in next 2dc, 3dc in next ch-3 sp**, 2dc in next ch-2 sp; rep from * twice more and from * to ** once again, join with sl st in 3rd ch of ch-3.

Fasten off and weave in ends.

Queen Anne's Lace

See page 16

A=Dawn Gray
B=Bleached

SPECIAL STITCHES

Beg cl (Beginning cluster): Work three dc sts to the last "yrh, pull through," yrh once again and draw through all four loops on the hook.

Cl (cluster): Work four dc sts to the last "yrh, pull through," yrh once again and draw through all five loops on the hook.

Foundation ring: Using color A, work 6 ch and join with sl st in first ch to form a ring.

Round 1: Ch 1, 12sc in ring, join with sl st in first sc.

Round 2: Ch4 (counts as 1dc and ch 1), [1dc in next sc, ch 1] 11 times, join with sl st in 3rd ch of ch-4.

Round 3: Sl st in next ch-1 sp, ch 3 (counts as 1dc), 2dc in same sp, ch 1, [3dc in next ch-1 sp, ch 1] 11 times, join with sl st in 3rd ch of ch-3.

Round 4: Sl st in next 2dc and in next ch-1 sp, ch 3 (counts as 1dc), beg cl in same sp, *ch 2, skip 1dc, 1dc in next dc, ch 2, cl in next ch-1 sp; rep from * a further 10 times, ch 2, join with sl st to top of beg cl.

Round 5: Sl st in next ch-2 sp, ch 1, 3sc in same sp, 3sc in every ch-2 sp to end of round, join with sl st in first sc.

Round 6: Ch 3 (counts as 1dc), [1dc, ch 2, 2dc] in same place, *[ch 2, skip next 3sc group, 1sc in sp between next two 3sc groups] five times, ch 2**, [2dc, ch 2, 2dc] in sp above next cl; rep from * twice more and from * to ** once again, join with sl st in 3rd ch of ch-3.

Round 7: Ch 3 (counts as 1dc), 1dc in next dc, *[2dc, ch 2, 2dc] in next ch-2 corner sp, 1dc in each of next 2dc, [1dc, 1hdc] in next ch-2 sp, 1hdc in next sc, [2sc in next ch-2 sp, 1sc in next sc] three times, 2sc in next ch-2 sp, 1hdc in next sc, [1hdc, 1dc] in next ch-2 sp**, 1dc in each of next 2dc; rep from * twice more and from * to ** once again, join with sl st in 3rd ch of ch-3. Break color A.

Round 8: Join color B 2 sts to the left of any corner st, ch 1, 1sc in same place, ch 1, skip next st, *[1sc in next st, ch 1, skip next st] to 2-ch corner sp, [1sc, ch 1, 1sc] in 2-ch corner sp, ch 1, skip next st; rep from * to end of round, join with sl st to first sc. Break color B.

Round 9: Join color A to any ch-1 corner sp, ch 3 (counts as 1dc), [1tr, 1dc] in same sp, *[ch 1, skip next sc, 1dc in next ch-1 sp] to corner**, [1dc, 1tr, 1dc] in ch-1 corner sp; rep from * twice more and from * to ** once again, ch 1, join with sl st to 3rd ch of ch-3.

Fasten off and weave in ends.

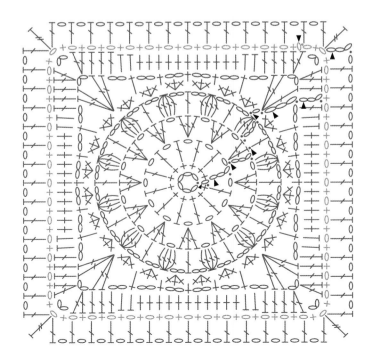

Eyelet Lace in the Round

See page 19

A=Lavender
B=Bleached
C=Dawn Gray

Foundation ring: Using color A, work 4 ch and join with sl st in first ch to form a ring.

Round 1: Ch 3 (counts as 1dc), 2dc in ring, ch 2, [3dc in ring, ch 2] 3 times, join with sl st in 3rd of ch-3. Break color A.

Round 2: Join color B to any ch-2 sp, ch 3 (counts as 1dc), [2dc, ch 3, 3dc] in same sp, [(3dc, ch 3, 3dc) in next ch-2 sp] 3 times, join with sl st in 3rd ch of ch-3.

Round 3: Sl st in next 2dc and in next ch-3 sp, ch 3 (counts as 1dc), [2dc, ch 3, 3dc] in same sp, *ch 1, skip next 2dc, 1dc in each of next 2dc, 1dc in next ch-1 sp, 1dc in next dc, ch 1, skip next 2dc**, [3dc, ch 3, 3dc] in next ch-3 sp; rep from * twice more and from * to ** once again, join with sl st in 3rd ch of ch-3.

Round 4: Sl st in next 2dc and in next ch-3 sp, ch 3 (counts as 1dc), [2dc, ch 3, 3dc] in same sp, *ch 1, skip next 2dc, 1dc in next dc, 1dc in next ch-1 sp, 1dc in each of next 2dc, 1dc in next ch-1 sp, 1dc in next dc, ch 1, skip next 2dc**, [3dc, ch 3, 3dc] in next ch-3 sp; rep from * twice more and from * to ** once again, join with sl st in 3rd ch of ch-3. Break color B.

Round 5: Join color C to any ch-3 corner sp, ch 3 (counts as 1dc), [2dc, ch 3, 3dc] in same sp, *ch 1, skip next 2dc, 1dc in next dc, ch 1, 1dc in next 6dc, ch 1, 1dc in next dc, ch 1, skip next 2dc**, [3dc, ch 3, 3dc] in next ch-3 sp; rep from * twice more and from * to ** once again, join with sl st in 3rd ch of ch-3.

Round 6: Sl st in next 2dc and in next ch-3 sp, ch 3 (counts as 1dc), [2dc, ch 3, 3dc] in same sp, *ch 1, skip next 2dc, 1dc in next dc, [ch 1, 1dc in next dc] twice, ch 1, skip next dc, 1dc in next dc, [ch 1, 1dc in next dc] twice, ch 1**, [3dc, ch 3, 3dc] in next ch-3 sp; rep from * twice more and from * to ** once again, join with sl st in 3rd ch of ch-3.

Round 7: Sl st in next 2dc and in next ch-3 sp, ch 3 (counts as 1dc), [2dc, ch 3, 3dc] in same sp, *1dc in each of next 3dc, [ch 1, 1dc in next dc] four times, [1dc in next dc, ch 1] four times, 1dc in each of next 3dc**, [3dc, ch 3, 3dc] in next ch-3 sp; rep from * twice more and from * to ** once again, join with sl st in 3rd ch of ch-3. Break color C.

Round 8: Join color B to any ch-3 corner sp, ch 3 (counts as 1dc), [2dc, ch 3, 3dc] in same sp, *ch 1, skip next 2dc, 1dc in next dc, [ch 1, 1dc in next dc] 4 times, [1dc in next dc, ch 1] 4 times, 1dc in each of next 4dc, ch 1**, [3dc, ch 3, 3dc] in next ch-3 sp; rep from * twice more and from * to ** once again, join with sl st in 3rd ch of ch-3. Break color B.

Round 9: Join color A to any dc from previous round, ch 2, 1hdc in every dc and ch-1 sp from previous round, working [1hdc, 1dc, 1hdc] in each ch-3 corner sp, join with a sl st in 2nd ch of ch-2.

Fasten off and weave in ends.

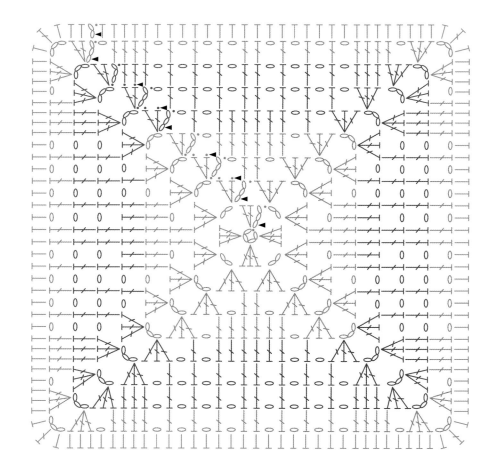

Pineapple Lace

See page 18

A=Bleached
B=Shell

Foundation ring: Using color A, work 4 ch and join with sl st to form a ring.

Round 1: Ch 3 (counts as 1dc), 2dc in ring, [ch 3, 3dc in ring] 3 times, ch 3, join with sl st in 3rd ch of ch-3.

Round 2: Sl st in next 2dc and in ch-3 sp, ch 3 (counts as 1dc), [2dc, ch 3, 3dc] in same sp, ch 1, *[3dc, ch 3, 3dc] in next ch-3 corner sp, ch 1; rep from * twice more, join with sl st in 3rd ch of ch-3.

Round 3: Sl st in next 2dc and ch-3 corner sp, ch 3 (counts as 1dc), [1dc, ch 3, 2dc] in same sp, *ch 2, [(1dc, ch 1) 5 times, 1dc in next ch-1 sp, ch 2**, [2dc, ch 3, 2dc] in next ch-3 sp; rep

from * twice more, then from * to ** again, join with sl st in 3rd ch of ch-3.

Round 4: Sl st in next 2dc and ch-3 corner sp, ch 3 (counts as 1dc), [1dc, ch 3, 2dc] in same sp, *1dc in next 2dc, ch 2, [1sc in next ch-1 sp, ch 3] 4 times, 1sc in next ch-1 sp, ch 2, 1dc in next 2dc**, [2dc, ch 3, 2dc] in ch-3 sp; rep from * twice more, then from * to ** once again, join with sl st in 3rd ch of ch-3. Break color A.

Round 5: Join color B to any ch-3 corner sp, ch 3 (counts as 1dc), 1dc in same sp, *1dc in next 4dc, ch 2, 1sc in next ch-1 sp, [ch 3, 1sc in next ch-1 sp] 3 times, ch 2, 1dc in next 4dc**,

[2dc, ch 3, 2dc] in next ch-3 sp; rep from * twice more, then from * to ** once again, 2dc in ch-3 sp, ch 3, join with sl st in 3rd ch of ch-3.

Round 6: Ch 3 (counts as 1dc), 1dc in same sp, *1dc in next 6dc, ch 2, [1sc in next ch-3 sp, ch 3] twice, 1sc in next ch-3 sp, ch 2, 1dc in next 6dc**, [2dc, ch 3, 2dc] in next ch-3 sp; rep from * twice more, then from * to ** once again, 2dc in ch-3 sp, ch 3, join with sl st in 3rd ch of ch-3.

Round 7: Ch 3 (counts as 1dc), 1dc in same sp, *1dc in next 8dc, ch 2, 1sc in next ch-3 sp, ch 3, 1sc in next ch-3 sp, ch 2, 1dc in next 8dc**, [2dc, ch 3,

2dc] in next ch-3 sp; rep from * twice more, then from * to ** once again, 2dc in ch-3 sp, ch 3, join with sl st in 3rd ch of ch-3.

Round 8: Ch 2 (counts as 1hdc), 1hdc in same sp, *1hdc in next 10dc, ch 3, 1sc in next ch-3 sp, ch 3, 1hdc in next 10dc**, [2hdc, ch 3, 2hdc] in next ch-3 sp; rep from * twice more, then from * to ** once again, 2hdc in ch-3 sp, ch 3, join with sl st in 2nd ch of ch-2.

Fasten off and weave in ends.

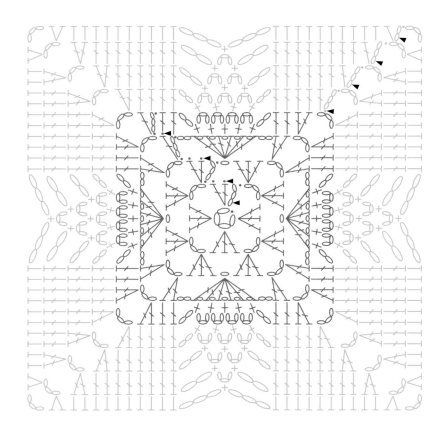

Butterfly Garden

See page 17

A=Rose
B=Bleached
C=Shell

Foundation ring: Using color A, ch 4 and join with sl st in first ch to form a ring.

Round 1: Ch 3 (counts as 1dc), 15dc into the ring, change to color B when joining with sl st in 3rd ch of ch-3.

Round 2: Ch 3 (counts as 1dc), [1dc, ch 2, 2dc] in same st, *1dc in each of next 3dc**, [2dc, ch 2, 2dc] in next dc; rep from * twice more and from * to ** once again, join with sl st in 3rd ch of ch-3. Break color B.

Round 3: Join color C in any 2ch-sp, ch 3, [1dc, ch 2, 2dc] in same sp, *ch 6, skip next 7dc**, [2dc, ch 2, 2dc] in next corner 2ch-sp; rep from * twice more and from * to ** once again, join with sl st in 3rd ch of ch-3.

Round 4: Sl st in next dc and in next 2ch-sp, ch 3, [1dc, ch 2, 2dc] in same sp, *1dc in each of next 2dc, ch 6, skip next 6ch-sp, 1dc in each of next 2dc**, [2dc, ch 2, 2dc] in next 2ch-sp; rep from * twice more and from * to ** once again, join with sl st in 3rd ch of ch-3.

Round 5: Sl st in next dc and in next 2ch-sp, ch 3, [1dc, ch 2, 2dc] in same sp, *1dc in each of next 4dc, ch 3, working over the ch-loops from Rounds 3 and 4, 1tr in 4th dc of next skipped 7 dc in Round 2, ch 3, 1dc in each of next 4dc**, [2dc, ch 2, 2dc] in next 2ch-sp; rep from * twice more and from * to ** once again, join with sl st in 3rd ch of ch-3.

Round 6: Sl st in next dc and in next 2ch-sp, ch 1, [1sc, ch 2, 1sc] in same sp, 1sc in each of next 6dc, 3sc in next 3ch-sp, 1sc in next tr, 3sc in next 3ch-sp, 1sc in each of next 6dc; rep from * to end of round, join with sl st in first sc. Break color C.

Round 7: Join color B in any 2ch-sp, ch 3, [1dc, ch 2, 2dc] in same sp, *ch 6, skip next 7sc, 1dc in each of next 7sc, ch 6, skip next 7sc**, [2dc, ch 2, 2dc] in next corner 2ch-sp; rep from * twice and from * to ** once more, join with sl st in 3rd ch of ch-3.

Round 8: Sl st in next dc and in next 2ch-sp, ch 3, [1dc, ch 2, 2dc] in same sp, *1dc in each of next 2dc, ch 6, skip next 6ch-sp, 1dc in each of next 7dc, ch 6, skip next 6ch-sp, 1dc in each of next 2dc**, [2dc, ch 2, 2dc] in next corner 2ch-sp; rep from * twice and from * to ** once more, join with sl st in 3rd ch of ch-3.

Round 9: Sl st in next dc and in next 2ch-sp, ch 3, [1dc, ch 2, 2dc] in same sp, *1dc in each of next 4dc, ch 3, working over the ch-loops from Rounds 7 and 8, 1tr in 4th sc of next skipped 7sc in Round 6, ch 3, 1dc in each of next 7dc, ch 3, working over the ch-loops from Rounds 7 and 8, 1tr in the 4th sc of next skipped 7sc in Round 6, ch 3, 1dc in each of next 4dc**, [2dc, ch 2, 2dc] in next corner 2ch-sp; rep from * twice more and from * to ** once again, join with sl st in 3rd ch of ch-3. Break color B.

Round 10: Join color A to any ch-2 corner sp, ch 1, [1sc, ch 2, 1sc] in same sp, 1sc in each of next 6dc, 3sc in next 3ch-sp, 1sc in next tr, 3sc in next 3ch-sp, 1sc in each of next 7dc, 3sc in next 3ch-sp, 1sc in next tr, 3sc in next 3ch-sp, 1sc in each of next 6dc; rep from * to end of round, join with sl st in first sc.

Fasten off and weave in ends.

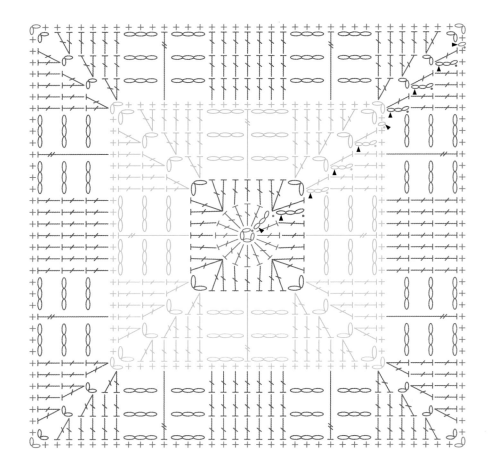

Isabella   See page 16

A=Shell Pink
B=Bleached
C=Rose

SPECIAL STITCHES

Dc2tog (work two double sts tog): [(Yoh) twice, draw up a loop in next st, (yoh, pull through 2 loops on hook) twice] twice, yoh and draw through all 3 loops on hook.

Dc3tog (work three double sts tog): [(Yoh) twice, draw up a loop in next st, (yoh, pull through 2 loops on hook) twice] 3 times, yoh and draw through all 4 loops on hook.

Foundation ring: Using color A, ch 6 and join with sl st in first ch to form a ring.

Round 1: Ch 1, 16sc into ring, change to color B when joining with sl st to first sc.

Round 2: Ch 4 (counts as 1dc, ch 1), 1dc in same st, ch 1, skip next sc, *[1dc, ch 1, 1dc] in next sc, ch 1, skip next sc; rep from * a further 6 times, join with sl st in 3rd ch of ch-3.

Round 3: Sl st in next 1ch-sp, dc2tog in same sp, ch 5, skip next 1ch-sp, *dc3tog in next 1ch-sp, ch 5, skip next 1ch-sp; rep from * to end of round, join with sl st in top of dc2tog. Break color B.

Round 4: Join color A to any 5ch-sp, ch 3 [counts as 1dc], 7dc in same ch-5 sp, 8dc in each ch-5 sp around, change to color B when joining with sl st in 3rd ch of ch-3.

Round 5: Ch 4 [counts as 1dc and ch 1], skip next dc, [1dc in next dc, ch 1, skip next st] around, join with sl st in 3rd ch of ch-4. (32 dc)

Round 6: Join color C to any 1ch-sp, ch 3, [1dc, ch 1, 2dc] in same 1ch-sp, *ch 1, skip next 1ch-sp**; [2dc, ch 1, 2dc] in next 1ch-sp; rep from * a further 14 times; rep from * to ** once more, join with sl st in 3rd ch of ch-3.

Round 7: Sl st into next dc and next 1ch-sp, ch 3, [2dc, ch 1, 3dc] in same 1ch-sp, *ch 1, skip next 1ch-sp **, [3dc, ch 1, 3dc] in next 1ch-sp (shell made); rep from * a further 14 times; rep from * to ** once more, join with sl st in 3rd ch of ch-3. Break color C.

Round 8: Join color A to 1ch-sp at center of any corner shell, ch 3 (counts as 1dc), [2dc, ch 3, 3dc] in same sp, (corner made), skip next ch-1 sp, *[ch 3, 1sc in ch-1 sp, ch 3, 1hdc in next ch-1 sp] 3 times, ch 3**, [3dc, ch 3, 3dc] in next 1ch-sp of next shell; rep from * twice more and from * to ** once again, join with sl st in 3rd ch of ch-3.

Round 9: Ch 1, 1sc in each of next 3dc, [2sc, ch 3, 2sc] in next ch-3 sp, 1sc in each of next 3sc, 3sc in each of next seven 3ch-sps; rep from * to end of round, join with sl st to first sc.

Fasten off and weave in ends.

 Filet Flower Square   See page 17

A=Shell
B=Bleached
C=Greengage

Foundation chain: Using color A, work 6 ch and join with sl st to form a ring.

Round 1: Ch 1, 12sc in the ring, join with sl st to first sc. (12 sc)

Round 2: Ch 3 (counts as 1dc), 4dc in same place, [ch 3, skip 2sc, 5dc in next sc] 3 times, ch 3, join with sl st in 3rd ch of ch-3.

Round 3: Ch 3 (counts as 1dc), 1dc in next dc, 5dc in next dc, 1dc in each of next 2dc, *ch 3, skip 3ch, 1dc in each of next 2dc, 5dc in next dc, 1dc in next 2dc; rep from * twice more, ch 3, skip 3ch, join with sl st in 3rd ch of ch-3.

Round 4: Ch 3 (counts as 1dc), 1dc in next 3dc, 5dc in next dc, 1dc in each of next 4dc, *ch 3, skip 3ch, 1dc in each of next 4dc, 5dc in next dc, 1dc in next 4dc; rep from * twice more, ch 3, skip 3ch, join with sl st in 3rd ch of ch-3 and change to color B.

Round 5: Ch 3, 1dc in next 4dc, *dc2tog over next 2dc, ch 5, dc2tog over last dc and next dc, 1dc in each of next 3dc, dc2tog over next 2dc, ch 5, skip 3ch**, dc2tog over next 2dc, 1dc in each of next 3dc; rep from *

twice more, then * to ** once, skip 3ch, join with sl st to first dc.

Round 6: Ch 3, 1dc in next 2dc, *dc2tog over next 2 sts, ch 3, skip 2ch, 1dc in next ch, ch 3, skip 1ch, 1dc in next ch, ch 3, skip 2ch, dc2tog over next 2 sts, 1dc in next dc, dc2tog over next 2 sts, ch 3, skip 2ch, 1dc in next ch, ch 3, skip 2ch**, dc2tog over next 2 sts; rep from * twice more, then * to ** once, join with sl st to first dc and change to color C.

Round 7: Ch 4 (counts as 1dc and ch 1), skip first 2dc, 1dc in dc2tog, ch 1, skip 1ch, 1dc in next ch, ch 1, skip 1ch, 1dc in next dc, *ch 5, skip 3ch, 1dc in next dc, [ch 1, skip 1 st, 1dc in next st] 10 times, ch 5, skip 3ch, 1dc in next dc, [ch 1, skip 1 st, 1dc in next st] 6 times, ch 1, skip 1 st, join with sl st in 3rd ch of ch-4.

Round 8: Ch 3 (counts as 1dc), *1dc in every dc and ch-1 sp to corner, [2dc, ch 3, 2dc] in every ch-5 sp; rep from * a further 3 times, 1dc in every remaining ch-2 sp and dc to end of round, join with a sl st to 3rd of ch-3.

Fasten off and weave in ends.

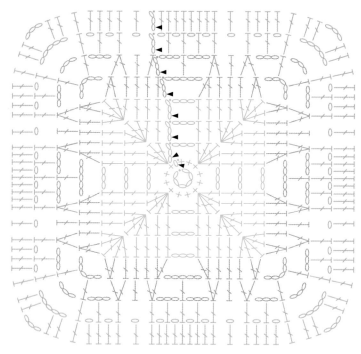

 ## Popcorns & Lace   *See page 19*

A=Dawn Gray

 ## Fleur   *See page 19*

A=Greengage

SPECIAL STITCHES

Beg cl (Beginning cluster): Ch 3, [(yarn round hook) twice, insert hook, yarn round hook, draw a loop through, yarn round hook, draw through 2 loops] 3 times in same stitch or space, yarn round hook, draw through all 4 loops on hook.

Cl (Cluster): [(Yarn round hook) twice, insert hook, yarn round hook, draw a loop through, yarn round hook, draw through 2 loops] 4 times in same stitch or space, yarn round hook, draw through all 5 loops on hook

Beg PC (Beginning popcorn): Ch 3 (counts as 1dc), 4dc in same stitch or space, remove hook from loop, insert hook in 3rd ch of beg ch-3, pick up the dropped loop and pull yarn through.

PC (Popcorn): 5dc in same stitch or space, remove hook from loop, insert hook into first of 5dc just made, pick up the dropped loop and pull yarn through.

Foundation chain: Using color A, ch 8 and join with sl st in first ch to form a ring.

Round 1: Beg cl in ring, *ch 3, cl into ring, ch 5**, cl into ring; rep from * twice more and from * to ** once again, join with sl st in 3rd ch of ch-3.

Round 2: Sl st in center of next ch-3 sp, ch 1, 1sc in same sp, *9dc in next ch-5 sp, 1sc in next ch-3 sp; rep from * to end of round, omitting last sc and join with sl st in first sc.

Round 3: Beg PC in first sc, *ch 2, skip next 2dc, 1dc in next dc, ch2, skip next dc, [2sc, ch3, 2sc] in next dc, ch 2, skip next dc, 1dc in next dc, ch 2, skip next 2dc**, 1PC in next sc; rep from * twice more and from * to ** once again, join with sl st in top of first PC.

Round 4: Ch 3 (counts as 1dc), *[2dc in ch-2 sp, 1dc in next dc] twice, 1dc in next dc, [2dc, ch 3, 2dc] in next ch-3 sp, 1dc in next dc, [1dc in next dc, 2dc in next ch-2 sp] twice**, 1dc in next PC; rep from * twice more and from * to ** once again, join with sl st in 3rd ch of ch-3.

Round 5: Ch 6 (counts as 1dc, ch3), 1dc in same st at base of ch 6, *skip next 2dc, 1dc in each of next 3dc, 1PC in next dc, 1dc in each of next 3dc, [2dc, ch 3, 2dc] in next ch-3 sp, 1dc in each of next 3dc, 1PC in next dc, 1dc in each of next 3dc, skip next 2dc**, [1dc, ch 3, 1dc] in next dc; rep from * twice more and from * to ** once again, join with sl st in 3rd ch of ch-6.

Round 6: Sl st to 2nd ch of next ch-3 sp, ch 4 (counts as 1dc, ch 1), skip next dc, *1dc in next dc, [ch 1, skip next st, 1dc in next st] 4 times, [2dc, ch 3, 2dc] in next ch-3 sp, [1dc in next dc, ch1, skip next st] 5 times**, 1dc in 2nd ch of next ch-3 sp, ch 1; rep from * twice more and from * to ** once again, join with sl st in 3rd ch of ch-4.
Fasten off and weave in ends.

Foundation ring: Using color A, ch6 and join with sl st in first ch to form a ring.

Round 1: Ch 1, [1sc, ch 3, 1tr, ch 3, 1tr, ch 3] 4 times into ring, join with sl st in first sc. (4 petals made)

Round 2: Sl st back in last tr made (to the left of any ch-3 sp), ch1, 1sc in same tr, *1sc in 3rd ch of next ch-3 sp, 2dc in next sc between petals, 1sc in 3rd ch of ch-3 sp, 1sc in next tr, 1sc in first ch of next ch-3 sp, ch 3, skip next ch, 1sc in next ch**, 1sc in next tr; rep from * twice more and from * to ** once again, join with sl st to first sc.

Round 3: Ch 3 (counts as 1dc), 1dc in each of next 6 sts, *[1dc, ch 3, 1dc] in next ch-3 sp (corner made)**, 1dc in each of next 8 sts; rep from * twice more and from * to ** once again, 1dc in next st, join with sl st in 3rd ch of ch-3.

Round 4: Sl st in next ch-3 corner sp, ch 3 (counts as 1dc), 2dc in same sp (half corner made), *[ch 2, skip next 2dc, 1dc in each of next 2dc] twice, ch 2, skip next 2dc**, [3dc, ch3, 3dc] in next ch-3 corner sp (corner made); rep from * twice more and from * to ** once again, 3dc in same ch-3 sp as first half corner, ch 3, join with sl st in 3rd ch of ch-3.

Round 5: Sl st in next ch-3 corner sp, ch 3 (counts as 1dc), 2dc in same sp (half corner made), *1dc in each of next 3dc, 2dc in ch-2 sp, [1dc in each of next 2dc, 2dc in next ch-2 sp] twice, 1dc in each of next 3dc**, [3dc, ch 3, 3dc] in next ch-3 sp (corner made); rep from * twice more and from * to ** once again, 3dc in same ch-3 sp as first half corner, ch 3, join with sl st in 3rd ch of ch-3.
Fasten off and weave in ends.

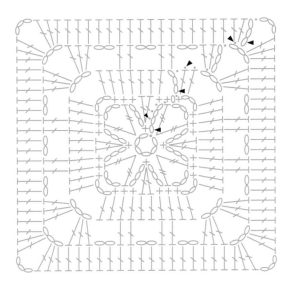

Picot Rose

See page 17

A=Dawn Gray

SPECIAL STITCHES

P (Picot): Ch4, sl st into 4th ch from hook.

Foundation ring: Using color A, ch4 and join with sl st in first ch to form a ring.

Round 1: Ch5 (counts as 1dc, ch2), [1dc, ch2] 7 times into ring, join with sl st in 3rd ch of ch-5. (8ch-2 sps, 8dc)

Round 2: Sl st in next ch-2 sp, ch4 (counts as 1dc, ch1), [picot, ch1] twice, [1dc in next ch-2 sp, [ch1, picot] twice, ch1] 7 times, join with sl st in 3rd ch ch-4.

Round 3: Sl st in next ch-1 sp between 2 picots, ch1, 1sc in same sp, *ch7, skip 2 picots**, 1sc in next ch-1 sp between 2 picots; rep from * 6 times more, then from * to ** once again, join with sl st in first sc.

Round 4: Sl st in next ch-7 sp, ch1, [1sc, 1hdc, 9dc, 1hdc, 1sc] in each ch-7 sp to end of round, join with sl st to first sc.

Round 5: Sl st in to next sp between 2sc in Round 4, ch4 (counts as 1tr), 1tr in same sp, (half corner made), *ch3, skip next 4 sts, 1sc in each of next 5dc, skip next 8 sts, 1sc in each of next 5dc, ch3 skip next 4 sts**, [2tr, ch3, 2tr] in space between last skipped and next sc (corner made); rep from * twice more and from * to ** once again, 2tr in same sp as first half corner, ch3, join with sl st in 3rd ch of ch-3.

Round 6: Ch1, 1sc in first tr, *[3sc in next ch-3 sp, 1sc in each of next 5sc] twice, 3sc in next ch-3 sp, 1sc in each of next 2tr, [2sc, ch3, 2sc] in next ch-3 sp**, 1sc in each of next 2tr; rep from * twice more and from * to ** once again, join with sl st in first sc.

Fasten off and weave in ends.

Popcorn Square

See page 18

A=Greengage

SPECIAL STITCHES

Beg PC (Beginning Popcorn): Ch2 (counts as 1hdc), 4hdc in same stitch or space, remove hook from loop, insert hook in 2ch of beg ch-2, pick up the dropped loop and pull yarn through.

PC (Popcorn): 5hdc in same stitch or space, remove hook from loop, insert hook into first of 5hdc just made, pick up the dropped loop and pull yarn through.

Foundation ring: Using A, ch10 and join with sl st in first ch to form a ring.

Round 1: Ch1, 16sc into ring, join with sl st in first sc. (16 sc)

Round 2: Beg PC in first sc, ch3, skip next sc, [PC in next sc, ch3, skip next sc] 7 times, join with a sl st in beg PC. (8PC, 8ch-3 sps)

Round 3: Sl st in top of next PC, ch1, 1sc in same st, [(ch6, 1sc) in each PC] 7 times, ch3, join with 1dc in first sc.

Round 4: Ch3, 4dc in same sp (half corner), *ch3, 1sc in next ch-6 sp, ch3**, [5dc, ch3, 5dc] in next ch-6 sp (corner); rep from * twice more and from * to ** once again, join with sl st in 3rd ch of ch-3.

Round 5: Ch7 (counts as 1dc, ch4), *1sc in next ch-3 sp, ch3, 1sc in next ch-3 sp, ch4**, [5dc, ch3, 5dc] in next ch-3 sp (corner made), ch4; rep from * twice more and from * to ** once again, [5dc, ch3, 4dc] in next ch-3 sp, join with sl st in 3rd ch of ch-6.

Round 6: Sl st back to last ch-3 corner sp, ch3, 2dc in same sp (half corner made), *[ch2, 3dc] in each of next ch-3 sp, ch2**, [3dc, ch3, 3dc] in next ch-3 sp (corner made); rep from * twice more and from * to ** once again, join with sl st in 3rd ch of ch-3.

Fasten off and weave in ends.

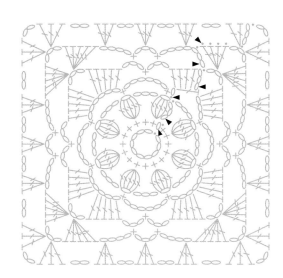

Sunshine Lace

See page 19

A=Lavender

Foundation ring: Using color A, work 8 ch and join with sl st in first ch to form a ring.

Round 1: Ch 1, 12sc in ring, join with sl st to first sc. (12 sc)

Round 2: Ch 6 (counts as 1tr and 2 ch), [1tr in next st, ch 2] 11 times, join with sl st in 4th ch of ch-6. (12 spaced tr)

Round 3: Ch 5 (counts as 1dc and 2 ch), *[1sc in next ch-2 sp, ch 2] twice, [3dc, ch 2, 3dc] in next ch-2 sp, ch 2; rep from * a further 3 times omitting 1dc, ch 2 at end of last rep, join with sl st in 3rd ch of ch-5.

Round 4: Ch 1, *[1sc in next ch-2 sp, ch 2] 3 times, [3dc, ch 2, 3dc] in ch-2 corner sp, ch 2; rep from * 3 more times, join with sl st to first sc.

Round 5: Sl st in first ch-2 sp, ch 1, 1sc in same sp, ch 2, [1sc in next ch-2 sp, ch 2] twice, *[3dc, ch 2, 3dc] in ch-2 corner sp, ch 2**, [1sc in next ch-2 sp, ch 2] 4 times; rep from * twice more and from * to ** once again, 1sc in next ch-2 sp, ch 2, join with sl st to first sc.

Round 6: Sl st in next ch-2 sp, ch 3 (counts as 1dc), 1dc in same sp, 2dc in each ch-2 sp on previous round, working 1dc in each dc and [3dc, ch 2, 3dc] in each ch-2 corner sp, join with sl st in 3rd ch of ch-3.

Round 7: Ch 3 (counts as 1dc), 1dc in each dc on previous round working 5dc in each ch-2 corner sp, join with a sl st in 3rd of ch-3.

Round 8: Ch 3 (counts as 1dc), 1dc in each dc on previous round working 3dc in 3rd dc of 5dc cluster on previous round, join with sl st in 3rd ch of ch-3.

Fasten off and weave in ends.

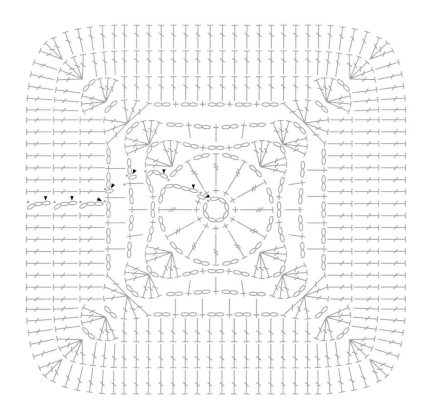

Daisy Chain Square

See page 18

A=Lavender
B=Ecru

Foundation ring: Using color A, work 5 ch and join with sl st to form a ring.

Round 1: Ch 4 (counts as 1dc and ch 1), [1dc in ring, ch 1] 7 times, sl st in 3rd ch of ch-4. (16 sts)

Round 2: Ch 4 (counts as 1dc and ch 1), [skip 1ch, 3dc in next dc, ch 1] 7 times, skip 1ch, 2dc in first ch sp, sl st in 3rd ch of ch-4. (8 groups)

Round 3: Sl st in ch-1 sp, ch 4 (counts as 1dc and ch 1), [1dc, ch 1, 1dc, ch1, 1dc] in same ch sp, *skip 3dc, [1dc, ch 1] 3 times in next ch sp, 1dc in same ch-sp; rep from * a further 6 times, join with sl st in 3rd ch of ch-4. Break color A. (8 shell groups)

Round 4: Join color B to 3rd ch sp of any shell group, ch 2, dc2tog over sp between next [2dc and first ch sp of next shell], *ch 3, sl st in next ch sp of same shell, ch 3, dc3tog over next [ch sp of same shell, sp between next 2dc and first ch sp of next shell]; rep from * a further 6 times, ch 3, sl st in next ch sp, ch 3, sl st in dc2tog at start of round.

Round 5: Ch 5, [1dc, ch 2] 3 times in dc2tog, 1dc in same place, *skip [ch 3, 1 sl st, ch 3], [1dc, ch 2] 4 times in dc3tog, 1dc in same place; rep from * a further 6 times, sl st in 3rd ch of ch-5. Break color B. (8 daisies)

Round 6: Rejoin color A to 4th ch sp of any daisy, ch 3 (counts as 1dc), [1dtr between next 2dc with 1tr in first ch-2 sp of next daisy], ch 6, 1sc in next ch sp, ch 1, 1sc in next ch sp, ch 2, dc3tog over [last ch sp of daisy, sp between 2dc and first ch sp of next daisy, ch 2, 1sc in next ch sp, ch 1, 1sc in next ch sp, ch6**, [1tr in last ch sp of daisy, tog with 1dtr between next 2dc and 1tr in first ch sp of next daisy]; rep from * twice more and then from * to ** once again, sl st tog the dtr and tr at start of round.

Round 7: Ch 5, 2dc in dc2tog, *ch 3, 1sc in ch-6 sp, ch 3 1dc in ch-1 sp, ch 3, 1sc in dc3tog, ch 3, 1dc in ch-1 sp, ch 3, 1sc in ch-6 sp, ch 3**, [2dc, 2ch, 2dc] in

3 sts tog at corner; rep from * twice more, then from * to ** once again, 1dc in same place as beg of round sl st in 3rd ch of ch-5.

Round 8: Ch 3 (counts as 1dc), *1dc in next dc, [1dc, ch 2, 1dc] in ch-2 corner sp, 1dc in next dc, 3dc in every ch-3 sp, 1dc in next dc; rep from * to end of round, omitting last dc, join with sl st to 3rd ch of ch-3.

Round 9: Ch 3 (counts as 1dc), 1dc in every dc of previous round, working 3dc in every ch-2 corner sp.

Fasten off and weave in ends.

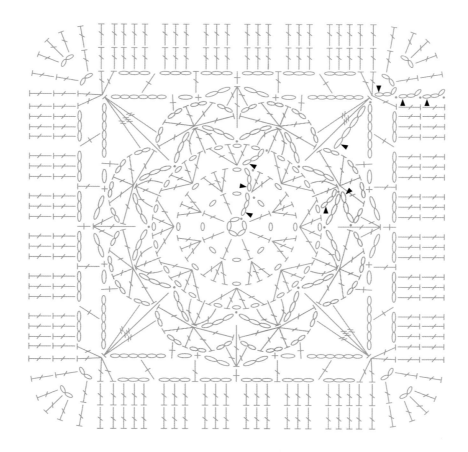

✪✪✪ *Spiraling Lace*

See page 16

A=Lavender
B=Nightshade

Foundation ring: Using color A, work 5 ch and join with sl st to form a ring.

Round 1: *Ch 3, 3sc in ring; rep from * a further 3 times, placing a marker in the last sc of the round. Move the marker up as you get to the end of each following round.

Round 2: *Ch 4, 2sc in next ch-3 sp, 1sc in each of the first 2 sc, skip next sc; rep from * a further 3 times.

Round 3: *Ch 4, 2sc in next ch-4 sp, 1sc in each of next 3 sc, skip next sc; rep from * a further 3 times.

Round 4: *Ch 4, 2sc in next ch-4 sp, 1sc in each of next 4 sc, skip next sc; rep from * a further 3 times.

Round 5: *Ch 4, 2sc in next ch-4 sp, 1sc in each of next 5 sc, skip next sc;

rep from * a further 3 times.

Round 6: *Ch 4, 2sc in next ch-4 sp, 1sc in each of next 6 sc, skip next sc; rep from * a further 3 times.

Round 7: *Ch 5, 2sc in next ch-4 sp, 1sc in each of next 7 sc, skip next sc; rep from * a further 3 times.

Round 8: *Ch 5, 2sc in next ch-5 sp, 1sc in each of next 8 sc, skip next sc; rep from * a further 3 times.

Round 9: *Ch 5, 2sc in next ch-5 sp, 1sc in each of next 9 sc, skip next sc; rep from * a further 3 times.

Round 10: *Ch 5, 2sc in next ch-5 sp, 1sc in each of next 10 sc, skip next sc; rep from * a further 3 times.

Round 11: *Ch 5, 2sc in next ch-5 sp, 1sc in each of next 11 sc, skip next sc;

rep from * a further 3 times.

Round 12: *Ch 8, skip next ch-5 sp and next 2sc, 1sc in each of next 10 sc, skip next sc; rep from * a further 3 times.

Round 13: *Ch 4, [1sc, ch 4, 1sc] in next ch-8 sp, ch 4, skip next 2sc, 1sc in each of the next 7 sc, skip next sc; rep from * a further 3 times.

Round 14: *Ch 4, 1sc in next ch-4 sp, ch 4, [1sc, ch 4, 1sc] in next ch-4 sp (corner made), ch 4, 1sc in next ch-4 sp, ch 4, skip next 2sc, 1sc in each of next 4 sc, skip next sc; rep from * a further 3 times.

Round 15: *4sc in each of next 2 ch-4 sp, [3sc, ch 2, 3sc] in next ch-4 sp (corner made), 4sc in next 2 ch-4 sp,

1sc in each of next 4 sc; rep from * a further 3 times, join with sl st in next sc.

Round 16: Ch 3 (counts as 1dc), 1dc in every sc of previous Round, working (3dc, ch2, 3dc) in each ch-2 corner sp, changing to color B when joining with sl st to 3rd ch of ch-3. Break color A.

Round 17: Ch 1, 1sc in every dc of previous Round, working 3sc in center dc of each 3dc corner, changing to color A when joining with sl st to first sc. Break color B.

Round 18: Ch 1, 1sc in every sc of previous Round, working 3sc in center sc of each 3sc corner, join with sl st to first sc.

Fasten off and weave in ends.

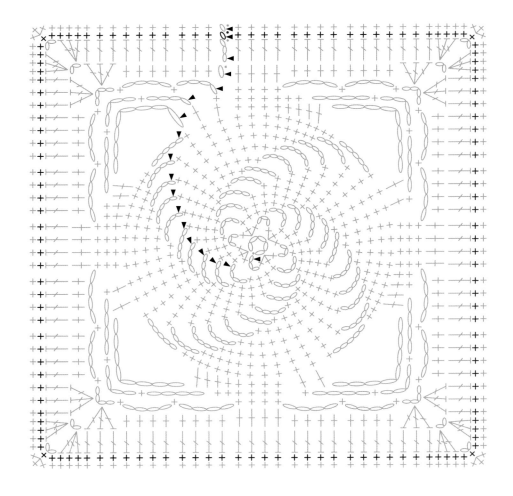

⭐ Double Filet Mesh

See page 19

A=Bleached
B=Shell
C=Greengage

Foundation ring: Using color A, work 6 ch and join with sl st to form a ring.

Round 1: Ch 3 (counts as 1dc), 2dc in ring, ch 2, [3dc in ring, ch 2] 3 times, join with sl st in 3rd ch of ch-3.

Round 2: Sl st in next 2dc and next ch-2 sp, ch 3 (counts as 1dc), [1dc, ch 3, 2dc] in same sp, *[1dc in next dc, ch 1] twice, 1dc in next dc, [2dc, ch 3, 2dc] in next ch-2 sp, 2dc in next dc, 1dc in next dc, 2dc in next dc**, 1dc in next dc, [2dc, ch 3, 2dc] in next ch-2 sp; rep from * to **, join with sl st in 3rd ch of ch-3.

Round 3: Sl st in next dc and next ch-3 sp, ch 3 (counts as 1dc), [1dc, ch 3, 2dc] in same sp, *ch 1, skip next dc, 1dc in next dc, [ch 1, 1dc in next dc] four times, 1dc in next dc, ch 1, skip next dc, [2dc, ch 3, 2dc in next ch-2 sp], 1dc in next dc, 2dc in next dc, 1dc in each of next 5dc, 2dc in next dc, 1dc in next dc**, [2dc, ch 3, 2dc in next ch-2 sp]; rep from * to **, join with sl st in 3rd ch of ch-3. Break color A.

Round 4: Join color B to next ch-3 sp, ch 3 (counts as 1dc), [1dc, ch 3, 2dc] in same sp, *[ch 1, 1dc in next dc] eight times, ch 1, skip next dc, [2dc, ch 3, 2dc in next ch-2 sp], 1dc in next dc, 2dc in next dc, 1dc in each of next 11dc, 2dc in next dc, 1dc in next dc**, [2dc, ch 3, 2dc in next ch-2 sp];

rep from * to **, join with sl st in 3rd ch ch-3.

Round 5: Sl st in next dc and next ch-3 sp, ch 3 (counts as 1dc), [1dc, ch 3, 2dc] in same sp, *[ch 1, 1dc in next dc] 11 times, ch 1, skip next dc, [2dc, ch 3, 2dc in next ch-2 sp], 1dc in next dc, 2dc in next dc, 1dc in each of next 17dc, 2dc in next dc, 1dc in next dc**, [2dc, ch 3, 2dc] in next ch-2 sp; rep from * to **, join with sl st in 3rd ch of ch-3. Break color B.

Round 6: Join color C to next ch-3 sp, ch 3 (counts as 1dc), [1dc, ch 3, 2dc] in same sp, *[ch 1, 1dc in next dc] 14 times, ch 1, skip next dc, [2dc, ch 3, 2dc in next ch-2 sp], 1dc in next dc, 2dc in next dc, 1dc in each of next 23dc, 2dc in next dc, 1dc in next dc**, [2dc, ch 3, 2dc] in next ch-2 sp; rep from * to **, join with sl st in 3rd ch of ch-3.

Round 7: Sl st in next dc and next ch-3 sp, ch 3 (counts as 1dc), [1dc, ch 3, 2dc] in same sp, *[ch 1, 1dc in next dc] 17 times, ch 1, skip next dc, [2dc, ch 3, 2dc] in next ch-2 sp, 1dc in next dc, 2dc in next dc, 1dc in each of next 29dc, 2dc in next dc, 1dc in next dc**, [2dc, ch 3, 2dc] in next ch-2 sp; rep from * to **, join with sl st in 3rd ch of ch-3.

Fasten off and weave in ends.

⭐ Filet Mesh Center

See page 18

A=Greengage
B=Bleached
C=Shell

Foundation chain: Using color A, work 12ch.

Row 1: 1dc in 6th ch from hook, [ch 1, skip next ch, 1dc in next ch] 3 times, turn. (4 ch-1 sp)

Row 2: Ch4, (counts as 1dc and ch 1), skip next ch-1 sp, [1dc, ch 1] in each of next 3dc, skip next ch, 1dc in 5th ch of ch-6, turn.

Rows 3-4: Ch 4, (counts as 1dc and ch 1), skip next ch-1 sp, [1dc, ch 1] in each of next 3dc, skip next ch, 1dc in 3rd ch of ch-4, turn.

Round 5: Ch 1, 2sc in first ch-1 sp (half corner made), [1sc in next dc, 1sc in next ch-1 sp] twice, 1sc in next dc, *[2sc, ch 2, 2sc] in next corner sp, 5sc worked across next 2 row-end sts**, [2sc, ch 2, 2sc] in next corner sp, working across opposite side of foundation ch, [1sc in next ch at base of dc, 1sc in next ch-1 sp] twice, 1sc in next ch at base of dc; rep from * to ** once more, 2sc in next corner sp, ch-2, join with sl st to first sc. Break color A.

Round 6: Join color B to any ch-2 corner sp, ch 3 (counts as 1dc), [2dc, ch 3, 3dc] in same sp, *ch 4, skip next 4sc, 1dc in next sc, ch 4, skip next 4sc**, [3dc, ch 3, 3dc] in next ch-2 corner sp; rep from * twice more, then from * to ** once again, join with sl st

in 3rd ch of ch-3.

Round 7: Sl st in next 2dc and next ch-3 sp, ch 3 (counts as 1dc), [2dc, ch 3, 3dc] in same sp, *ch 4, skip next 4sc, 3dc in next dc, ch 4, skip next 4sc**, [3dc, ch 3, 3dc] in next ch-2 corner sp; rep from * twice more, then from * to ** once again, join with sl st in 3rd ch of ch-3. Break color B.

Round 8: Join color C to any ch-3 corner sp, ch 3 (counts as 1dc), [2dc, ch 3, 3dc] in same sp, *ch 2, 1dc in first of ch-4 from previous round, ch 2, 1dc in next dc, ch 2, skip next dc, 1dc in next dc, ch 2, 1dc in 4th ch of ch-4 from previous round, ch 2**, [3dc, ch 3, 3dc] in next ch-2 corner sp; rep from * twice more, then from * to ** once again, join with sl st in 3rd ch of ch-3.

Round 9: Sl st in next 2dc and next ch-3 sp, ch 3 (counts as 1dc), [2dc, ch 3, 3dc] in same sp, *ch 3, 3dc in each of 4dc, ch 3**, [3dc, ch 3, 3dc] in next ch-2 corner sp; rep from * twice more, then from * to ** once again, join with sl st in 3rd ch of ch-3.

Round 10: Ch 3 (counts as 1dc), 1dc in every dc and 3tr in every ch-3 sp along sides and [1dc, 1tr, 1dc] in ch-3 corner sps, join with sl st in 3rd ch of ch-3.

Fasten off and weave in ends.

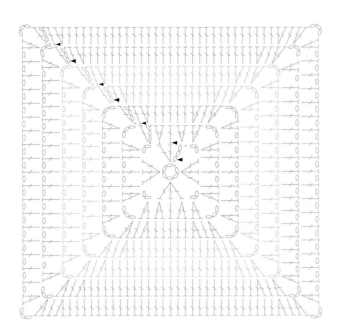

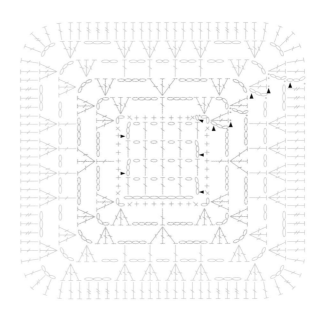

⭐ *Spinner*

See page 20

A=Persimmon
B=Bleached
C=Aqua
D=Winsor

Foundation chain: Using color A, work 4 ch and join with sl st to form a ring.

Round 1: Ch 3 (counts as 1dc), 15dc in ring, join with sl st in 3rd ch of ch-3.

Round 2: Sl st in space between ch 3 and first dc from previous row, ch 3 (counts as 1dc), 1dc in same sp, 2dc in each remaining space between dc, break color A and join color B with sl st in 3rd ch of ch-3.

Round 3: Ch 3 (counts as 1dc), 1dc in same place, 1dc in next dc, [2dc in next dc, 1dc in next dc] 15 times, join with sl st in 3rd ch of ch-3. Break color B.

Round 4: Join color C to any dc, ch 4 (counts as 1tr), [2dc, ch 2, 2dc, 1tr] in same place, *skip next 2dc, 1hdc in next 2dc, 1sc in next 3dc, 1hdc in next 2dc, skip next 2dc**, [1tr, 2dc, ch 2, 2dc, 1tr] in next dc; rep from * twice more and from * to ** once again, join with sl st to 4th ch of ch-4.

Round 5: Join color D to any ch-2 corner sp, ch 3 (counts as 1dc), [2tr, ch 2, 2tr, 1dc] in same sp, *1dc in every st along side of square**, [1dc, 2tr, ch 2, 2tr, 1dc] in next ch-2 corner sp; rep from * twice more and from * to ** once again, join with sl st in 3rd ch of ch-3. Break color D.

Round 6: Join color B to any ch-2 corner sp, ch 3 (counts as 1dc), [1dc, ch 2, 2dc] in same sp, *1dc in every st along side of square**, [2dc, ch 2, 2dc] in next ch-2 corner sp; rep from * twice and from * to ** once again, join with sl st in 3rd ch of ch-3. Break color B.

Round 7: Using color A, work as Round 6, changing to color D when joining with sl st to 3rd ch of ch 3. Break color A.

Round 8: Ch 2 (counts as 1hdc), 1hdc in every dc to end of round, working [1hdc, 1dc, 1hdc] in every ch-2 corner sp, join with sl st to 2nd ch of ch-2.

Fasten off and weave in ends.

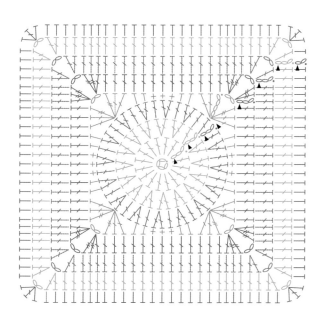

⭐ *Circle in a Square*

See page 23

A=Aqua
B=Winsor
C=Bleached
D=Persimmon

Foundation ring: Using color A, work 8 ch and join with sl st to form a ring.

Round 1: Ch 3 (counts as 1dc), 15dc in ring, changing to color B when joining with sl st in 3rd ch of ch-3.

Round 2: Ch 5 (counts as 1dc and ch 2), [1dc in next dc, ch 2] 15 times, join with sl st in 3rd ch of ch-5. Break color B.

Round 3: Join color C to any ch-2 sp, ch 3 (counts as 1dc), 2dc in same sp, ch 1, *[3dc, ch 1] in next ch-2 sp; rep from * to end of round, join with sl st in 3rd ch of ch-3. Break color C.

Round 4: Join color D to any ch-1 sp, *[ch 3, 1sc in next ch-1 sp] 3 times, ch 6 (corner-sp made), 1sc in next ch-1 sp; rep from * to end of round, join with sl st in base of ch-3.

Round 5: Ch 3 (counts as 1dc), 2dc in first ch-3 sp, 3dc in each of next two ch-3 sps, *[5dc, ch 3, 5dc] in ch-6 corner sp, 3dc in each ch-3 sp to corner; rep from * to end of round, changing to color C when joining with sl st in 3rd ch of ch-3.

Round 6: Ch 3 (counts as 1dc), 1dc in every dc of previous round, working [1dc, 1tr, 1dc] in each ch-2 corner sp, changing to color A when joining with sl st in 3rd ch of ch-3.

Round 7: Ch 3 (counts as 1dc), 1dc in every dc of previous round, working 3dc in each corner tr, join with sl st in 3rd ch of ch-3. Break color A.

Round 8: Join color B to any sp between 2dc, ch 3 (counts as 1dc), *1dc between every 2dc of previous round, working ch 3, between first and third dc of dc3 cluster in each corner, join with sl st in 3rd ch of ch-3.

Fasten off and weave in ends.

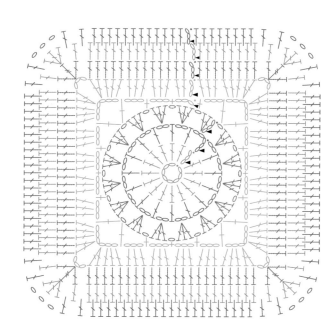

★★ Squaring the Circle

See page 22

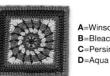

A=Winsor
B=Bleached
C=Persimmon
D=Aqua

Foundation ring: Using color A, make a magic ring.
Round 1: Ch 1, 8sc in ring, changing to color B when joining with sl st to first sc.
Round 2: Ch 1, 1sc in same place, [ch 2, 1sc in next st] 7 times, ch 2, join with sl st to first sc. Break color B.
Round 3: Join color C to any ch-2 sp, ch 3 (counts as 1dc), 2dc in same sp, [ch 1, 3dc in next ch-2 sp] 7 times, ch 1, join with sl st to 3rd ch of ch-3. Break color C.
Round 4: Join color B to any ch-1 sp, ch 3 (counts as 1dc), 1dc in same place, [ch 1, miss next st, 2dc in next st, ch 1, miss next st, 2dc in ch-1 sp] 7 times, ch 1, miss next st, 2dc in next st, ch 1, miss next st, join with sl st to 3rd ch of ch-3. Break color B.
Round 5: Join color A to any ch-1 sp, ch 1, 1sc in same sp, [ch 2, 1sc in next ch-1 sp] 15 times, ch 2, join with sl st to first sc. Break color A.
Round 6: Join color D to any ch-2 sp, ch 3 (counts as 1dc), 2dc in same sp, [ch 1, 3dc in ch-2 sp] 15 times, ch 1, join with sl st to 3rd ch of ch-3. Break color D.
Round 7: Join color A to any ch-1 sp,

ch 1, 1sc in same sp, [ch 3, 1sc in next ch-1 sp] 15 times, ch 2, join with sl st to first sc. Break color A.
Round 8: Join color B to any ch-3 sp, ch 1, 4sc in same sp, *[1hdc, 3dc] in next ch-3 sp, [1tr, ch 2, 1tr] in next sc, [3dc, 1hdc], in next ch-3 sp, 4sc in next ch-3 sp**, 4sc in next ch-3 sp; rep from * twice more and from * to ** once again, join with sl st in first sc. Break color B.
Round 9: Join color C to any ch-2 corner sp, ch 3 (counts as 1dc), [1tr, 1dc] in same sp, 1dc in every·st, working [1dc, 1tr, 1dc] in every ch-2 corner sp to end of round, changing to color A when joining with sl st to 3rd ch of ch-3.
Round 10: Ch 3 (counts as 1dc), *[1dc, 1tr, 1dc] in next tr, 1dc in every dc to corner tr; rep from * to end of round, changing to color D when joining with sl st to 3rd ch of ch-3.
Round 11: Ch 3 (counts as 1dc), 1dc in next dc, *[1dc, 1tr, 1dc] in next tr, 1dc in every dc to corner tr; rep from * to end of round, join with sl st to 3rd ch of ch-3.
Fasten off and weave in ends.

★★ Starburst in a Square

See page 21

A=Bleached
B=Aqua
C=Winsor
D=Persimmon

SPECIAL STITCHES
Dc2tog: Work 2dc sts together.
Dc3tog: Work 3dc sts together.

Foundation ring:
Using color A, make a magic loop.
Round 1: Ch 3 (counts as 1dc), 23dc in center of loop, join with sl st to 3rd ch of ch-3.
Round 2: Ch 3 (counts as 1dc), 1dc in next 2dc, ch 3, [1dc in next 3dc, ch 3] 7 times, changing to color B when joining with sl st to 3rd ch of ch-3. Break color A.
Round 3: Ch 2, dc2tog over next 2dc, [ch 3, 1dc in next 3-ch sp, ch 3, dc3tog over next 3dc] 7 times, ch 3, 1dc in next 3-ch sp, ch 3, join with sl st to 3rd ch of ch-3. Break color B.
Round 4: Join color C to any ch-3 sp before a single dc, ch 4 (counts as 1dc and ch 1), [3dc in next ch-3 sp, ch 1] 15 times, 2dc in first ch-sp, join with sl st to 3rd ch of ch-4. Break color C.
Round 5: Join color D to any ch-1 sp,

ch 4 (counts as 1dc and ch 1), [4dc in next ch-3 sp, ch 1] 15 times, 3dc in first ch-sp, join with sl st to 3rd ch of ch-4. Break color D.
Round 6: Join color A to any ch-1 sp, ch 4 (counts as 1dc and ch 1), [5dc in next ch-3 sp, ch 1] 15 times, 4dc in first ch-sp, join with sl st to 3rd ch of ch-4. Break color A.
Round 7: Join color B to first dc in any 5dc cluster, ch 1, 1sc in same place, 1sc in next 10dc, 1hdc in next 2dc, 1dc in next 2dc, *[1dc, 1tr, 1dc], in next ch-1 sp, 1dc in next 2dc, 1hdc in next 2 dc**, 1sc in next 12dc, 1hdc in next 2dc, 1dc in next 2dc; rep from * twice more and from * to ** once again, 1sc in next dc, change to color D when joining with sl st in first sc. Break color B.
Round 8: Ch 2 (counts as 1hdc), 1hdc in every st, working [1hdc, 1dc, 1hdc] in every tr corner st to end of round, join with sl st to 2nd ch of ch-2.
Fasten off and weave in ends.

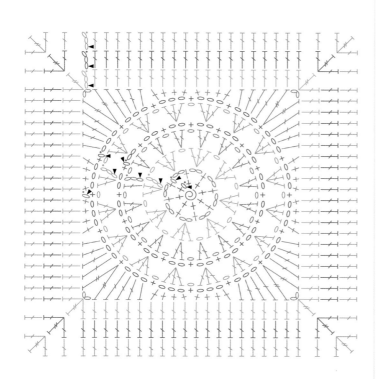

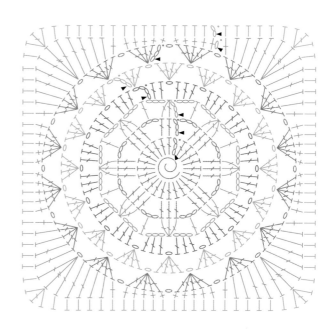

✪✪ Fretwork Circle

See page 21

A=Dawn Gray
B=Bleached
C=Persimmon

SPECIAL STITCHES

Beg cl: Work two double sts tog: [yoh draw up a loop in next st, (yoh, pull through 2 loops on hook) twice] twice, yoh and draw through all 3 loops on hook.

Cl: Work three double sts tog: [yoh draw up a loop in next st, (yoh, pull through 2 loops on hook) twice] three times, yoh and draw through all 4 loops on hook.

Foundation ring: Using color A, work 6 ch and join with sl st to form a ring.
Round 1: Ch 1, 12sc in ring, join with sl st to first sc.
Round 2: Ch 4 (counts as 1dc and ch 1), [1dc in next sc, ch 1] 11 times, join with sl st to 3rd ch of ch-4. Break color A.
Round 3: Join color B to any ch-1 sp, ch 3 (counts as 1dc), beg cl in same sp, ch 3, *cl in next ch-1 sp, ch 3; rep from * a further 10 times, join with a sl st to top of beg cl. Break color B.
Round 4: Join color C to any ch-3 sp, ch 1, 4sc in same sp, 4sc in every ch-3 sp to end, join with sl st to first sc. Break color C.
Round 5: Join color A to top of any cl, ch 3 (counts as 1dc), [1dc, ch 2, 2dc] in same place*, ch 2, skip next 4sc group, 2sc in sp above next cl, ch 3,

skip next 4sc group**, [2dc, ch 2, 2dc] in sp above next cl; rep from * twice more and from * to ** once again, join with sl st to 3rd ch of ch-3.
Round 6: Ch 3 (counts as 1dc), 1dc in next dc, *[2dc, ch 2, 2dc] in ch-2 corner sp, 1dc in next 2dc, ch 2, 1dc in next 2sc, ch 3, 1dc in next 2sc, ch 2**, 1dc in next 2dc; rep from * twice more and from * to ** once again, join with sl st to 3rd ch of ch-3.
Round 7: Ch 3 (counts as 1dc), 1dc in next 3dc, *[2dc, ch 2, 2dc] in ch-2 corner sp, 1dc in next 4dc, ch 2, 1dc in next 2dc, ch 3, 1dc in next 2dc, ch 2**, 1dc in next 4dc; rep from * twice more and from * to ** once again, join with sl st to 3rd ch of ch-3.
Round 8: Ch 3 (counts as 1dc), 1dc in next 5dc, *[2dc, ch 2, 2dc] in ch-2 corner sp, 1dc in next 6dc, ch 2, 1dc in next 2dc, ch 3, 1dc in next 2dc, ch 2**, 1dc in next 6dc; rep from * twice more and from * to ** once again, changing to color C when joining with sl st in 3rd ch of ch-3.
Round 9: Ch 3 (counts as 1dc), 1dc in every dc and ch from previous round, working 3dc in every ch-2 corner sp, join with sl st to 3rd ch of ch-3.
Fasten off and weave in ends.

✪✪ Cluster Circle

See page 20

A=Bleached
B=Persimmon
C=Dawn Gray

SPECIAL STITCHES

Beg cl: Work three double sts tog: [yoh draw up a loop in next st, (yoh, pull through 2 loops on hook) twice] twice, yoh and draw through all 4 loops on hook.

Cl: Work four double sts tog: [yoh draw up a loop in next st, (yoh, pull through 2 loops on hook) twice] three times, yoh and draw through all 5 loops on hook.

Foundation ring: Using color A, work 6 ch and join with sl st to form a ring.
Round 1: Ch1, 12dc in ring, join with sl st to first dc.
Round 2: Ch 4 (counts as 1dc and ch1), [1dc in next dc, ch1] 11 times, join with sl st to 3rd ch of ch-4. Break A.
Round 3: Sl st in next ch-1 sp, ch 3 (counts as 1dc), beg cl in same sp, ch 3, *cl in next ch-1 sp, ch 3; rep from * a further 10 times, join with a sl st to top of beg cl. Break color A.
Round 4: Join color B to any ch-3 sp, ch 3 (counts as 1dc), beg cl in same sp, *ch 2, 1dc in next cl, ch 2**, cl in next ch-3 sp; rep from * a further 10 times, then from * to ** once, join with a sl st to top of beg cl.
Round 5: Sl st in next ch-2 sp, ch 1, 3dc in same sp, 3dc in every ch-2 sp

to end of round, join with sl st in first dc. Break color B.
Round 6: Join color A in to top of any cl, ch 3 (counts as 1dc), [1dc, ch 2, 2dc] in same place, *[ch 2, skip next 3dc group, 1dc in sp between next two 3dc groups] 5 times, ch 2**, [2dc, ch 2, 2dc] in sp above next cl; rep from * twice more and from * to ** once again, join with sl st to 3rd ch of ch-3.
Round 7: Ch 3 (counts as 1dc), 1dc in next dc, *[2dc, ch 2, 2dc] in ch-2 corner sp, 1dc in next dc, ch 2, 1dc in next dc, [ch 2, 1dc in next dc] 3 times, ch 2, 1dc in next dc, ch 2**, 1dc in next 2dc; rep from * twice more and from * to ** once again, changing to color C when joining with sl st in 3rd ch of ch-3. Break color A.
Round 8: Ch 3 (counts as 1dc), 1dc in next 3dc, *[2dc, ch 2, 2dc] in ch-2 corner sp, 1dc in next 4dc, ch 2, 1dc in next dc, [ch 2, 1dc in next dc] 3 times, ch 2, 1 dc in next dc, ch 2**, 1dc in next 4dc; rep from * twice more and from * to ** once again, join with sl st to 3rd ch of ch-3.
Round 9: Ch 3 (counts as 1dc), 1dc in every dc and ch from previous round, working 3dc in every ch-2 corner sp, join with sl st to 3rd ch of ch-3.
Fasten off and weave in ends.

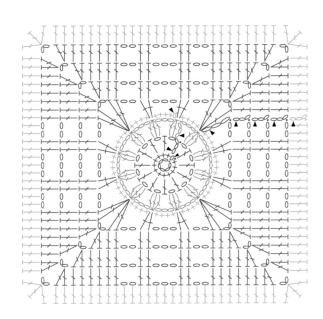

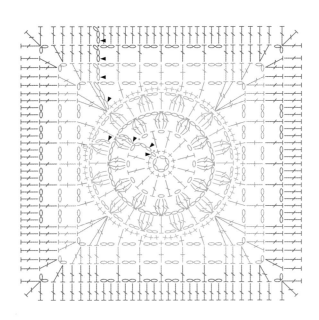

★★ *Starflower Circle*

See page 20

A=Persimmon
B=Bleached
C=Dawn Gray

SPECIAL STITCHES

Tr2tog (work two treble sts tog):
[Yoh (twice) draw up a loop in next st, (yoh, pull through 2 loops on hook) twice] twice, yoh and draw through all 3 loops on hook.

Foundation chain: Using color A, ch 4 and join with a sl st to form a ring.
Round 1: Ch 4, 1tr into the ring (counts as tr2tog), ch 3, [tr2tog, ch 3] 7 times into the ring, join with sl st in 4th ch of ch 4. Break A.
Round 2: Join color B to any 3ch-sp, ch 1, 1sc in same sp, *[ch 5, 1sc] in each of next seven 3ch-sps, ch 5, join with sl st in first sc.
Round 3: Sl st in first 3 ch sts of next 5ch-sp ch 4 (counts as 1tr and ch 1), *[tr2tog, ch 1] 5 times in next 5ch-sp **, 1dc in next 5ch-sp, ch 1; rep from * twice and then from * to ** once, change to color C when joining with sl st in 3rd ch of ch-4.
Round 4: Ch 4 (counts as 1tr), 1tr in same st, ch 1, *[1dc, ch 1] in each of next four 1ch-sps**, [2tr, ch 2, 2tr] in next tr; rep from * twice more and from * to ** once again, 2tr in same sp as first half corner, ch 2, join with sl st in 3rd ch of ch-3.

Round 5: Sl st in next tr and next 1ch-sp, ch 3 (counts as 1dc), *[1dc in next dc, 1dc in next ch-1 sp] 4 times, 1dc in each of next 2tr, [2tr, ch 2, 2tr] in ch-2 corner sp, 1dc in each of next 2tr**, 1dc in next 1ch-sp; rep from * twice more and from * to ** once again, change to color B when joining with sl st in 3rd ch of ch-3.
Round 6: Ch 2 (counts as 1hdc), 1hdc in every dc and [2dc, ch 2, 2dc] in every ch-2 corner sp to end of round, change to color A when joining with sl st in 2nd ch of ch-2.

Round 7: Ch 3 (counts as 1dc), 1dc in every hdc and [2tr, ch 2, 2tr] in every ch-2 corner sp to end of round, change to color B when joining with sl st to 3rd of ch-3.
Round 8: Ch 1 (does not count as st), 1sc in every dc and [2hdc, ch 2, 2hdc] in every ch-2 corner sp to end of round, change to color C when joining with sl st to first sc.
Round 9: Ch 2 (counts as 1hdc), 1hdc in every sc and 3dc in every ch-2 corner sp to end of round, join with sl st in 2nd ch of ch-2.
Fasten off and weave in ends.

★★ *Framed Circle*

See page 20

A=Winsor
B=Dawn Gray
C=Bleached
D=Aqua

SPECIAL STITCHES

BPdc: Work a dc in the back post of designated stitch.

Foundation chain: Using color A, work 4 ch and join with sl st to form a ring.

Round 1: Ch 3 (counts as 1dc), 11dc in the ring, changing to color B when joining with sl st to 3rd ch of ch-3. Break color A.

Round 2: Ch 3 (counts as 1dc), 1dc in same place, 2dc in every dc to end of round, changing to color C when joining with sl st to 3rd ch of ch-3. Break color B.

Round 3: Ch 3 (counts as 1dc), 1dc in same place, [1dc in next dc, 2dc in next dc] 11 times, changing to color A when joining with sl st to 3rd ch of ch-3. Break color C.

Round 4: Ch 1, 1sc in same place, [ch 3, skip 2 dc, 1sc in next dc] 11 times, ch 3, changing to color D when joining with sl st to first sc. Break color A.

Round 5: Sl st in next ch-3 sp, [1sc, 1hdc, 1dc, ch 3, 1dc, 1hdc, 1sc] in same ch-3 sp, *[1sc, 1hdc, 2dc, 1hdc, 1sc] in next 2 ch-3 sp**, [1sc, 1hdc, 1dc, ch 3, 1dc, 1hdc, 1sc] in next ch-3 sp; rep from * twice more, then from * to ** once again, join with sl st to first sc. Break color D.

Round 6: Join color C to any ch-3 corner sp, ch 1, 1sc in same sp, *ch 2, [1BPdc around sc from Round 4, ch 3] twice, 1BPdc around next sc from Round 4, ch 2**, [1sc, 1hdc, 1dc, 1hdc, 1sc] in ch-3 sp from Round 5; rep from * to ** once more, [1sc, 1hdc, 1dc, 1hdc] in ch-3 sp from Round 5, join with sl st to first sc.

Round 7: Ch 3 (counts as 1dc), 2dc in ch-2 sp, 1dc in next dc, [3dc in ch-3 sp, 1dc in next dc] twice, 2dc in ch-2 sp, 1dc in next 2sts, [1dc, 1tr, 1dc] in next st**, 1dc in next 2sts; rep from * twice and then from * to ** once more, 1dc in next st, changing to color B when joining with sl st to 3rd ch of ch-3. Break color C.

Round 8: Ch 3 (counts as 1dc), 1dc in every dc, working [1dc, 1tr, 1dc] in every corner tr, changing to color A when joining with sl st to 3rd ch of ch-3. Break color B.

Round 9: Ch 3 (counts as 1dc), 1dc in every dc, working [1dc, 1tr, 1dc] in every corner tr, changing to color D when joining with sl st to 3rd ch of ch-3. Break color A.

Round 10: Ch 3 (counts as 1dc), 1dc in every dc, working [1dc, 1tr, 1dc] in every corner tr, join with sl st to 3rd ch of ch-3.

Fasten off and weave in ends.

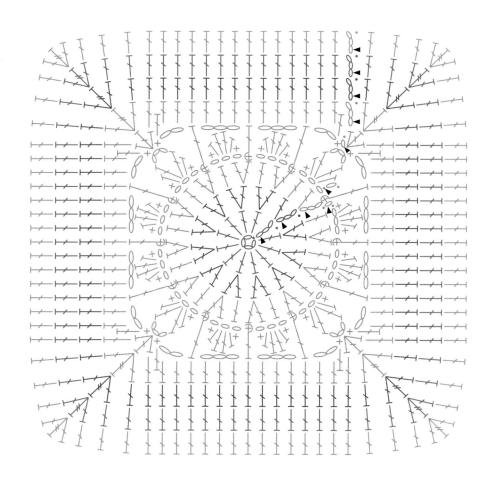

★★ Flower in a Web

See page 21

A=Aqua
B=Bleached
C=Winsor
D=Dawn Gray

SPECIAL STITCHES

Beg cl: Work two double sts tog: [yoh draw up a loop in next st, (yoh, pull through 2 loops on hook) twice] twice, yoh and draw through all 3 loops on hook.
Cl: Work three double sts tog: [yoh draw up a loop in next st, (yoh, pull through 2 loops on hook) twice] three times, yoh and draw through all 4 loops on hook.

Foundation ring: Using color A, work 4 ch and join with sl st to form a ring.
Round 1: Ch 3, (counts as 1dc), 2dc in ring, ch 3, [3dc in ring, ch 3] 3 times, ch 3, join with sl st to 3rd ch of ch-3. Break color A.
Round 2: Join color B to any ch-3 sp, ch 3 (counts as 1dc), [1dc, ch 2, 2dc, ch 2, 2dc] in same sp, *[2dc, ch 2, 2dc, ch 2, 2dc] in next ch-3 sp; rep from * twice more, join with sl st to 3rd ch of ch-3. Break color B.
Round 3: Join color C to 2nd dc of any 3dc cluster from Round 1, ch 5 (counts as 1dc and ch 2), *[1sc in ch-2 sp, ch 2] twice**, 1dc in 2nd dc of next 3dc cluster from Round 1, ch 2; rep from * twice more and from * to ** once again.
Round 4: Ch7 (counts as 1dc and ch 4), *1sc in next sc, 3sc in next ch-2 sp, 1sc in next sc, ch 4**, 1dc in next dc, ch 4; rep from * twice more and then from * to ** once again, changing to color D when joining with a sl st to 3rd

ch of ch-7. Break color C.
Round 5: Ch 3, (counts as 1dc), 1tr, 1dc in same place, *5dc in ch-4 sp, 1dc in next 5 sts, 5dc in ch-4 sp**, [1dc, 1tr, 1dc] in corner dc; rep from * twice more and then from * to ** once again, join with sl st to 3rd ch of ch-3. Break color D.
Round 6: Join color B to any dc 2 sts to the left of a tr from Round 5. Ch 3 (counts as 1dc), 1dc in next 2 sts, *[ch 3, skip 3 sts, 1dc in next 3 sts] to 1 st before next tr, ch 3, skip 1 st, 1dc in corner tr, ch 3, skip 1 st**, 1dc in next 3 sts; rep from * twice and from * to ** once more, join with sl st to 3rd ch of ch-3.
Round 7: Ch 3 (counts as 1dc), 1dc in next 2 sts, ch 3, [1dc in next 3 sts, ch 3] to corner st, 5dc in corner st, ch 3; rep from * to end of round, changing to color A when joining with a sl st to 3rd ch of ch-3. Break color B.
Round 8: Ch 3 (counts as 1dc), 1dc in next 2 sts, ch 3, [1dc in next 3 sts, ch 3] to 5dc corner group, 1dc in next 2dc, [1dc, ch 3, 1dc] in next dc, 1dc in next 2dc, ch 3; rep from * to end of round, changing to color C when joining with a sl st to 3rd ch of ch-3. Break color A.
Round 9: Ch 1, 1sc in same place, 1sc in every dc and 3sc in every ch-3 sp from previous round, join with sl st to first sc.
Fasten off and weave in ends.

★★ Snowflake in a Square

See page 23

A=Bleached
B=Aqua
C=Winsor
D=Persimmon

SPECIAL STITCHES

Beg cl: Work three double sts tog: [yoh draw up a loop in next st, (yoh, pull through 2 loops on hook) twice] three times, yoh and draw through all 4 loops on hook.
Cl: Work four double sts tog: [yoh draw up a loop in next st, (yoh, pull through 2 loops on hook) twice] four times, yoh and draw through all 5 loops on hook.

Foundation ring: Using color A, work 8 ch and join with sl st to form a ring.
Round 1: Ch 3 (counts as 1dc), 2dc in ring, ch 7, [3dc, ch 7] 7 times in ring, join with sl st to 3rd ch of ch-3.
Round 2: Sl st in next 2dc and next ch-7 sp, ch 3 (counts as 1dc), beg cl in first ch-7 sp, [ch 9, cl in next ch-7 sp] 7 times, ch 9, join with sl st in top of beg cl.
Round 3: Ch 1, *[2sc, ch 5, 2sc] in next ch-9 sp, ch 7, [cl, ch 5, cl], in next ch-9 sp, ch 7; rep from * a further 3 times, join with sl st in first sc. Break color A.
Round 4: Join color B to ch-5 sp, between 2 groups of 2sc, ch 1, 2sc in

same loop, *ch 5, 2sc in next ch-7 sp, ch 5, [cl, ch 5, cl] in next ch-5 sp, ch 5, 2sc in ch-7 sp, ch 5**, 2sc in next ch-5 sp; rep from * twice more and from * to ** once again, join with sl st in first sc.
Round 5: Ch 2 (counts as 1hdc), 1hdc in next sc, 3sc in next ch-5 sp, 1hdc in next 2sc, 3sc in next ch-5 sp, *1sc in top of next cl, [1sc, 1hdc, 1dc, 1hdc, 1sc] in next ch-5 corner sp, 1sc in next cl**, [3sc in next ch-5 sp, 1hdc in next 2sc] 3 times, 3sc in next ch-5 sp; rep from * twice more and from * to ** once again, 3sc in next ch-5sp, 1hdc in next 2sc, 3sc in next ch-5 sp, changing to color C when joining with sl st to 2nd ch of ch-2. Break color B.
Round 6: Ch 2 (counts as 1hdc), 1hdc in every st from previous round, working 5hdc in center st of each corner group, change to color D when joining with sl st to 2nd of ch-2. Break color C.
Round 7: Ch 1, 1sc in same place, 1sc in every st from previous round, working 3sc in center st of each corner group, join with sl st to first sc.
Fasten off and weave in ends.

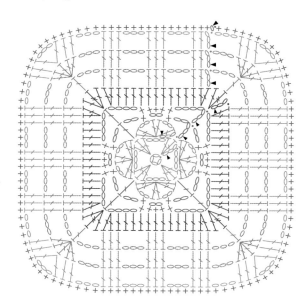

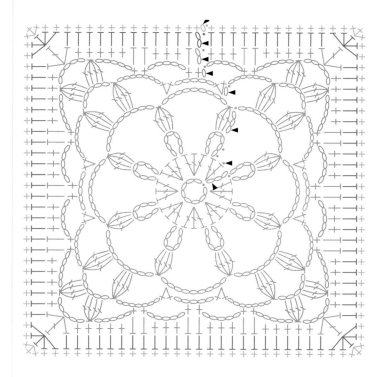

⭐⭐ *Star in a Square*

See page 21

A=Persimmon
B=Winsor
C=Aqua

Foundation ring: Using color A, work 4 ch and join with sl st to form a ring.

Round 1: Ch 1, 8sc in ring, join with sl st to first sc.

Round 2: *Ch 6, 1sc in 3rd and 4th ch from hook, 1hdc in 5th and 6th ch from hook, sl st in next sc (spike made); rep from * a further 7 times, join with sl st in first ch of ch-6. Break color A.

Round 3: Join color B to the tip of any spike, ch 5 (counts as 1dc and ch 2), 1dc in same place (corner made), ch 4, sl st in top of next spike, ch 4, *[1dc, ch 2, 1dc] in tip of next spike (corner made), ch 4, sl st in tip of next spike, ch 4; rep from * twice, join with sl st to 3rd ch of ch-5.

Round 4: Sl st in ch-2 corner space, ch 3 (counts as 1dc), [2dc, ch 2, 3dc] in same ch-2 sp, 4dc in each of next 2 ch-4 sp, *[3dc, ch 2, 3dc] in next ch 2 corner sp, 4dc in each of next 2 ch-4 sp; rep from * twice more, join with sl st to 3rd ch of ch-3.

Round 5: Ch 3 (counts as 1dc), 1dc in every dc of previous round, working [3dc, ch 2, 3dc] in every ch-2 corner sp, changing to color B when joining with sl st to 3rd ch of ch-3. Break color A.

Round 6: Ch 3 (counts as 1dc), 1dc in every dc of previous round, working [3dc, ch 2, 3dc] in every ch-2 corner sp, changing to color C when joining with sl st to 3rd ch of ch-3. Break color B.

Round 7: Ch 3 (counts as 1dc), 1dc in every dc of previous round, working [3dc, ch 2, 3dc] in every ch-2 corner sp, changing to color C when joining with sl st to 3rd ch of ch-3. Break color B.

Round 8: Ch 2 (counts as 1hdc), 1hdc in every dc of previous round, working 3hdc in every ch-2 corner sp, join with sl st to 2nd ch of ch-2.

Fasten off and weave in ends.

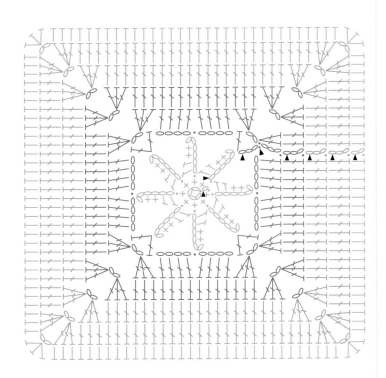

⭐ *Diamond in a Square*

See page 23

A=Winsor
B=Aqua
C=Bleached
D=Persimmon

Foundation ring: Using color A, work 4 ch and join with sl st to form a ring.

Round 1: Ch 6 (counts as 1dc and 3 ch), [3dc in ring, ch 3] 3 times, 2dc in ring, join with sl st in 3rd ch of ch-6.

Round 2: Sl st in next ch-3 sp, ch 3 (counts as 1dc), [2dc, ch 2, 3dc] in same sp, *1dc in each of next 3dc, [3dc, ch 3, 3dc] in next ch-3 sp; rep from * twice more, 1dc in each of next 3dc, join with sl st in 3rd ch of ch-3. Break color A.

Round 3: Join color B to any ch-2 sp, *ch 6, skip 4dc, 1tr in next dc, ch 6, skip 4dc, sl st in next ch-2 sp; rep from * a further 3 times, join with sl st to in first ch.

Round 4: Ch 1, *7sc in next ch-6 sp, [1hdc, ch 2, 1hdc] in next tr (corner made), 7sc in next ch-6 sp, 1sc in ch-2 sp from Round 2; rep from * a further 3 times, join with sl st in first sc.

Round 5: Ch 2 (counts as 1hdc), 1hdc in next 6sc, 1dc in next hdc, *[2dc, ch 2, 2dc] in next ch-2 corner sp, 1dc in next hdc, 1hdc in next 7sc, 1dc in next sc**, 1hdc in next 7sc; rep from * twice more and from * to ** once again, join with sl st to 2nd ch of ch-2. Break color B.

Round 6: Join color C to a center dc along one side of the square, ch 3 (counts as 1dc), *1dc in each of next 7hdc, 1hdc, in next 3dc, [2dc, ch 2, 2dc] in next ch-2 corner sp, 1hdc in each of next 3dc, 1dc in next dc; rep from * a further 3 times, 1dc in each of next 7hdc, changing to color D when joining with sl st to 3rd ch of ch-3. Break color C.

Round 7: Ch 3 (counts as 1dc), 1dc in every st from previous round, working 3dc in each ch-2 corner sp, changing to color A when joining with sl st to 3rd ch of ch-3. Break color D.

Round 8: Ch 3 (counts as 1dc), 1dc in every st from previous round, working 3dc in 2nd dc of 3dc corner group to end of round, join with sl st to 3rd ch of ch-3.

Fasten off and weave in ends.

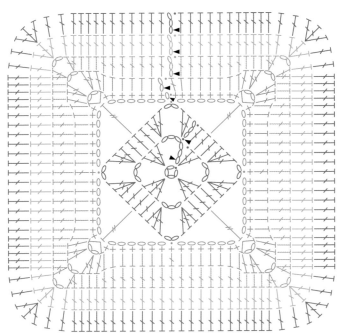

✪✪ Edwardian Fancy

See page 22

A=Dawn Gray
B=Winsor
C=Bleached

Foundation chain: Using color A, work 4 ch and join with sl st to form a ring.

Round 1: Ch 3 (counts as 1dc), 11dc in ring, changing to color B when joining with sl st to 3rd ch of ch-3. Break color A.

Round 2: Ch 5 (counts as 1dc and ch 2), [1dc in next dc, ch 2] 11 times, changing to color C when joining with sl st to 3rd ch of ch-5. Break color B.

Round 3: Sl st in next ch-2 sp, ch 1, 3sc in same sp, *3sc in next ch-2 sp; rep from * to end of round, join with sl st to first sc.

Round 4: Sl st in next 2sc, ch 1, 1sc in same place (2nd of 2sc), 1sc in next sc, [2sc in next sc, 1sc in next 2sc] 11 times, 2sc in next sc, join with sl st in first sc.

Round 5: Ch 1, [1sc, 1dc] in same place, ch 1, [1dc, 1sc] in next sc, *sl st in each of next 2sc, [1sc, 1dc] in next sc, ch 1, [1dc, 1sc] in next sc; rep from * a further 10 times, sl st in each of next 2sc, join with sl st in first sc. Break color C.

Round 6: Join color D to any ch-1 sp, ch 1, 1sc in same sp, ch 5, [1sc in next ch-1 sp, ch 5] 11 times, join with sl st in first sc.

Round 7: Sl st in next ch-5 sp, ch 1, [1sc, 1hdc, 2dc, ch 2, 2dc, 1hdc, 1sc] in same sp (corner made), *1sc in next sc, [4sc in next ch-5 sp, 1sc in next sc] twice**, [1sc, 1hdc, 2dc, ch 2, 2dc, 1hdc, 1sc] in next ch-5 sp (corner made); rep from * twice more and from * to ** once again, join with sl st in first sc.

Round 8: Ch 3 (counts as 1dc), 1dc in every st of previous round, working 3dc in each ch-2 corner sp, join with sl st in 3rd ch of ch-3. Break color D.

Round 9: Join color B to 2nd dc of any 3dc corner group, ch 3 (counts as 1dc), [1dc, ch 1, 2dc] in same place, *1dc in next dc, ch 1, skip next dc, [1dc in next dc, ch 1, skip 1dc] 9 times, 1dc in next dc**, [2dc, ch 1, 2dc] in next dc; rep from * twice and from * to ** once again, changing to color A when joining with sl st to 3rd ch of ch-3. Break color B.

Round 10: Ch 3 (counts as 1dc), 1dc in every st and ch-1 sp of previous round, working 3dc in each ch-1 corner sp, changing to color B when joining with sl st to 3rd ch of ch-3. Break color A.

Round 11: Ch 1, 1sc in same place, 1sc in every dc from previous round, working 3sc in 2nd dc of each 3dc corner group. Join with sl st to first sc.

Fasten off and weave in ends.

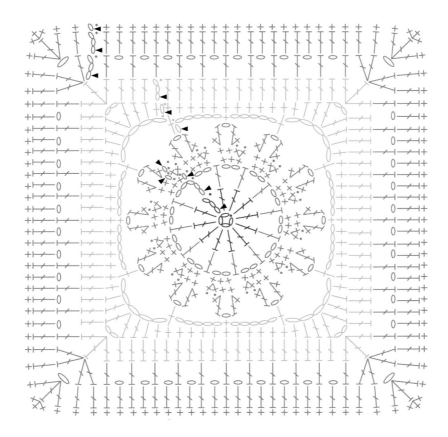

⭐ Octagon Tile

See page 23

A=Dawn Gray
B=Persimmon
C=Bleached
D=Windsor

SPECIAL STITCHES

Dc2tog (work two double sts tog):
[Yoh draw up a loop in next st, (yoh, pull through 2 loops on hook) twice] twice, yoh and draw through all 3 loops on hook.

Foundation ring: Using color A, ch 8 and join with sl st in first ch to form a ring.

Round 1: Ch 3, (counts as 1dc), 1dc into ring, [ch 1, 2dc into ring] 7 times, ch 1, change to color B when joining with sl st in 3rd ch of ch-3. (16 sts and 8 ch-sps)

Round 2: Ch 3 (counts as 1dc), 1dc in next st, [(1dc, ch 2, 1dc) in 1ch-sp, 1dc in each of next 2 sts] 7 times, [1dc, ch 2, 1dc] in next 1ch-sp, change to color B when joining with sl st in 3rd ch of ch-3. (32 sts and 8 ch-sps)

Round 3: Ch 1, 1sc in same place, [1sc in each st to 2ch-sp, 3sc in 2ch-sp] 8 times, 1sc in next st, change to color D when joining with sl st into first sc. (56 sts)

Round 4: Ch 1, 1sc in same place, 1sc in each of next 3 sts, [3sc in next st, 1sc in next 6 sts] 7 times, 3sc in next sc, 1sc in each of next 2 sts, change to color A when joining with sl st in first sc. (72 sts)

Round 5: Ch 1, 1sc in same place, 1sc in each of next 5 sts, 1hdc in next st, 1dc in each of next 2 sts, *2tr in next st, ch 2, 2tr in next st, 1dc in each of next 2 sts, 1hdc in next st**, 1sc in each of next 10 sts, 1hdc in next st, 1dc in each of next 2 sts; rep from * twice more and from * to ** once again, 1sc in each of next 4 sts, change to color D when joining with sl st in first sc. (80 sts and 4 ch-sps)

Round 6: Ch 3 (counts as first dc), *1dc in each st to corner, [1dc, 1tr, 1dc] in 2ch-corner sp; rep from * 3 times, 1dc in each st to end of round, change to color B when joining with sl st in first st. (92 sts)

Round 7: Ch 3 (counts as 1dc), 1dc in every st from previous round, working 3dc in center st of each corner group, change to color C when joining with sl st to 2nd of ch-2.

Round 8: Ch 1, 1sc in same place, 1sc in each st from previous round, working 3sc in center st of each corner group, change to color A when joining with sl st in first sc.

Round 9: Ch 2 (counts as 1hdc), 1hdc in every st from previous round, working 3hdc in center st of each corner group, join with sl st in 2nd ch of ch-2.

Fasten off and weave in ends.

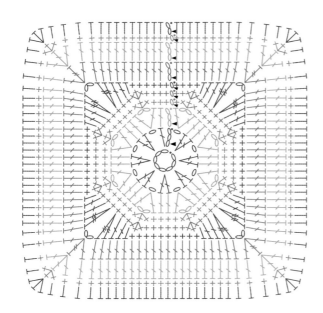

⭐⭐ Octagon Framed Flower

See page 22

A=Bleached
B=Persimmon
C=Dawn Gray
D=Windsor

SPECIAL STITCHES

Cl: Work 1dc in each of next 3 sts, leaving last 2 loops of each st on hook, (7 loops on hook), yoh, pull through all loops on hook, ch 1 to close the cluster. (The ch 1 counts as the top of the stitch).

Foundation ring: Using color A, work 6 ch and join with sl st to form a ring.

Round 1: Ch 1, 16sc in ring, change to color B when joining with sl st to first sc. Break color A.

Round 2: Ch 3 (counts as 1dc), 2dc in same sp, *ch 3, skip next sc, 3dc in next st; rep from * a further 6 times, ch 3, join with a sl st to 3rd ch of ch-3.

Round 3: Ch 3, *cl over next 3 sts, ch 3, sl st in ch-3 sp**, ch 3: rep from * a further 6 times, then from * to ** once again, changing to color A when joining with sl st in last ch-3 sp. Break color B.

Round 4: Ch 4 (counts as 1tr), 2dc in same sp, *1sc in top of cl, [2dc, 1tr, 2dc] in next ch-3 sp of Round 2; rep from * a further 6 times, 1sc in top of next cl, 2dc in ch-3 sp of Round 2, change to color C when joining with sl st to to 4th ch of ch-4. Break color A.

Round 5: Ch 3 (counts as 1dc), 2dc in same place, 1dc in every st to next tr, 3dc in next tr; rep from * a further 6 times, 1dc in each st to end of round, changing to color D when joining with sl st to 3rd ch of ch-3. Break color C.

Round 6: Sl st in next dc, ch 1, 1sc in same st, 1sc in next st, *1hdc in next st, 1dc in next, 1tr in next st, [1tr, ch 3, 1tr] in next st, 1tr in next st, 1dc in next st, 1hdc in next st**, 1sc in next 9 sts; rep from * twice more and then from * to ** once again, 1sc in next 7 sts, join with sl st to first sc.

Round 7: Ch 3, 1dc in every st from previous round, working 5dc in ch-3 corner spaces and changing to color A when joining with sl st to 3rd ch of ch-3. Break color D.

Round 8: Ch 3, 1dc in every st from previous round, working 3dc in center dc of 5dc corner group and changing to color C when joining with sl st to 3rd ch of ch-3. Break color A.

Round 9: Ch 2, 1hdc in every st from previous round, working 3hdc in center dc of 3dc corner group, join with sl st to 2nd of ch-2.

Fasten off and weave in ends.

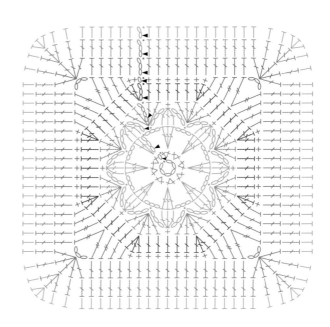

Diamonds *See page 22*

A=Winsor
B=Bleached
C=Persimmon
D=Dawn Gray

Foundation ring: Using color A, work 6 ch and join with sl st to form a ring.
Round 1: Ch 4 (counts as tr), [4dc in the ring, 1tr in the ring] 3 times, 4dc in the ring, changing to color B when joining with sl st to 4th ch of ch 4. Break color A.
Round 2: Ch 1, 1sc in same place, *skip next st, [2dc, 1tr] in next st, ch 1, [1tr, 2dc] in next st, skip next st**, 1sc in next st; rep from * twice and from * to ** once more, change to color C when joining with sl st to first sc. Break color B.
Round 3: Ch 4 (counts as tr), 3tr in same st, *1sc in ch-1 sp, [4tr, ch 1, 4tr] in next sc; rep from * twice more, 1sc in ch-1 sp, 4tr in sc at beg of round, ch 1, changing to color D when joining with sl st to 4th ch of ch 4. Break color C.
Round 4: Ch 2 (counts as 1hdc), *1dc in next 2 sts, 1tr in next st, [2tr, ch 2, 2tr] in next st, 1tr in next st, 1dc in next 2 sts, 1hdc in next st, 1sc in ch-1 sp**, 1hdc in next st; rep from * twice more and from * to ** once again,

change to color A when joining with sl st to first sc. Break color D.
Round 5: Ch 3 (counts as 1dc), 1dc in every st, working [2dc, ch 2, 2dc] in each ch-2 corner sp, changing to color B when joining with sl st to 3rd of ch-3. Break color A.
Round 6: Ch 2 (counts as 1hdc), 1hdc in every st, working 5hdc in each ch-2 corner sp, changing to color C when joining with sl st to 2nd of ch-2. Break color B.
Round 7: Ch 4 (counts as 1dc and ch 1), skip next st, [1dc in next st, ch 1, skip next st] 4 times, *3dc in next st, ch 1, skip next st, [1dc in next st, ch 1, skip next st] 10 times; rep from * twice more, 3dc in next st, ch 1, skip next st, [1dc in next st, ch 1, skip next st] 5 times, changing to color D when joining with sl st to 3rd ch of ch-3. Break color C.
Round 8: Ch 3 (counts as 1dc), [1dc in every st and ch-1sp, working 3dc in 2nd st of 3dc corner cluster, join with sl st to 3rd of ch-3.
Fasten off and weave in ends.

 Mitered Curve *See page 23*

A=Persimmon
B=Bleached
C=Windsor
D=Dawn Gray

SPECIAL STITCHES
Picot: Ch 3, sl st in first ch.

Foundation ring: Using color A, make a Magic Ring.
Row 1: Ch 1, 3sc in ring, turn. (3 sts)
Row 2: Ch 1, 1sc in first st, 2sc in next st, 1sc in next st, turn. (4 sts)
Row 3: Ch 1, 1sc in first st, 2sc in next 2 sts, 1sc in next st, turn. (6 sts)
Row 4: Ch 1, 2sc in first st, 1sc in next 4 sts, 2sc in next st, turn. (8 sts)
Row 5: Ch 3 (counts as 1dc), 1dc in first st, 1dc in next 6 sts, 2dc in last st, turn. (10 sts)
Row 6: Ch 3 (counts as 1dc), 1dc in first st, 1dc in next st, 2dc in next st, 1dc in next 4 sts, 2dc in next st, 1dc in next st, changing to color B at the end of 2nd dc when working 2dc in 3rd ch of ch-3, turn. (14 sts)
Row 7: Ch 1, 1sc in every st to the end, turn.
Row 8: Ch 1, 1sc in first st, skip next st, [2dc, 1tr, picot, 1tr, 2dc] in next st, skip 1 st, 1sc in next st, skip next st, [2dc, 2tr, picot] in next st, [2tr, 2dc] in next st, skip 1 st, 1sc in next st, skip next st, [2dc, 1tr, picot, 1tr, 2dc] in next st, skip next st, changing to color C when working 1sc in last st, turn.
Row 9: Ch 3 (counts as 1dc), 2dc in first st, 1sc in picot, [(2tr, 2dc, 2tr) in

next sc, 1sc in picot] twice, changing to color D when working 3rd of 3dc in last sc, turn. (21 sts)
Row 10: Ch 1, 1sc in first st, 1sc in next 2 sts, 1hdc in next 3 sts, 1dc in next 2 sts, 1tr in next 2 sts, [2dtr, ch 2, 2dtr] in next st, 1tr in next 2 sts, 1dc in next 2 sts, 1hdc in next 3 sts, 1sc in next 2 sts, changing to color B when working last sc in 3rd ch of ch-3, turn. (24 sts)
Row 11: Ch 1, 1sc in every st to ch-2 sp, [2sc, 1hdc, 2sc] in ch-2 sp (corner made), 1sc in every st to end, changing to A when working last sc, turn. (29 sts)
Row 12: Ch 3 (counts as 1dc), skip first st, 1dc in every st to hdc, [1dc, 1tr, 1dc] in hdc, 1dc in every st to end of row, turn. (31 sts)
Row 13: Ch 3 (counts as 1dc), skip first st, 1dc in every dc to tr, [1dc, 1tr, 1dc] in tr, 1dc in every dc to end of row, turn. (33 sts)
Row 14: As Row 13.
Row 15: As Row 13, changing to color C when working last dc in 3rd ch of ch-3.
Row 16: As Row 13, changing to color D when working last dc in 3rd ch of ch-3.
Rows 17-18: As Row 13.
Fasten off and weave in ends.

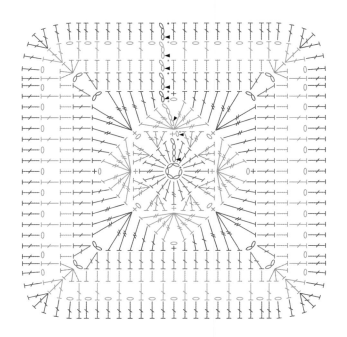

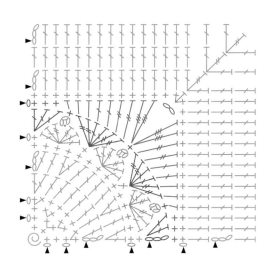

Hexagon in a Square

See page 22

A=Persimmon
B=Bleached
C=Aqua
D=Windsor

Foundation ring: Using color A, work 4 ch and join with sl st to form a ring.

Round 1: Ch 3 (counts as 1dc), 1dc in the ring, [ch 1, 2dc in ring] 5 times, ch 1, join with sl st to 3rd ch of ch-3. Break color A.

Round 2: Join color B to any ch-1 sp with a sl st, ch 3 (counts as 1dc), [1dc, ch 1, 2dc] in same sp, [2dc, ch 1, 2dc] in every ch-1 sp, join with sl st to 3rd ch of ch-3. Break color B.

Round 3: Join color C to any ch-1 sp with a sl st, ch 3 (counts as 1dc), 6dc in same sp, 7dc in every ch-1 sp, join with sl st to 3rd ch of ch-3. Break color C.

Round 4: Join color D to first dc of any shell, ch 1, 1sc in same place, 1sc in next 6dc, *1dc in sp between two shells from Round 2, 1sc in next 7dc; rep from * to end, changing to color B when joining with sl st to first sc. Break color D.

Round 5: Ch 1, 1sc in same place, 1sc in next 6sc, *[1dc, ch 2, 1dc] in next st**, 1sc in next 11sc; rep from * twice more and from * to ** once again, 1sc in next 4sc, join with sl st to first sc.

Round 6: Ch 1, 1sc in same place, 1sc in next 3sc, 1hdc in next 4sc, *[2dc, ch 3, 2dc] in next ch-2 sp, 1hdc in next 4sc**, 1sc in next 5sc, 1hdc in next 4sc; rep from * twice more and from * to ** once again, 1sc in next sc, join with sl st to first sc.

Round 7: Ch 3 (counts as 1dc), 1dc in next 9 sts, *[2dc, ch 3, 2dc] in next ch-3 sp**, 1dc in next 17 sts; rep from * twice more and from * to ** once again, 1dc in next 7 sts, changing to color C when joining with sl st to 3rd ch of ch-3. Break color B.

Round 8: Ch 3 (counts as 1dc), 1dc in next 13 sts, *[2dc, ch 3, 2dc] in next ch-3 sp**, 1dc in next 21 sts; rep from * twice more and from * to ** once again, 1dc in next 11 sts, changing to color D when joining with sl st to 3rd ch of ch-3. Break color C.

Round 9: Ch 3 (counts as 1dc), 1dc in next 17 sts, *[2dc, ch 2, 2dc] in next ch-3 sp**, 1dc in next 25 sts; rep from * twice more and from * to ** once again, 1dc in next 15 sts, changing to color A when joining with sl st to 3rd ch of ch-3. Break color D.

Round 10: Ch 1, 1sc in next 21 sts, *3sc in ch-2 sp**, 1sc in next 29 sts; rep from * twice more and from * to ** once again, 1sc in next 19 sts, join with sl st to first sc.

Fasten off and weave in ends.

Circle in a Hexagon

See page 20

A=Winsor
B=Aqua
C=Bleached
D=Persimmon

Foundation ring: Using color A, ch 8 and join with sl st in first ch to form a ring.

Round 1: Ch 3 (counts as 1dc), 23dc into the ring, change to yarn B when joining with sl st in 3rd ch of ch-3. Break color A.

Round 2: Ch 3 (counts as 1dc, 1dc in each of next 2dc, ch 5, skip next dc, *1dc in each of next 3dc, ch 5, skip next dc; rep from * a further 4 times, join with sl st in 3rd ch of ch-3.

Round 3: Ch 1, 1sc in same place, 1sc in each of next 2dc, *[2sc, ch 2, 2sc] in next ch-5 sp; rep from * 5 more times, change to color C when joining with sl st in first sc.

Round 4: Ch 3 (counts as 1dc), 1dc in each of next 4sc, 3dc in 2ch-sp, *1dc in each of next 7sc, 3dc in next 2ch-sp; rep from * a further 5 times, 1dc in each of next 2sc, join with sl st in 3rd ch of ch-3.

Round 5: Ch 3 (counts as 1dc), 1dc in each of next 3dc, ch 5, skip next 5dc, *1dc in each of next 5dc, ch 5, skip next 5dc; rep from * 4 more times, change to color D when joining with sl st in 3rd ch of ch-3.

Round 6: Ch 1, 1sc in same place, 1sc in each of next 4dc, *[2sc in next ch-5 sp, working over 5ch-sp, 1sc in in center dc from 3dc group in Round 3, 2sc in same ch-5 sp], (2hdc, ch 2, 2hdc) in next dc, 1sc in each of next 4dc, rep between [ ] once, 1sc in each of next 4dc, (2hdc, ch 2, 2hdc) in next dc, rep between [ ] once more*, 1sc in each of next 5dc; rep from * once more, 1sc in next sc, join with sl st in first sc. Break color D.

Round 7: Join color C to any ch-2 corner sp, ch 1, *[2sc, ch 1, 2sc] in ch-2 corner sp, 1sc in every sc to next ch-2 corner sp; rep from * a further 3 times, change to color B when joining with sl st in first sc.

Round 8: Ch 3 (counts as 1dc), 1dc in every st and 3dc in every 1ch-sp to end of round, change to color A when joining with sl st in 3rd ch of ch-3.

Round 9: Ch 3 (counts as 1dc), 1dc in every st and 3dc in center dc of every 3dc corner cluster to end of round, change to color D when joining with sl st in 3rd ch of ch-3.

Round 10: Ch 1, 1sc in every st and [1sc, 1hdc, 1sc] in center dc of every 3dc corner cluster to end of round, join with sl st in first sc.

Fasten off and weave in ends.

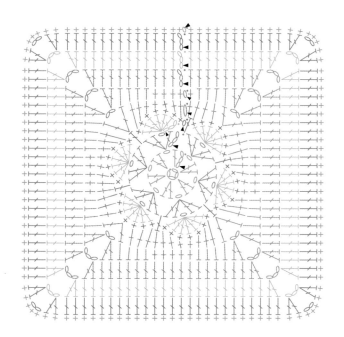

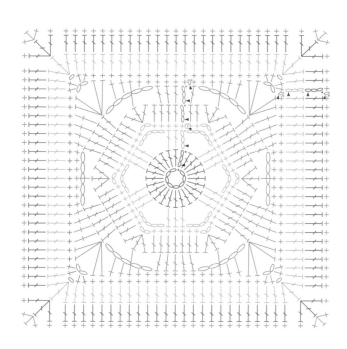

Double Diamonds

See page 21

A=Bleached
B=Dawn Gray
C=Persimmon

SPECIAL STITCHES

PS (Puff Stitch): Yoh, insert hook into designated stitch, [yoh, pull up a loop to the height of a hdc] 3 times, yoh and pull through all 7 loops on hook.

Foundation ring: Using color A, ch 6 and join with sl st in first ch to form a ring.

Round 1: Ch 4 (counts as 1tr), [5dc into the ring, 1tr into the ring] 3 times, 5dc into the ring, change to color B when joining with sl st in 4th ch of ch-4.

Round 2: Ch 1, 1sc in same place, *skip 2dc, [3dc, ch 3, 3dc] in next st, skip 2 sts**, 1sc in next dc; rep from * twice more, then from * to ** once more, join with sl st in first sc. Fasten off color B.

Round 3: Join color A to any 3ch-sp, ch 4 (counts as 1tr), [1tr, 3dc, ch 2, 3dc, 2tr] in same 3ch-sp, skip 3 sts, sl st in next sc, *[2tr, 3dc, ch 2, 3dc, 2tr] in same 3ch-sp, skip 3 sts, sl st in next sc**; rep from * once again and then from * to ** once more, 1tr in first ch-3 corner sp, join with sl st in 4th ch of ch-4. Fasten off color A.

Round 4: Join color C to any 2ch-sp, ch 1, 3sc in 2ch-sp, 1sc in each of next 5 sts, 1sc in sc from Round 2, 1sc in each of next 5 sts; rep from * 3 more times, change to color A when joining with sl st in first sc.

Round 5: Ch 1, 1sc in same place, *3sc in next sc, 1sc in each of next 3 sts, 1hdc in each of next 2 sts, 1dc in each of next 3sc, 1hdc in each of next 2 sts**, 1sc in each of next 3 sts; rep from * twice more and from * to ** once more, 1sc into each of next 2sc, join with sl st to first sc, Fasten off color A.

Round 6: Join color C to 2nd sc of 3sc corner cluster, ch 4 (counts as 1hdc and ch 2), 1hdc in same place, *[ch 1, skip 1 st, PS in next st] 7 times, ch 1**, skip 1 st, [1hdc, ch 2, 1hdc] in next st; rep from * twice more and then from * to ** once more, join with sl st in 2nd ch of ch-4. Fasten off color C.

Round 7: Join color A in 2ch-sp, ch 4 (counts as 1hdc and ch 2), 1hdc in same place, 1sc in hdc, [1sc over ch-sp and into corresponding st from Round 5, 1sc in PS] 7 times, 1sc over ch-sp and into corresponding st from Round 5**, 1hdc in hdc, ch 2, 1hdc in hdc; rep from * twice more and from * to ** once more, join with sl st in 2nd ch of ch-4. Fasten off color A.

Round 8: Join color B to any sc, ch 3 (counts as 1dc), 1dc in every sc and hdc from previous round and [2tr, ch 2, 2tr] in every ch-2 corner sp to end of round, change to color A when joining with sl st in 3rd ch of ch-3.

Round 9: Ch 2 (counts as 1hdc), 1hdc in every hdc and dc around and [2dc, ch 2, 2dc] in every ch-2 corner sp to end of round, change to color C when joining with sl st in 2nd ch of ch-2.

Round 10: Ch 2 (counts as 1hdc), 1hdc in every hdc and dc around and 3dc in every ch-2 corner sp to end of round, join with sl st in 2nd ch of ch-2. **Fasten off and weave in ends.**

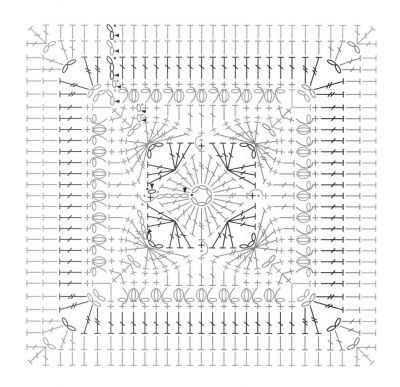

⭐ Lacy Cross
See page 25

A=Greengage

Foundation ring: Ch 6 and join with sl st in first ch to form a ring.
Round 1: Ch 3 (counts as 1dc throughout), 15dc into ring, join with sl st in 3rd ch of ch-3.
Round 2: Ch 3, 2dc in same place, ch 2, skip 1dc, 1dc in next dc, ch 2, skip 1dc, *3dc in next dc, ch 2, skip 1dc, 1dc in next dc, ch 2, skip 1dc; rep from * twice more, join with sl st in 3rd ch of ch-3.
Round 3: Ch 3, 5dc in next dc, *1dc in next dc, [ch 2, 1dc in next dc] twice, 5dc in next dc; rep from * twice more, [1dc in next dc, ch 2] twice, join with sl st in 3rd ch of ch-3.
Round 4: Ch 3, 1dc in each of next 2dc, 5dc in next dc, *1dc in each of next 3dc, ch 2, 1dc in next dc, ch 2, 1dc in each of next 3dc, 5dc in next dc; rep from * twice more, 1dc in each of next 3dc, ch 2, 1dc in next dc, ch 2, join with sl st in 3rd ch of ch-3.
Round 5: Ch 3, 1dc in each of next 4dc, 5dc in next dc, *1dc in each of next 5dc, ch 2, 1dc in next dc, ch 2, 1dc in to each of next 5dc, 5dc in next dc; rep from * twice more, 1dc in each of next 5dc, ch 2, 1dc in next dc, ch 2, join with sl st in 3rd ch of ch-3.
Round 6: Ch 3, 1dc in each of next 6dc, 5dc in next dc, *1dc in each of next 7dc, ch 2, 1dc in next dc, ch 2, 1dc in each of next 7dc, 5dc in next dc; rep from * twice more, 1dc in each of next 7dc, ch 2, 1dc in next dc, ch 2, join with sl st in 3rd ch of ch-3.
Round 7: Ch 3, 1dc in each dc and 2dc in each ch-2 sp of previous round, working [2dc, ch 1, 2dc] in centere of each 5dc corner group, join with sl st in 3rd ch of ch-3.
Fasten off and weave in ends.

⭐ Criss Cross
See page 27

A=Oyster

Foundation ring: Using color A, ch6 and join with sl st in first ch to form a ring.
Round 1: Ch3 (counts as 1dc), 3dc in ring, ch3, [4dc in ring, ch3] 3 times, join with sl st in 3rd ch of ch-3.
Round 2: Ch5 (counts as 1dc, 2ch), *skip 2dc, 1dc in next dc, [2dc, ch3, 2dc] in next ch-3 sp**, 1dc in next dc, ch2; rep from * twice more and then from * to ** once again, join with sl st in 3rd ch of ch-5.
Round 3: Ch5 (counts as 1dc, 2ch), *1dc in each of next 3dc, [2dc, ch3, 2dc] in next ch-3 sp**, 1dc in each of next 3dc, ch2; rep from * twice more and then from * to ** once again, 1dc in each of next 2dc, join with sl st in 3rd ch of ch-5.
Round 4: Ch5 (counts as 1dc, 2ch), *1dc in each of next 5dc, [2dc, ch3, 2dc in next dc] in next ch-3 sp**, 1dc in each of next 5dc, ch2; rep from * twice more and from * to ** once again, 1dc in each of next 4dc, join with sl st in 3rd ch of ch-5.
Round 5: Ch5 (counts as 1dc, ch2), *1dc in each of next 7dc, [2dc, ch3, 2dc in next dc] in next ch-3 sp**, 1dc in each of next 7dc, ch2; rep from * twice more and from * to ** once again, 1dc in each of next 6dc, join with sl st in 3rd ch of ch-5.
Round 6: Ch5 (counts as 1dc, ch2), *1dc in each of next 9dc, [2dc, ch3, 2dc in next dc] in next ch-3 sp**, 1dc in each of next 9dc, ch2; rep from * twice more and from * to ** once again, 1dc in each of next 8dc, join with sl st in 3rd ch of ch-5.
Round 7: Ch1, 1sc in same place, 1sc in each dc and 2sc in each ch-2 sp of previous round, working [2sc, ch1, 2sc] in each ch-3 corner sp, join with sl st to first sc.
Fasten off and weave in ends.

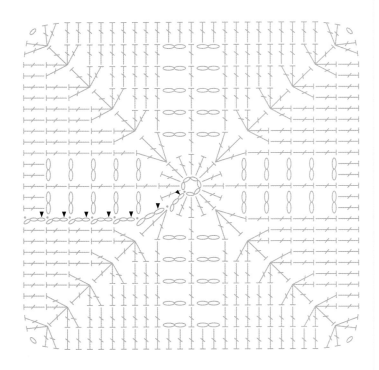

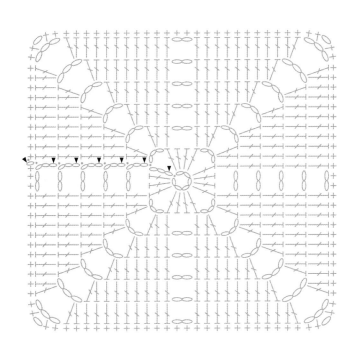

Sunray Cross

See page 24

A=Greengage

Foundation ring: Using color A, ch6 and join with sl st in first ch to form a ring.

Round 1: Ch4 (counts as 1tr), 1tr into ring, ch2, [2tr into ring, ch2] 7 times, join with sl st in 4th ch of ch-4.

Round 2: Ch3 (counts as 1dc), 2 dc in next tr, ch2, [1dc in next tr, 2dc in next tr, ch2] 7 times, join with sl st in 3rd ch of ch-3.

Round 3: Ch3 (counts as 1dc), 3dc in next dc, 1dc in next dc, ch2, *1dc in next dc, 3dc in next dc, 1dc in next dc, ch2; rep from * a further 6 times, join with sl st in 3rd ch of ch-3.

Round 4: Ch3 (counts as 1dc), 2hdc in next dc, 1sc in each of next 3dc, 2sc in next ch-2 sp, 1sc in each of next 3dc, 2hdc in next dc, 1dc in next dc, *ch3 (corner sp made), 1dc in next dc, 2hdc in next dc, 1sc in each of next 3dc, 2sc in next ch-2 sp, 1sc in each of next 3dc, 2hdc in next dc, 1dc

in next dc; rep from * twice, ch3 (corner sp made), join with sl st in 3rd ch of ch-3.

Round 5: Ch3 (counts as 1dc), 2dc in same place, *1hdc in each of next 5 sts, skip 1 st, ch2, 1dc in each of next 5 sts, 3dc in next st, ch3**, 3dc in next st; rep from * twice more and from * to ** once again, join with sl st in 3rd ch of ch-3.

Round 6: Ch3 (counts as 1dc), 1dc in each of next 7sts, *2dc in next ch-2 sp, 1dc in each of next 8 sts, 5dc in next ch-3 corner sp**, 1dc in each of next 8 sts; rep from * twice more and from * to ** once again, join with sl st in 3rd ch of ch-3.

Round 7: Ch2 (counts as 1hdc), 1hdc in each dc of previous round, working 3hdc in center st of each 5dc group, join with sl st in 2nd ch of ch-2.

Fasten off and weave in ends.

Popcorn Cross

See page 26

A=Oyster

SPECIAL STITCHES

Beg PC (Beginning Popcorn): Ch3, work 4dc in same place, remove hook from working loop and insert under both loops of first dc in the group. Pick up the working loop with the hook and draw it through to fold the group of sts together and close it at the top.

PC (Popcorn): Work 5dc in same place, remove hook from working loop and insert under both loops of first dc in the group. Pick up the working loop with the hook and draw it through to fold the group of sts together and close it at the top.

Foundation ring: Using color A, ch8 and join with sl st in first ch to form a ring.

Round 1: Beg PC into ring, [ch5, PC in ring] 3 times, ch 5, join with sl st in top of beg PC.

Round 2: Ch3 (counts as 1dc), *[2dc, ch2, PC, ch2, 2dc] in next ch-5 sp**, 1dc in next PC; rep from * twice more and from * to ** once again, join with sl st in 3rd ch of ch-3.

Round 3: Ch3 (counts as 1dc), 1dc in each of next 2 sts, *2dc in next ch-2 sp, ch2, PC in next PC, ch2, 2dc in

next ch-2 sp**, 1dc in each of next 5dc; rep from * twice more and from * to ** once again, 1dc in each of last 2 sts, join with sl st in 3rd ch of ch-3.

Round 4: Ch3 (counts as 1dc), 1dc in each of next 4dc, *2dc in next ch-2 sp, ch2, PC in next PC, ch2, 2dc in next ch-2 sp**, 1dc in each of next 9dc; rep from * twice more and from * to **once again, 1dc in each of last 4dc, join with sl st in 3rd ch of ch-3.

Round 5: Ch3 (counts as 1dc), 1dc in each of next 6dc, *2dc in next ch-2 sp, ch2, PC in next PC, ch2, 2dc in next ch-2 sp**, 1dc in each of next 13dc; rep from * to ** once again, 1dc in each of last 6dc, join with sl st in 3rd ch of ch-3.

Round 6: Ch3 (counts as 1dc), 1dc in each of next 8dc, *2dc in next ch-2 sp, ch2, PC in next PC, ch2, 2dc in next ch-2 sp**, 1dc in each of next 17dc; rep from * twice more and from * to ** once again, 1dc in each of last 8dc, join with sl st in 3rd ch of ch-3.

Round 7: Ch1, 1sc in every st of previous round, working 3sc in each ch-2 sp and [1hdc, 1dc, 1hdc] in top of each PC, join with sl st to first sc.

Fasten off and weave in ends.

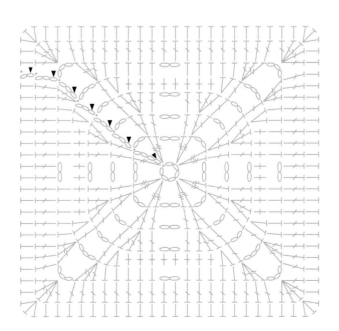

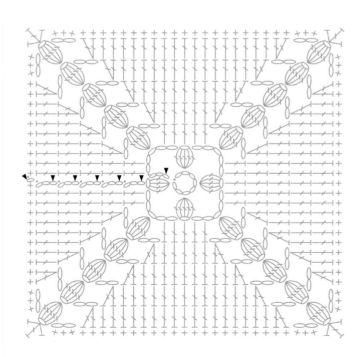

✪✪ Anemone

See page 27

A=Blood Orange
B=Garnet
C=Ecru
D=Oyster

Foundation ring: Using color A, ch4 and join sl st in first ch to form a ring.

Round 1: Ch3 (counts as 1dc), 3dc into ring, ch1, *4dc into ring, ch1; rep from * twice more, join with sl st in 3rd ch of ch-3. Break color A.

Round 2: Join color B to any ch-1 sp, ch3 (counts as 1dc), [3dc, ch1, 4dc] in next ch-1 sp (corner made), ch1, *[4dc, ch1, 4dc] in next ch-1 sp, ch1; rep from * twice more, change to color C when joining with sl st in 3rd ch of ch-3. Break color B.

Round 3: Ch1, 1sc in same place, 1sc in each dc and ch-1 sp from previous round, join with sl st to first sc.

Round 4: Join color D to any corner sc, ch3 (counts as 1dc), [2dc, ch1,

3dc] in same sc, ch1, *skip 4sc, [2dc, ch1, 2dc] in next sc, ch1, skip 4sc**, [4dc, ch1, 4dc] in next sc, ch1; rep from * twice more and from * to ** once again, join with sl st in 3rd ch of ch-3. Break color D.

Round 5: Join color A to first dc of any corner group, ch3 (counts as 1dc), 1dc in every dc and ch-1 sp along the edges of previous round and [2dc, ch1, 2dc] in each ch-1 corner sp, join with sl st in 3rd ch of ch-3.

Rounds 6-8: Ch3 (counts as 1dc), 1dc in every dc of previous round and [2dc, ch1, 2dc] in each ch-1 corner sp, join with sl st in 3rd ch of ch-3.

Fasten off and weave in ends.

✪✪ Seville

See page 25

A=Blood Orange
B=Oyster
C=Garnet

Foundation ring: Using color A, ch8 and join with sl st in first ch to form a ring.

Round 1: Ch3 (counts as 1dc), 2dc in the ring, ch7, [3dc in ring, ch7] 7 times, change to color B when joining with sl st in 3rd ch of ch-3.

Round 2: Sl st in next 2dc and ch-7 sp, ch3 (counts as 1dc), [2dc, ch2, 3dc] in same sp, *ch7, skip next ch-7 sp, [3dc, ch2, 3dc] in next ch-7 sp; rep from * twice more, ch7, skip next ch-7 sp, join with sl st in 3rd ch of ch-3.

Round 3: Ch3 (counts as 1dc), 1dc in each of next 2dc, *[2dc, ch2, 2dc] in ch-2 corner sp, 1dc in each of next 3dc, ch7**, 1dc in each of next 3dc; rep from * twice more and from * to ** once more, join with sl st in 3rd ch of ch-3.

Round 4: Ch3 (counts as 1dc), 1dc in each of next 4dc, *[2dc, ch2, 3dc] in ch-2 corner sp, 1dc in each of next 5dc, ch4, 1sc in skipped ch-7 sp from Round 1 enclosing ch made on Rounds 2 and 3, ch4**, 1dc in each of next 5dc; rep from * twice more and from * to ** once more, join with sl st

in 3rd ch of ch-3.

Round 5: Ch1, 1sc in same place, 1sc in each of next 6dc, *3sc in next ch-2 corner sp, 1sc in each of next 7dc, 1sc in next ch-4 sp, ch3, 1sc in next ch-4 sp**, 1sc in each of next 7dc; rep from * twice more and from * to ** once again, change to color C when joining with sl st in first sc.

Round 6: Ch4 (counts as 1dc and ch1), *[skip 1sc, 1dc in next sc, ch1] 3 times, 5dc in center st of next 3sc corner group, ch1, [skip 1 sc, 1dc in next sc, ch1] 3 times, skip next sc, 1 dc in each of next 2sc, 2dc in next ch-3 sp**, 1dc in each of next 2sc; rep from * twice more and from * to ** once again, 1dc in next sc, join with sl st in 3rd ch of ch-4.

Round 7: Ch4 (counts as 1dc and ch1), *[1dc in next dc, ch1] 3 times, 1dc in each of next 2dc, 3dc in center st of 5dc corner group, 1dc in each of next 2dc, ch1, [1dc in next dc, ch1] 3 times**, 1dc in each of next 6dc; rep from * twice more and from * to ** once again, 1dc in each of next 5dc, join with sl st in 3rd ch of ch-4.

Fasten off and weave in ends.

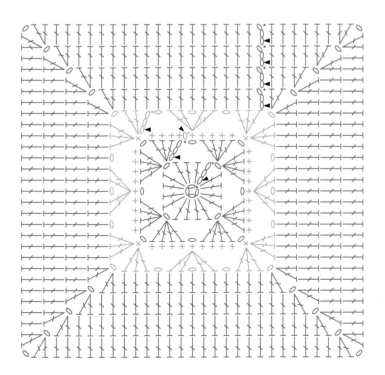

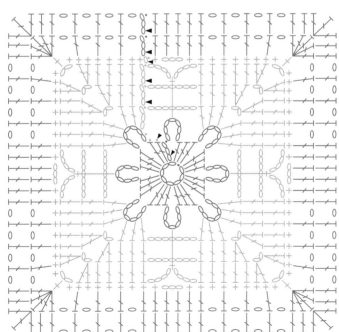

✪ ✪ *Italian Cross*

See page 24

A=Blackcurrant
B=Oyster
C=Garnet

SPECIAL STITCHES

hdc3tog (beg pf): Work three half double sts tog: [yoh, draw up a loop in next st] 3 times, yoh and draw through all 7 loops on hook.

hdc4tog (pf): Work four half double sts tog: [yoh, draw up a loop in next st] 4 times, yoh and draw through all 5 loops on hook.

Foundation ring: Using color A, ch 4 and join with sl st in first ch to form a ring.

Round 1: Ch 3 (counts as 1dc), 11dc into the ring, change to color B when joining with sl st in 3rd ch of ch-3. Break color A.

Round 2: Ch 2 (counts as 1hdc), beg pf in same place, *[ch 1, pf in next st] twice, ch 5**, pf in next st; rep from * twice more and from * to ** once again, join with sl st in top of beg pf.

Round 3: Sl st in next 1ch-sp, ch 2 (counts as 1hdc), beg pf in same sp, *pf in next sp, ch 2, 5dc in next 5ch-sp, ch 2**, pf in next 1ch-sp; rep from * twice more and from * to ** once again, join with sl st in top of beg pf.

Round 4: Sl st in next 1ch-sp, ch 2 (counts as 1hdc), beg pf in same sp, *ch 3, skip 2ch, [1dc in next dc, ch 1] twice, [1dc, (ch 1, 1dc) twice] in next dc, [ch 1, 1dc in next dc] twice, ch 3, skip 2ch**, pf in next 1ch-sp; rep from * twice more and from * to ** once again, join with sl st to top of beg pf. Break color B.

Round 5: Join color C to first dc of any 7dc corner group, ch 4 (counts as 1dc and ch 1), *[1dc in next dc, ch 1] twice, [1dc, (ch 1, 1dc) twice] in next dc, [ch 1, 1dc in next dc] 3 times, 3dc in next 3ch-sp, ch 1, 3dc in next 3ch-sp**, 1dc in next dc, ch 1; rep from * twice more and from * to ** once again, change to color A when joining with sl st in 3rd ch of ch-4.

Round 6: Ch 4 (counts as 1dc and ch 1), *[1dc in next dc, ch 1] 3 times, [1dc, (ch 1, 1dc) twice] in next dc, [ch 1, 1dc in next dc] 4 times, 1dc in each of next 3dc, 1dc in 1ch-sp, 1dc in each of next 3dc**, 1dc in next dc, ch 1; rep from * twice more and from * to ** once again, change to color C when joining with sl st in 3rd ch of ch-4.

Round 7: Ch 4 (counts as 1dc and ch 1), *[1dc in next dc, ch 1] 4 times, [1dc, (ch 1, 1dc) twice] in next dc, [ch 1, 1dc in next dc] 5 times**, 1dc in each of next 8dc, ch 1; rep from * twice more and from * to ** once again, 1dc in each of next 7dc, join with sl st in 3rd ch of ch-4.

Round 8: Ch 4 (counts as 1dc and ch 1), *[1dc in next dc, ch 1] 5 times, [1dc, (ch 1, 1dc) twice] in next dc, [ch 1, 1dc in next dc] 6 times**, 1dc in each of next 8dc, ch 1; rep from * twice more and from * to ** once again, 1dc in each of next 7dc, join with sl st in 3rd ch of ch-4.

Fasten off and weave in ends.

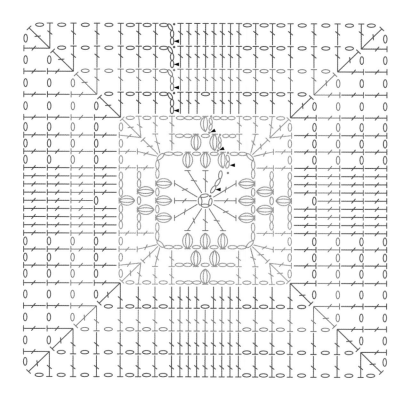

✪ ✪ *Looped Cross*

See page 26

A=Oyster
B=Greengage
C=Ecru
D=Dark Forest

Chain section: Using color A, ch 4 and join with sl st in first ch to form a ring, ch 16, *1sc into the ring, ch 15; rep from * twice more, join with a sl st in first ch. Fasten off.

Center motif: Using color B, ch 4 and join with sl st in first ch to form a ring, ch 3, (counts as 1dc), 2dc into the ring, ch 3, *3dc into the ring, ch 3; rep from * twice more, join with sl st in 3rd ch of ch-3. Fasten off. Hold the center motif in front of the chain section and pull each 15ch-loop through a corresponding 3ch-sp from the center motif.

Round 1: Join color B to any 15ch-sp, ch 1, [1sc, ch 3, 1sc] in same 15ch-sp, ch 8, *[1sc, ch 3, 1sc] in next 15ch-sp, ch 8; rep from * twice more, join with sl st in first sc.

Round 2: Ch 3 (counts as 1dc), *[1dc, ch 3, 1dc] in next 3ch-sp, 1dc in next sc, 8dc in 8ch-sp, 1dc in next sc; rep from * to end of round, omitting last dc, join with sl st in 3rd ch of ch-3.

Round 3: Ch 1, 1sc in same place, 1sc in next dc, *[(1sc, ch 1) twice, 1sc] in next 3ch-sp**, 1sc in each dc to corner; rep from * twice more and from * to ** again, 1sc in every dc to end of round, change to color C when joining with sl st in first sc.

Round 4: Ch 1, 1sc in same place, 1sc in in each of next 2sc, *1sc in next 1ch-sp, [1sc, ch 1, 1sc] in next sc, 1sc in next 1ch-sp**, 1sc in each of next 14 sc; rep from * twice more and from * to ** again, 1sc in every sc to end of round, change to color D when joining with sl st in first sc.

Round 5: Ch 1, 1sc in same place, *1sc in every sc to corner, [1sc, ch 1, 1sc] in 1ch-corner sp; rep from * a further 3 times, 1sc in every sc to end of round, join with sl st in first sc.
Fasten off and weave in ends.

✪ ✪ *Interlocking Cross*

See page 25

A=Dark Forest
B=Ecru
C=Greengage
D=Oyster

Foundation ring: Using color A, ch 4 and join with sl st in first ch to form a ring.

Round 1: Ch 1, [3sc into ring, ch 10] 4 times, change to color B when joining with sl st in first sc.

Round 2: Ch 2 (counts as 1hdc), 1hdc in same st, 1hdc in next sc, 2hdc in next sc, ch 12, *2hdc in next sc, 1hdc in in next sc, 2hdc in next sc, ch 12; rep from * twice more, change to color C when joining with sl st in 2nd ch of ch-2.

Round 3: Ch 3 (counts as 1dc), 1dc in same st, 1dc in each of next 3hdc, 2dc in next hdc, ch 12, *2dc in next sc, 1dc in each of next 3hdc, 2dc in next hdc, ch 12; rep from * twice more, change to color D when joining with sl st in 3rd ch of ch-3.

Round 4: Ch 3 (counts as 1dc), 1dc in same st, 1dc in each of next 5dc, 2dc in next dc, ch 12, *2dc in next dc, 1dc in each of next 5dc, 2dc in next dc, ch 12; rep from * twice more, change to color B when joining with sl st in 3rd ch of ch-3. Drop loop from hook. Form the corner chain links by slipping the loop from Round 1 over the loop from Round 2, slip Round 2 loop over Round 3 loop, and Round 3 loop over Round 4 loop. Insert hook back into dropped loop and continue with following round.

Round 5: Ch 3 (counts as 1dc), 1dc in same st, 1dc in each of next 7dc, 2dc in next dc, 5dc in 12ch-loop from Round 4, *2dc in next dc, 1dc in each of next 5dc, 2dc in next dc, 5dc in 12ch-loop from Round 4; rep from * twice more, join with sl st in 3rd ch of ch-3.
Fasten off and weave in ends.

Center motif

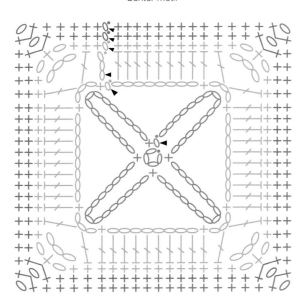

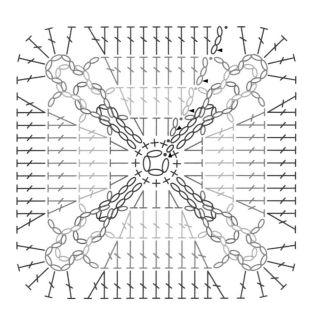

Crossroads   See page 27

A=Greengage

SPECIAL STITCHES

dc2tog (work 2 double sts tog):
Work two dc sts to the last "yoh, pull through," yoh once again and draw through all three loops on the hook.

dc3tog (work 3 double sts tog):
Work three dc sts to the last "yoh, pull through," yoh once again and draw through all four loops on the hook.

Foundation ring: Using color A, ch 4 and join with sl st in first ch to form a ring.

Round 1: Ch 3 (counts as 1dc), dc2tog into the ring, ch 1, dc3tog into the ring, ch 3, *dc3tog into ring, ch 1, dc3tog into ring, ch 3; rep from * twice more, join with sl st in top of first cluster.

Round 2: Sl st to next 1ch-sp, [ch 3, dc2tog, ch 1, dc3tog] in same sp, *ch 3, [(1dc, ch 3) twice in next 3ch-sp**, [dc3tog, ch 1, dc3tog] in next 1ch-sp;

rep from * twice more and from * to ** once again, join with sl st in top of first cluster.

Round 3: Sl st to next 1ch-sp, [ch 3, dc2tog, ch 1, dc3tog] in same sp, ch 1, *1dc in next 3ch-sp, ch 3 [(1dc, ch 3) twice in 3ch-corner sp, 1dc in next 3ch-sp, ch 1**, [(dc3tog, ch 1) twice] in next 1ch-sp; rep from * twice more and from * to ** once again, join with sl st to top of first cluster.

Round 4: Sl st to next 1ch-sp, [ch 3, dc2tog, ch 1, dc3tog] in same sp, *ch 3, skip next 1ch-sp, 1dc in next 3ch-sp, ch 3 [(1dc, ch 3) twice in 3ch-corner sp, 1dc in next 3ch-sp, ch 3, skip next 1ch-sp**, [dc3tog, ch 1, dc3tog] twice in next 1ch-sp; rep from * twice more and from * to ** once again, join with sl st to top of first cluster.

Fasten off and weave in ends.

 Embossed Cross   See page 24

A=Oyster
B=Ecru
C=Greengage
D=Dark Forest

SPECIAL STITCHES

dc5tog (cluster): Work five double sts tog: [Yoh , draw up a loop in next st, (yoh, pull through 2 loops on hook) twice] 5 times, yoh and draw through all 6 loops on hook.

Spiked dc: Yarn round hook, insert hook into stitch one round below the next stitch and pull loop through up to the level of current round, [yarn round hook and pull through two loops on hook] twice.

Foundation ring: Using color A, ch 6 and join with sl st in first ch to form a ring.

Round 1: Ch 3 (counts as 1dc), 15dc into the ring, change to color B when joining with sl st in 3rd ch of ch-3.

Round 2: Ch 1, 1sc in same place, *dc5tog in next sc, 1sc in each of next 3dc; rep from * to end of round, omitting last sc and joining with a sl st in first sc. Break color B.

Round 3: Join color A to top of any cluster from previous round, ch 3 (counts as 1dc), 4dc in same stitch, 1spiked dc in row below in each of next 3 sts, *5dc in top of corner cluster, 1spiked dc in row below in each of next 3 sts; rep from * twice

more, change to color C when joining with sl st in 3rd ch of ch-3.

Round 4: Ch 1, 1sc in same place, *1sc in next st, dc5tog in next st, 1sc in each of next 6 sts; rep from * to end of round, omitting last sc and joining with a sl st in first sc. Break color C.

Round 5: Join color A to top of any cluster from previous round, ch 3 (counts as 1dc), 4dc in same stitch, 1spiked dc in row below in each of next 7 sts, *5dc in corner cluster, 1spiked dc in row below in each of next 7 sts; rep from * twice more, change to color D when joining with sl st in 3rd ch of ch-3.

Round 6: Ch 1, 1sc in same place, *1sc in next st, dc5tog in next st, 1sc in each of next 10 sts; rep from * to end of round, omitting last sc and joining with a sl st in first sc. Break color D.

Round 7: Join color A to top of any cluster from previous round, ch 3 (counts as 1dc), 4dc in same stitch, 1spiked dc in row below in each of next 11 sts, *5dc in corner cluster, 1spiked dc in row below in each of next 11 sts; rep from * twice more, join with sl st in 3rd ch of ch-3.

Fasten off and weave in ends.

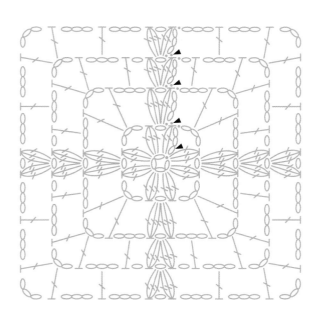

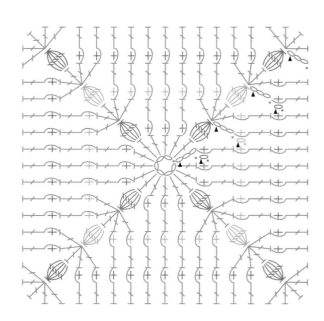

Catherine Wheel

See page 26

A=Garnet
B=Oyster
C=Ecru
D=Greengage

Foundation ring: Using color A, ch6 and join with sl st in first ch to form a ring.

Round 1: Ch3 (counts as 1dc), work 19dc in ring, changing to color B when joining with sl st to 3rd ch of ch-3. (20 dc)

Round 2: Ch4 (counts as 1dc, ch1), [1dc in next dc, ch1] 19 times, changing to color C when joining with sl st in 3rd ch of ch-3. (20 dc)

Round 3: Sl st in next ch-sp, ch3 (counts as 1dc), 2dc in same sp, [3dc in next ch-sp] 3 times, ch5, *skip next ch-sp, [3dc in next ch-sp] 4 times, ch5; rep from * twice more and change to color A when joining with sl st in 3rd ch of ch-3.

Round 4: Ch3 (counts as 1dc), 1dc in every dc of previous round, working [3dc, ch2, 3dc] in each ch-5 corner sp, and change to color C when joining with sl st to 3rd ch of ch-3.

Round 5: Join yarn C to next ch-2 corner sp, ch3 (counts as 1dc), [2dc, ch3, 3dc] in same sp, *[ch2, skip 2dc, 1dc in next dc] 3 times, [1dc in next dc, ch2, skip 2dc] 3 times**, [3dc,

ch2, 3dc] in next ch-2 corner sp; rep from * twice more and from * to ** once again, and change to color B when joining with sl st in 3rd ch of ch-3.

Round 6: Ch3 (counts as 1dc), 1dc in each of next 2dc, *[3dc, ch2, 3dc] in same sp, [ch2, 1dc in next dc] 3 times, [1dc in next dc, ch2] 3 times**, 1dc in each of next 3dc; rep from * twice more and from * to ** once again, join with sl st in 3rd ch of ch-3.

Round 7: Ch3 (counts as 1dc), 1dc in each of next 2dc *[3dc, ch2, 3dc] in same dc, [ch2, 1dc in next dc] 3 times, [1dc in next dc, ch2] 3 times**, 1dc in each of next 6dc; rep from * twice more and from * to ** once again, and change to color D when joining with sl st in 3rd ch of ch-3.

Round 8: Ch1, 1sc in each dc of previous round, working 2sc in each ch2-sp along sides of the square and 3sc in each ch-2 corner sp, join with sl st in first sc.

Fasten off and weave in ends.

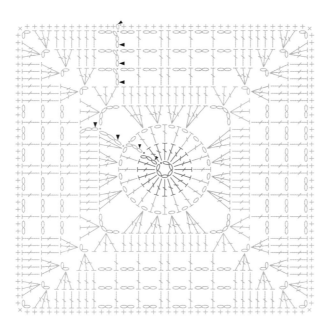

Gothic Square

See page 25

A=Ecru
B=Oyster
C=Garnet
D=Greengage

SPECIAL STITCHES

Beg cl (Beginning cluster): Ch3, [Yarn round hook, insert hook, yarn round hook, draw a loop through, yarn round hook, draw through 2 loops] twice in same stitch or space, yarn round hook and draw through all 3 loops on hook.

Cl (Cluster): [Yarn round hook, insert hook, yarn round hook, draw a loop through, yarn round hook, draw through 2 loops] three times in same stitch or space, yarn round hook and draw through all 4 loops on hook.

Foundation ring: Using color A, ch4 and join with sl st in first ch to form a ring.

Round 1: Ch4, (counts as 1dc, ch1), [1dc into ring, ch1] 11 times, change to color B when joining with sl st in 3rd ch of ch-4. (12 spaced dc)

Round 2: Ch3 (counts as 1dc), beg cl in same sp, [ch3, cl in ch-1 sp] 11 times, ch3, join with sl st to top of beg cl.

Round 3: Sl st in top of beg cl and center st of next ch-3 sp, ch1, 1sc in same sp, [ch5, 1sc in next ch-3 sp] 11 times, ch5, join with sl st to first sc. Break color B.

Round 4: Join color C to center st of any ch-5 sp, ch3 (counts as 1dc), 4dc in same sp, *ch1, 1sc in next ch-5 sp, ch5, 1sc in next ch-5 sp, ch1**, [5dc, ch3, 5dc] in next ch-5 sp; rep from * twice more and from * to ** once again, 5dc in next ch-5 sp, ch3, join with sl st in 3rd ch of ch-3. Break color C.

Round 5: Join color D to any ch-3 sp,

ch3 (counts as 1dc), [1dc, ch2, 2dc] in same sp, *1dc in each of next 4dc, ch5, 1sc in next ch-5 sp, ch4, skip next dc, 1dc in each of next 4dc**, [2dc, ch2, 2dc in next ch-3 sp; from * twice more and from * to ** once again, 5dc in next ch-5 sp, ch3, join with sl st in 3rd ch of ch-3.

Round 6: Ch3 (counts as 1dc), [1dc, ch2, 1dc] in same sp, *1dc in each of next 4dc, [ch4, 1sc in next ch-5 sp] twice, ch4, skip next dc, 1dc in each of next 4dc**, [2dc, ch2, 2dc in next ch-3 sp]; from * twice more and from * to ** once again, 5dc in next ch-5 sp, ch3, change to color A when joining with sl st in 3rd ch of ch-3.

Round 7: Ch3 (counts as 1dc), [1dc, ch2, 1dc] in same sp, *1dc in each of next 4dc, [ch4, 1sc in next ch-5 sp] 3 times, ch4, skip next dc, 1dc in each of next 4dc**, [2dc, ch2, 2dc] in next ch-3 sp; from * twice more and from * to ** once again, 5dc in next ch-5 sp, ch3, change to color B when joining with sl st in 3rd ch of ch-3.

Round 8: Ch2 (counts as 1hdc), 1hdc in next dc, *3hdc in next ch-2 corner sp, 1hdc in each of next 6dc, 4hdc in each of next ch-4 sp**, 1hdc in each of next 6dc; rep from * twice more and from * to ** once again, 1hdc in each of next 4dc, change to color C when joining with sl st to 2nd of ch-2.

Round 9: Ch1, 1sc in every st from previous round, working 3sc in center st of every 3hdc cluster, to end of round, join with sl st to first sc.

Fasten off and weave in ends.

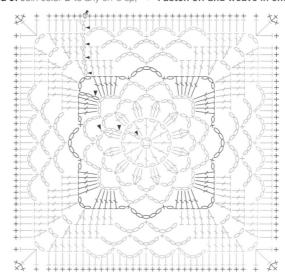

Treble Cross

See page 26

A=Greengage
B=Ecru
C=Oyster
D=Blackcurrant

SPECIAL STITCHES

dc2tog (work two double sts tog):
[Yoh draw up a loop in next st, (yoh, pull through 2 loops on hook) twice] twice, yoh and draw through all 3 loops on hook.

Foundation ring: Using color A, ch 8 and join with sl st in first ch to form a ring.
Round 1: Ch 1, 16sc into the ring, join with sl st in first sc.
Round 2: Ch 1, 1sc in same place, [ch7, skip 3sc, 1sc in next sc] 3 times, ch7, skip 3sc, join with sl st in first sc.
Round 3: Sl st to 3rd ch of next 7ch-sp, ch 3 (counts as 1dc), 1dc in same place, *ch 3, 2dc in same sp, ch 3, dc2tog inserting hook into same sp for first leg and into next 7ch-sp for second leg, ch 3, 2dc in next sp; rep from * a further 3 times, omitting 2dc at end of last rep, join with sl st in 3rd ch of ch 3. Break color A.
Round 4: Join color B to next 3ch-corner sp, ch 3 (counts as 1dc), 1dc in same place, *ch 3, 2dc in same 3ch-sp, ch 3, skip 2dc, 3dc in next 3ch-sp, 1dc in top of cluster, 3dc in next 3ch-sp, ch 3, skip 2dc, 2dc in next 3ch-sp; rep from * a further 3 times, omitting 2dc at end of last rep, join with sl st in 3rd ch of ch 3. Break color B.
Round 5: Join color C to next 3ch-corner sp, ch 3 (counts as 1dc), 2dc in same sp, *ch 3, 3dc in same 3ch-sp, ch2, 2dc in next 3ch-sp, ch2, skip 1dc, 1dc in each of next 5dc, ch 2, 2dc in next 3ch-sp, ch 2, 3dc in next 3ch-sp; rep from * a further 3 times, omitting 3dc at end of last rep, change to color D when joining with sl st in 3rd ch of ch 3. Break color C.
Round 6: Ch 3 (counts as 1dc), 1 dc in each of next 2dc, *[3dc, ch 3, 3dc] in next 3ch-sp, 1dc in each of next 3dc, ch 2, 2dc in each of 2dc, ch 2, skip 1dc, 1dc in each of next 3dc, ch 2, 1dc in each of next 2dc, ch 2, 1dc in each of next 3dc; rep from * a further 3 times, omitting 3dc at end of last rep, change to color C when joining with sl st in 3rd ch of ch 3. Break color D.
Round 7: Ch 3 (counts as 1dc), 1dc in each of next 5dc, *[3dc, ch 3, 3dc] in next 3ch-sp, 1dc in each of next 6dc, ch2, 1dc in each of next 2dc, ch2, skip 1dc, 1dc in next dc, skip 1dc, ch 2, 1dc in each of next 2dc, ch2, 1dc in each of next 6dc; rep from * a further 3 times, omitting 6dc at end of last rep, change to color B when joining with sl st in 3rd ch of ch 3. Break color C.
Round 8: Ch 3 (counts as 1dc), 1dc in every dc of previous round, working 2dc in every 2ch-sp and [3dc, ch 3, 3dc] in next 3ch-sp to end of round, change to color A when joining with sl st in 3rd ch of ch-3. Break color B.
Round 9: Ch 1, 1sc in every dc of previous round, working 3sc in every 3ch-corner sp, join with sl st in first sc.
Fasten off and weave in ends.

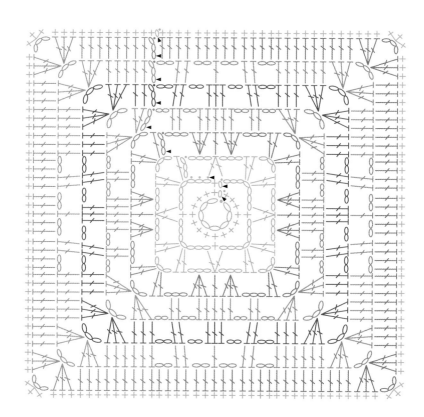

Compass Cross

See page 26

A=Garnet

Foundation ring: Using color A, ch 6 and join with sl st in first ch to form a ring.

Round 1: Ch 3 (counts as 1dc), 4dc into the ring, ch 8, [5dc, ch 8] 3 times into the ring, join with sl st in 3rd ch of ch-3.

Round 2: Sl st in next 4dc and in 8ch-sp, ch 3, [2dc, ch 3, 3dc] in same sp, ch 5, *[3dc, ch 3, 3dc] in next 8ch-sp, ch 5; rep from * twice more, join with sl st in 3rd ch of ch-3.

Round 3: Ch 3, 1dc in each of next 2dc, *[3dc, ch 3, 3dc] in next 3ch-sp, 1dc in each of next 3dc, ch 2, 1sc in 3rd ch of next 5ch-sp, ch 2**, 1dc in each of next 3dc; rep from * twice more and from * to ** once again, join with sl st in 3rd ch of ch-3.

Round 4: Ch 3, 1dc in each of next 5dc, *[3dc, ch 3, 3dc] in next 3ch-sp, 1dc in each of next 6dc, 5ch-sp, skip next two 2ch-sps**, 1dc in each of next 6dc; rep from * twice more and from * to ** once again, join with sl st in 3rd ch of ch-3.

Round 5: Ch 3, 1dc in each of next 8dc, *[3dc, ch 3, 3dc] in next 3ch-sp, 1dc in each of next 9dc, ch 2, 1sc in 3rd ch of next 5ch-sp, ch 2**, 1dc in each of next 9dc; rep from * twice more and from * to ** once again, join with sl st in 3rd ch of ch-3.

Round 6: Ch 3, 1dc in each of next 11dc, *[3dc, ch 3, 3dc] in next 3ch-sp, 1dc in each of next 12dc, 5ch-sp, skip next two 2ch-sps**, 1dc in each of next 12dc; rep from * twice more and from * to ** once again, join with sl st in 3rd ch of ch-3.

Round 7: Ch 2 (counts as 1hdc), work 1hdc in every dc, [2ch, 1sc, ch 2] in each in 5ch-sp , and 3hdc in every 3ch-corner sp around, join with sl st in 2nd ch of ch-2.

Fasten off and weave in ends.

Double Popcorn Cross

See page 25

A=Persimmon

SPECIAL STITCHES
PC (Popcorn): Work 5hdc into designated stitch, remove hook from last loop, place hook from front to back in top of the first of the last 5 hdc, pick up dropped loop, draw through loop on hook to complete the stitch.

Foundation ring: Using color A, ch 6 and join with sl st in first ch to form a ring.

Round 1: Ch 3 (counts as 1dc), 1dc into the ring, [ch 3, 3dc into the ring] 3 times, ch 3, 1dc into the ring, join with sl st in 3rd ch of ch-3.

Round 2: Ch 3 (counts as 1dc), *1pc in next st, 5dc in next ch-3 sp, 1pc in next dc**, 1dc in next dc; rep from * twice more and from * to ** once again, join with sl st in 3rd ch of ch-3.

Round 3: Ch 5 (counts as 1dc and ch 2), *skip next pc, 1pc in next dc, 1dc in next dc, 3dc in next dc, 1dc in next dc, 1pc in next dc, ch 2, skip next pc**, 1dc in next dc, ch 2; rep from * twice more and from * to ** once again, join with sl st in 3rd ch of ch-5.

Round 4: Sl st in next 2ch-sp, ch 5 (counts as 1dc and ch 2), *skip next pc, 1pc in next dc, 1dc in next dc, 3dc in next dc, 1dc in next dc, 1pc in next dc, ch 2, skip next pc**, [1dc in next 2ch-sp, ch 2] twice; rep from * twice more and from * to ** once again, 1dc in next 2ch-sp, ch 2, join with sl st in 3rd ch of ch-5.

Round 5: Sl st in next 2ch-sp, ch 5 (counts as 1dc and ch 2), *skip next pc, 1pc in next dc, 1dc in next dc, 3dc in next dc, 1dc in next dc, 1pc in next dc, ch 2, skip next pc**, [1dc in next 2ch-sp, ch 2] 3 times; rep from * twice more and from * to ** once again, [1dc in next 2ch-sp, ch 2] twice, join with sl st in 3rd ch of ch-5.

Round 6: Sl st in next 2ch-sp, ch 5 (counts as 1dc and ch 2), *skip next pc, 1pc in next dc, 1dc in next dc, 3dc in next dc, 1dc in next dc, 1pc in next dc, ch 2, skip next pc**, [1dc in next 2ch-sp, ch 2] 4 times; rep from * twice more and from * to ** once again, [1dc in next 2ch-sp, ch 2] 3 times, join with sl st in 3rd ch of ch-5.

Round 7: Sl st in next 2ch-sp, ch 5 (counts as 1dc and ch 2), *skip next pc, 1pc in next dc, 1dc in next dc, 3dc in next dc, 1dc in next dc, 1pc in next dc, ch 2, skip next pc**, [1dc in next 2ch-sp, ch 2] 5 times; rep from * twice more and from * to ** once again, [1dc in next 2ch-sp, ch 2] 4 times, join with sl st in 3rd ch of ch-5.

Round 8: Sl st in next 2ch-sp, ch 5 (counts as 1dc and ch 2), *skip next pc, 1pc in next dc, 1dc in next dc, 3dc in next dc, 1dc in next dc, 1pc in next dc, ch 2, skip next pc**, [1dc in next 2ch-sp, ch 2] 6 times; rep from * twice more and from * to ** once again, [1dc in next 2ch-sp, ch 2] 5 times, join with sl st in 3rd ch of ch-5.

Round 9: Ch 3 (counts as 1dc), *2dc in next 2ch-sp, 1dc in next pc, 1dc in each of next 2dc, 3dc in next dc, 1dc in each of next 2dc, 1dc in next pc, [2dc in next 2ch-sp, 1dc in next st] 6 times; rep from * a further 3 times, omitting last dc on final repeat, join with sl st in 3rd ch of ch-3.

Fasten off and weave in ends.

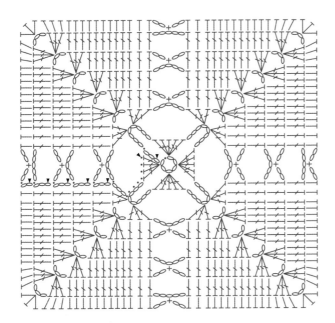

 **Wisteria**

See page 24

A=Oyster
B=Garnet
C=Ecru
D=Blood Orange

SPECIAL STITCHES

Beg cl (Beginning cluster): Work two double crochet stitches together: [yarn over hook, pull through a loop in next st, yarn over hook, pull through 2 loops on the hook] twice, yarn over hook and pull through all 3 loops on hook.

Cl (Cluster): Work three double crochet stitches together: [yarn round hook, pull through a loop in next st, yarn round hook, pull through 2 loops on the hook] three times, yarn round hook and pull through all 4 loops on hook.

Foundation ring: Using color A, ch4 and join with sl st in first ch to form a ring.

Round 1: Ch3 (counts as 1dc), beg cl in ring, ch5, *cl in ring, ch2**, [cl in ring, ch2**, cl in ring, ch5; rep from * twice more and from * to ** once again, join with sl st in 3rd ch of ch-3. Break color A.

Round 2: Join color B to any ch-5 corner sp, ch3 (counts as 1dc), [beg cl, ch2, cl] in same sp, *ch2, 3dc in next ch-2 sp, ch2**, [cl, ch2, cl] in next ch-5 sp; rep from * twice more and from * to ** once again, join with sl st in 3rd ch of ch-3.

Round 3: Sl st in next ch-2 corner sp, ch3 (counts as 1dc), [beg cl, ch2, cl] in same sp, *ch2, 2dc in next ch-2 sp, 1dc in each of next 3dc, 2dc in next ch-2 sp, ch2**, [cl, ch2, cl] in next ch-2 sp; rep from * twice more and from * to ** once again, join with sl st in 3rd ch of ch-3. Break color B.

Round 4: Join color C in next ch-2 corner sp, ch3 (counts as 1dc), [beg cl, ch2, cl] in same sp, *ch2, 2dc in next ch-2 sp, 1dc in each of next 7dc, 2dc in next ch-2 sp, ch2**, [cl, ch2, cl] in next ch-2 sp; rep from * twice more and from * to ** once again, join with sl st in 3rd ch of ch-3. Break color C.

Round 5: Join color D in next ch-2 corner sp, ch3 (counts as 1dc), [beg cl, ch2, cl] in same sp, *ch2, 2dc in next ch-2 sp, 1dc in each of next 11dc, 2dc in next ch-2 sp, ch2**, [cl, ch2, cl] in next ch-2 sp; rep from * twice more and from * to ** once again, join with sl st in 3rd ch of ch-3.

Round 6: Sl st in top of cl and next ch-2 corner sp, ch3 (counts as 1dc), [beg cl, ch2, cl] in same sp, *ch2, 2dc in next ch-2 sp, 1dc in each of next 15dc, 2dc in next ch-2 sp, ch2**, [cl, ch2, cl] in next ch-2 sp; rep from * twice more and from * to ** once again, join with sl st in 3rd ch of ch-3.

Round 7: Ch1, 1sc in same place, 1sc in every dc and cluster top of previous round, working 2sc in each ch-2 sp and [2sc, ch1, 2sc] in each ch-2 corner sp, join with sl st to first sc.

Fasten off and weave in ends.

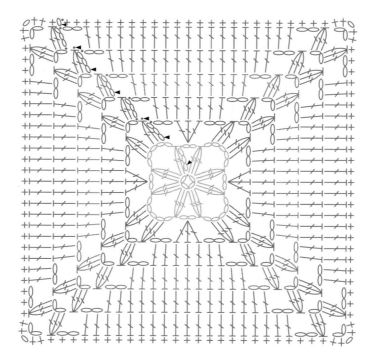

★ ★ *Danish Diamond*

See page 27

A=Greengage
B=Ecru
C=Persimmon
D=Oyster
E=Blood Orange

Foundation ring: Using color A, ch 10 and join with sl st to form a ring.
Round 1: Ch 1, 20sc into ring, join with sl st to first sc. (20 sc)
Round 2: Ch 1, 1sc, ch 8, *skip 4sc, 1sc in next sc, ch 8; rep from * twice more, join with sl st in first sc.
Round 3: Ch 1, 1sc in same place, [9sc in next 8ch-sp, 1sc in next sc] 3 times, 9sc in next 8ch-sp, join with sl st in first sc. Break color A.
Round 4: Join yarn B to 5th of 9sc corner group, ch 1, 2sc in same place, [1sc in each of next 9sc, 2sc in next sc] 3 times, 1sc in each of next 9sc, change to yarn C when joining with sl st in first sc.

Round 5: Ch 1, 2sc in same place, [1sc in each of next 10sc, 2sc in next sc] 3 times, 1sc in each of next 10sc, change to yarn D when joining with sl st in first sc.
Round 6: Ch 4 (counts as 1dc and ch 1], 1dc in same place, *ch 1, [1dc in next sc, ch 1, skip 1sc] 5 times, 1dc in next sc, ch1**, [1dc, ch 1, 1dc] in next sc; rep from * twice and from * to ** once again, join with sl st in 3rd ch of ch-4.
Round 7: Sl st in next 1ch-sp, 3sc in same place, 1sc in next dc, *[1sc in 1ch-sp, 1sc in next dc] 7 times, 3sc in

next 1ch-corner-sp, 1sc in next dc; rep from * twice more, [1sc in 1ch-sp, 1sc in next dc] 6 times, change to yarn E when joining with sl st in first sc. Break color D.
Round 8: Ch 3 (counts as 1dc), 1dc in every st to end of the round working 3dc in center sc of every 3sc corner cluster, change to yarn C when joining with sl st in 3rd ch of ch-3.
Round 9: Ch 3 (counts as 1dc), 1dc in every st to end of round working [1dc, ch 2, 1dc] in center dc of every 3dc corner cluster, change to yarn D when joining with sl st in 3rd ch of ch-3.
Round 10: Ch 3 (counts as 1dc), 1dc

in every st to the end of the round working [1dc, ch 2, 1dc] in each 2ch-corner-sp, change to yarn B when joining with sl st in 3rd ch of ch-3.
Round 11: Ch 1, 1sc in every st to end of round working [1sc, ch 2, 1sc] in each 2ch-corner-sp, change to yarn A when joining to first sc.
Round 12: Ch 2 (counts as 1hdc), 1hdc in every st to end of round working [1hdc, ch 2, 1hdc] in each 2ch-corner-sp, join with sl st in 2nd of ch-2.
Fasten off and weave in ends.

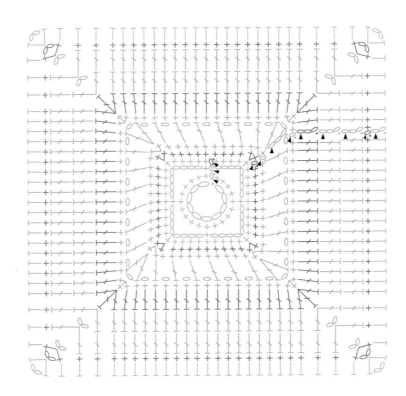

Tricolor Square

See page 27

A=Persimmon
B=Oyster
C=Garnet
D=Ecru

SPECIAL STITCHES

Beg cl (Beginning cluster): Work 5 treble sts together [yarn round hook twice, draw up a loop in next st, (yarn round hook, pull through 2 loops on hook) over next 5 sts, yarn round hook and draw through all 6 loops on hook.

Cl (Cluster): Work 6 treble sts together [yarn round hook twice, draw up a loop in next st, (yarn round hook, pull through 2 loops on hook) over next 6 sts, yarn round hook and draw through all 7 loops on hook.

Foundation ring: Using color A, ch8 and and join with sl st in first ch to form a ring.

Round 1: Ch4, (counts as 1 tr), 5tr, [ch3, 6tr in ring] 3 times, ch3, join with sl st in 4th ch of ch-4.

Round 2: Ch4, (counts as1tr), beg cl in each of next 5tr, *ch5, sl st in 2nd ch of ch-3, ch5**, Cl over next 6tr; rep from * twice more and from * to ** once again, join with sl st in 4th ch of ch-4. Break color A.

Round 3: Join color B to top of any cl, *[3tr, ch1, 3tr, ch2, 3tr, ch1, 3tr] in next ch-3 sp of Round 1, sl st in top of next cl; rep from * 3 times, join with sl st to top of first cl. Break color B.

Round 4: Join color C to sl st at top of cl, ch4 (counts as 1tr), 5tr in same place, *[6tr, ch2, 6tr] in next ch-2 sp**, 6tr in sl st at top of next cl; rep from * twice more and from * to ** once again, join with sl st in 4th ch of ch-4. Break color C.

Round 5: Join color A to last sl st of previous round, ch1, 1sc in each of next 6tr, 1dc in ch-1 sp between groups of tr worked on Round 3, *1sc in each of next 6tr, 3sc in ch-2 corner sp**, [1sc in each of next 6tr, 1dc in ch-1 sp between groups of tr worked on Round 3] twice; rep from * twice more and from * to ** once again, 1sc in each of next 6dc, 1dc in ch-1 sp between groups of tr worked on Round 3, change to color D when joining with sl st to first sc. Break color A.

Round 6: Ch3 (counts as 1dc), 1dc in every st from previous round, working 3dc in center st of each 3sc corner group, change to color B when joining with sl st to first sc. Break color D.

Round 7: Ch3 (counts as 1dc), 1dc in every st from previous round, working 3dc in center st of each 3dc corner group, join with sl st in 3rd ch of ch-3.
Fasten off and weave in ends.

 ## St. Petersburg

See page 24

A=Blood Orange
B=Oyster
C=Ecru
D=Greengage
E=Persimmon

SPECIAL STITCHES

FRdc (Front Raised double crochet): Yarn over hook, insert hook from front to back around the post of designated stitch, yarn over hook, pull up a loop, [yarn over hook, pull through two loops on the hook] twice more.

BRdc (Back Raised double crochet): Yarn over hook, insert hook from back to front around the post of designated stitch, yarn over hook, pull up a loop, [yarn over hook, pull through two loops on the hook] twice more.

Foundation ring: Using color A, ch8 and join with sl st in first ch to form a ring.

Round 1: Ch3 (counts as 1dc), 2dc into ring, ch3, [3dc into ring, ch3] 3 times, join with sl st in 3rd ch of ch-3. Break color A.

Round 2: Join color B to any ch-3 corner sp, ch3 (counts as 1dc), 2dc in same sp, *1FRdc round each of next 3dc**, [3dc, ch3, 3dc] in next ch-3 corner sp; rep from * twice more and from * to ** once again, [3dc, ch3] in next ch-3 corner sp, join with sl st in 3rd ch of ch-3. Break color B.

Round 3: Join color C to any ch-3 corner sp, ch6 (counts as 1dc, ch3), 3dc in same sp, *1BRdc around each of next 3dc, 1FRdc around each of next 3 sts, 1BRdc around each of next 3dc**, [3dc, ch3, 3dc] in next ch-3 corner sp; rep from * twice more and from * to ** once again, 2dc in next ch-3 corner sp, join with sl st in 3rd ch of ch-3, Break color C.

Round 4: Join color D to any ch-3 corner sp, ch3 (counts as 1dc,) 2dc in same sp, *[1FRdc around each of next 3 sts, 1BRdc round each of next 3 sts] twice, 1FRdc round each of next 3 sts**, [3dc, ch3, 3dc] in next ch-3 corner sp; rep from * twice more and from * to ** once again, [3dc, ch3] in next ch-3 corner sp, join with sl st in 3rd ch of ch-3. Break color D.

Round 5: Join color E to any ch-3 corner sp, ch1, *[2sc, ch2, 2sc] in same sp, 1sc in each of next 3dc, 1hdc in each of next 15 sts, 1sc in each of next 3dc; rep from * a further 3 times, join with sl st to first sc. Break color E.

Round 6: Join color A to any ch-2corner sp, ch2, (counts as 1hdc), 2hdc in same sp, *1hdc in each of next 5sc, 1dc in each of next 15hdc, 1hdc in each of next 5sc**, 3hdc in next ch-2 corner sp; rep from * twice more and from * to ** once again, join with sl st in 2nd ch of ch2. Break color A.

Round 7: Join color B to any hdc, ch3 (counts as 1dc), 1dc in every st of previous round, working 3dc in center hdc of each 3hdc corner cluster, join with sl st in 3rd ch of ch-3.
Fasten off and weave in ends.

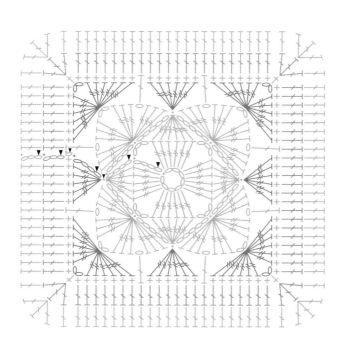

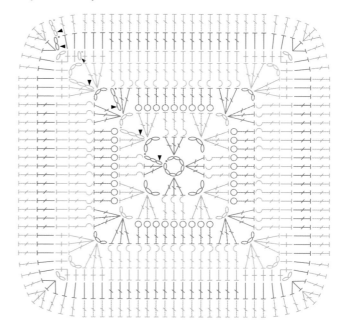

⭐⭐ Quartet

See page 30

A=Cobalt
B=Nightshade
C=Blood Orange
D=Oyster

Foundation chain: Using color A, work 29 ch.

The center of the block is worked entirely from the chart.

Each square on the chart represents one stitch, but does not show any turning chain. Charts are read from bottom to top and the first row will count as a RS row and be read from right to left. The following row is a WS row and therefore read from left to right. This is illustrated by start-of-row indicators.

Change colors at the last stage of the preceding stitch. When you are changing color on a WS row you will need to take the old color forward and take the new one to the back, looping the old yarn around the new one so that you prevent a hole from occurring. Fasten off.

Border

Round 1: Join color C to LH row edge of Row 17 with a sl st, ch 1, 1sc in same place, *work 12sc evenly along this row-end edge to corner, [1sc, 1hdc, 1sc] in corner, 1sc in each of next 25 ch, [1sc, 1hdc, 1sc] in corner**, work 12sc evenly along RH lower row-end edge, changing to color B at end of Row 17; rep from * to ** once more working 25sc across the top sts, 12sc evenly along upper LH edge, changing to color A when joining with sl st in first sc.

Round 2: Ch 2 (counts as 1hdc), 1hdc in every sc and [1hdc, 1dc, 1hdc] in every corner hdc from previous round, change to color D when joining with sl st in 2nd ch of ch-2.

Round 3: Ch 2 (counts as 1hdc), 1hdc in every sc and [1hdc, 1dc, 1hdc] in every hdc from previous round, join with sl st in 2nd ch of ch-2.

Fasten off and weave in ends.

⭐⭐ Intarsia Steps

See page 28

A=Cobalt
B=Nightshade
C=Blood Orange
D=Oyster

Foundation chain: Using color A, work 29 ch.

The center of the block is worked entirely from the chart.

Each square on the chart represents one stitch, but does not show any turning chain. Charts are read from bottom to top and the first row will count as a RS row and be read from right to left. The following row is a WS row and therefore read from left to right. This is illustrated by start-of-row indicators.

Change colors at the last stage of the preceding stitch. When you are changing color on a WS row you will need to take the old color forward and take the new one to the back, looping the old yarn around the new one so that you prevent a hole from occurring. Fasten off.

Border

Round 1: Join color C to any ch along Foundation edge with a sl st, ch 1, 1sc in same place, 1sc in every ch to corner, *[1sc, 1hdc, 1sc] in corner, work 21sc evenly along row-end edge to corner, [1sc, 1hdc, 1sc] in corner**, 1sc in each of next 26 sts, rep from * to ** once more, 1sc in every ch to end of round, join with sl st in first sc.

Round 2: Ch 2 (counts as 1hdc), 1hdc in every sc and [1hdc, 1dc, 1hdc] in every hdc from previous round, changing to color D when joining with sl st in 2nd ch of ch-2.

Round 3: Ch 2 (counts as 1hdc), 1hdc in every hdc and [1hdc, 1dc, 1hdc] in every dc from previous round, join with sl st in 2nd of ch-2.

Fasten off and weave in ends.

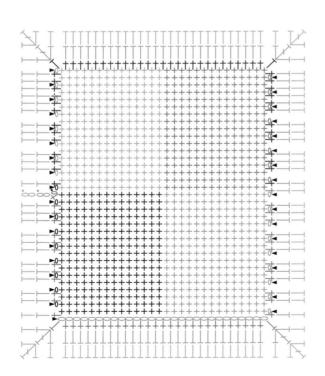

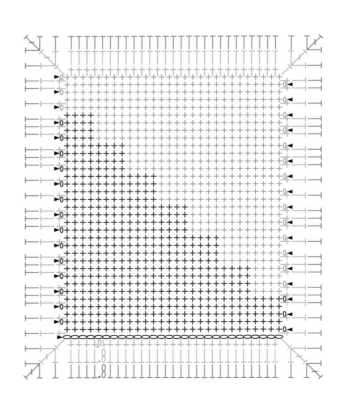

★★ Zig Zag

See page 31

A=Cobalt
B=Nightshade
C=Blood Orange
D=Oyster

Foundation chain: Using color A, work 29ch.

The center of the block is worked entirely from the chart.

Each square on the chart represents one stitch, but does not show any turning chain. Charts are read from bottom to top and the first row will count as a RS row and be read from right to left. The following row is a WS row and therefore read from left to right. This is illustrated by start-of-row indicators.

Change colors at the last stage of the preceding stitch. When you are changing color on a WS row you will need to take the old color forward and take the new one to the back, looping the old yarn around the new one so

that you prevent a hole from occurring. Fasten off.

Border

Round 1: Join color D to any ch along Foundation edge with a sl st, ch 1, 1sc in same place, 1sc in every ch to corner, *[1sc, 1hdc, 1sc] in corner, work 25sc evenly along row-end edge to corner, [1sc, 1hdc, 1sc] in corner**, 1sc in each of next 26 sts; rep from * to ** once more, 1sc in every ch to end of round, change to color B when joining with sl st in first sc.

Round 2: Ch 1, 1sc in every sc and [1sc, 1dc, 1sc] in every corner hdc from previous round, join with sl st in first sc.

Fasten off and weave in ends.

★★ Random Patches

See page 28

A=Cobalt
B=Sky
C=Nightshade
D=Bleached
E=Blood Orange
F=Oyster

Foundation chain: Using color A, work 29 ch.

The center of the block is worked entirely from the chart.

Each square on the chart represents one stitch, but does not show any turning chain. Charts are read from bottom to top and the first row will count as a RS row and be read from right to left. The following row is a WS row and therefore read from left to right. This is illustrated by start-of-row indicators.

Change colors at the last stage of the preceding stitch. When you are changing color on a WS row you will need to take the old color forward and take the new one to the back, looping the old yarn around the new one so

that you prevent a hole from occurring. Fasten off.

Border

Round 1: Join color D to any ch along Foundation edge with a sl st, ch 1, 1sc in same place, 1sc in every ch to corner, work 22sc evenly along row-end edge to corner, [1sc, 1hdc, 1sc] in corner, *[1sc, 1hdc, 1sc] in corner, 1sc in each of next 26 sts; rep from * to ** once more, 1sc in every ch to end of round, change to color F when joining with sl st in first sc.

Round 2: Ch 2 (counts as 1hdc), 1hdc in every sc and [1hdc, 1dc, 1hdc] in every hdc from previous round, join with sl st in 2nd ch of ch-2.

Fasten off and weave in ends.

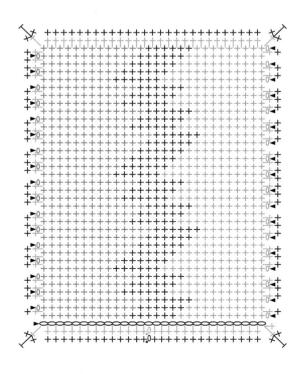

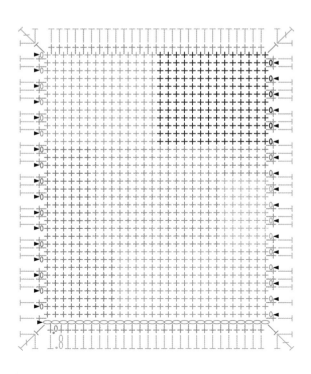

Seminole

See page 28

A=Blood Orange
B=Sky
C=Nightshade
D=Cobalt
E=Bleached
F=Oyster
G=Cadmium

Foundation chain: Using color A, make 29ch.

The center of the block is worked entirely from the chart.

Each square on the chart represents one stitch, but does not show any turning chain. Charts are read from bottom to top and the first row will count as a RS row and be read from right to left. The following row is a WS row and therefore read from left to right. This is illustrated by start-of-row indicators.

Change colors at the last stage of the preceding stitch. When you are changing color on a WS row you will need to take the old color forward and take the new one to the back, looping the old yarn around the new one so that you prevent a hole from occurring. Fasten off.

Border

Round 1: Join color F to the 14th ch (last one worked in color A), of Foundation chain with a sl st, ch 1, 1sc in same place, 1sc in every ch to corner, *[1sc, 1hdc, 1sc] in corner, work 25sc evenly along row-end edge to corner, [1sc, 1hdc, 1sc] in corner**, 1sc in each of next 12 sts, change to color C when working sc in last ch in color A, (do not break color F), continue to work 1sc in every st to corner; rep from * to ** once more, 1sc in every ch to end of round, join with sl st in first sc.

Round 2: Ch 2 (counts as 1hdc), 1hdc in every sc previously worked in color F and [1hdc, 1dc, 1hdc] in every hdc from previous round, continue as set to end of round, changing to color F when you reach the first sc in color C from previous round, join with sl st in 2nd ch of ch-2.

Fasten off and weave in ends.

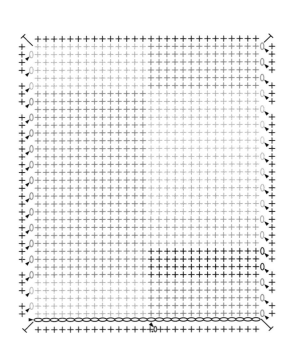

Interlocking Stripes

See page 31

A=Nightshade
B=Oyster
C=Cobalt
D=Bleached

E=Sky
F=Winsor
G=Cadmium
H=Blood Orange

Foundation chain: Using color A, work 29 ch.

The center of the block is worked entirely from the chart.

Each square on the chart represents one stitch, but does not show any turning chain. Charts are read from bottom to top and the first row will count as a RS row and be read from right to left. The following row is a WS row and therefore read from left to right. This is illustrated by start-of-row indicators.

Change colors at the last stage of the preceding stitch. When you are changing color on a WS row you will need to take the old color forward and take the new one to the back, looping the old yarn around the new one so that you prevent a hole from occurring. Fasten off.

Border

Round 1: Join color D to any ch along Foundation edge with a sl st, ch 1, 1sc in same place, 1sc in every ch to corner, *[1sc, 1hdc, 1sc] in corner, work 25sc evenly along row-end edge to corner, [1sc, 1hdc, 1sc] in corner**, 1sc in each of next 26 sts; rep from * to ** once more, 1sc in every ch to end of round, change to color C when joining with sl st in first sc.

Round 2: Ch 2 (counts as 1hdc), 1hdc in every sc and [1hdc, 1dc, 1hdc] in every hdc from previous round, join with sl st in 2nd ch of ch-2.

Fasten off and weave in ends.

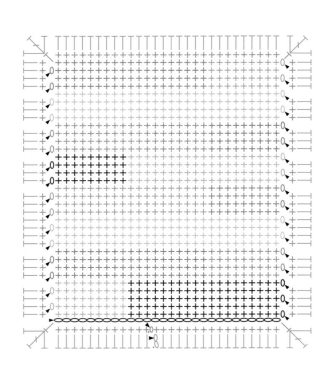

✪✪ *Jaguard Stripes*   *See page 29*

A=Blood Orange
B=Oyster
C=Cobalt
D=Nightshade

Foundation chain: Using color A, make 29 ch.
The center of the block is worked by repeating Rows 1–2 of the chart, 14 times.
Remember that RS rows (odd numbers) are worked from right to left and WS rows (even numbers) are worked from left to right. Fasten off.
Border
Round 1: Join color C to any ch along Foundation edge with a sl st, ch 1, 1sc in same place, 1sc in every ch to corner, *[1sc, 1hdc, 1sc] in corner, work 21sc evenly along row-end edge to corner, [1sc, 1hdc, 1sc] in corner**,

1sc in each of next 26 sts; rep from * to ** once more, 1sc in every ch to end of round, change to color D when joining with sl st in first sc.
Round 2: Ch 2 (counts as 1hdc), 1hdc in every sc and [1hdc, 1dc, 1hdc] in every hdc from previous round, change to color B when joining with sl st in 2nd ch of ch-2.
Round 3: Ch 1, 1sc in every hdc and [1sc, 1hdc, 1sc] in every dc from previous round, join with sl st in first sc.
Fasten off and weave in ends.

 ✪✪ *Jaguard Checks*   *See page 31*

A=Nightshade
B=Oyster
C=Blood Orange

Foundation chain: Using color A, make 29ch.
The center of the block is worked entirely from the chart working Rows 2–9 a total of 3 times, then repeat Rows 2–5 once more.
Each square on the chart represents one stitch, but does not show any turning chain. Charts are read from bottom to top and the first row will count as a RS row and be read from right to left. The following row is a WS row and therefore read from left to right. This is illustrated by start-of-row indicators.
Change colors at the last stage of the preceding stitch. When you are changing color on a WS row you will need to take the old color forward and take the new one to the back, looping the old yarn around the new one so that you prevent a hole from occurring. Fasten off.

Border
Round 1: Join color C to any ch along Foundation edge with a sl st. Ch1, 1sc in same place, 1sc in every ch to corner, *[1sc, 1hdc, 1sc] in corner, work 21sc evenly along row-end edge to corner, [1sc, 1hdc, 1sc] in corner**, 1sc in each of next 26 sts; rep from * to ** once more, 1sc in every ch to end of round, change to color A when joining with sl st in first sc.
Round 2: Ch 2 (counts as 1hdc), 1hdc in every sc and [1hdc, 1dc, 1hdc] in every hdc from previous round, change to color B when joining with sl st in 2nd ch of ch-2.
Round 3: Ch 1, 1sc in every hdc and [1sc, 1hdc, 1sc] in every dc from previous round, join with sl st in first sc.
Fasten off and weave in ends.

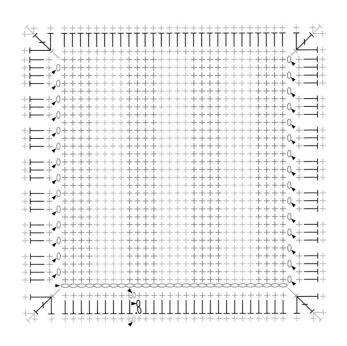

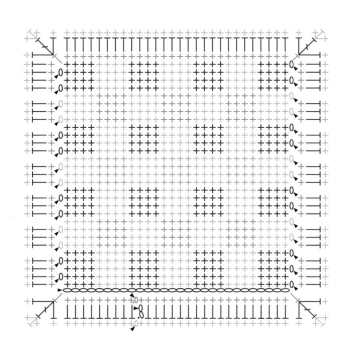

⭐⭐ *Darts*
See page 30

A=Nightshade
B=Bleached
C=Cobalt
D=Blood Orange
E=Oyster

Foundation chain: Using color A, ch 21, do not break A, but join in B for a further ch. (22ch)

The center of the block is worked entirely from the chart working Rows 1–24 once.

Each square on the chart represents one stitch. Charts are read from bottom to top and the first row will count as a RS row and be read from right to left. The following row is a WS row and therefore read from left to right. This is illustrated by start-of-row indicators.

Change colors at the last stage of the preceding stitch. When you are changing color on a WS row you will need to take the old color forward and take the new one to the back, looping the old yarn around the new one so that you prevent a hole from occurring. Fasten off.

Border

Round 1: Join color E to any ch along Foundation edge with a sl st. Ch 1, 1sc in same place, 1sc in every ch to corner, [1sc, 1hdc, 1sc] in corner, work 16sc evenly along row-end edge to corner, *[1sc, 1hdc, 1sc] in corner, 1sc in each of next 20sts, [1sc, 1hdc, 1sc] in corner**, work 16sc evenly along next row-end edge; rep from * to **, work 1sc in every ch to end of round, join with sl st in first sc.

Round 2: Ch2 (counts as 1hdc), 1hdc in every sc and [3hdc] in every hdc from previous round, change to color C when joining with sl st in 2nd ch of ch-2.

Round 3: As Round 2 in C.
Round 4: As Round 2 in E.
Round 5: As Round 2 in D.
Round 6: As Round 2 in A.
Fasten off and weave in ends.

⭐⭐ *Half and Half*
See page 29

A=Blood Orange
B=Sky
C=Nightshade

Foundation chain: Using color A, make 2ch.

Foundation row (WS): 3sc in 2nd ch from hook, turn. (3 sc)

Row 1: Ch 1, 2sc in first sc, 1sc in next sc, 2sc in last sc, turn. (5 sc)

Rows 2–4: Ch 1, 2sc in first sc, 1sc in each sc to last sc, 2sc in last sc, turn. (2 sts increased)

Row 5: Ch 1, 1sc in every sc to end, turn.

Rep Rows 2–5 a further 5 times, changing to color B in the last sc of the final Row 5 repeat. (41 sc) Break color A.

Next row: Ch 1, 1sc in every sc to end, turn.

Next 3 rows: Ch 1, skip first sc, 1sc in each sc to last 2sc, skip 1sc, 1sc in last sc, turn. (2 sts decreased)

Rep last 4 rows a further 5 times. (5 sc)

Next row: Ch 1, skip first sc, 1sc in each of next 2sc, skip 1sc, 1sc in last sc, turn. (3 sc)

Next row: Ch 1, sc3tog over next 3sc. Fasten off.

Border

Round 1: Join color C to any corner with a sl st, 1ch, *[1sc, 1hdc, 1sc] in corner, 25sc evenly along row-end edge to corner; rep from * 3 more times, join with sl st in first sc.

Fasten off and weave in ends.

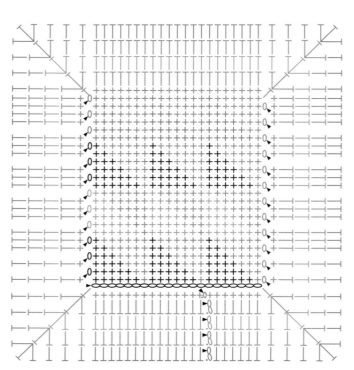

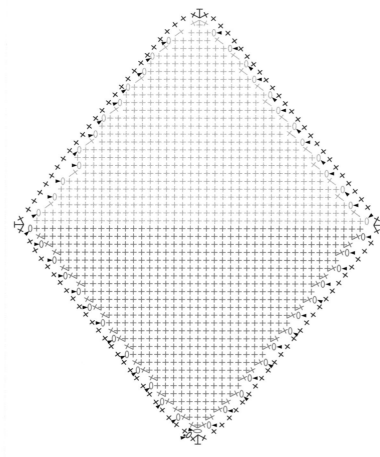

Trio

See page 29

A=Nightshade
B=Cobalt
C=Sky
D=Bleached

Foundation chain: Using color A, make 29 ch.

The center of the block is worked entirely from the chart.

Each square on the chart represents one stitch, but does not show any turning chain. Charts are read from bottom to top and the first row will count as a RS row and be read from right to left. The following row is a WS row and therefore read from left to right. This is illustrated by start-of-row indicators.

Change colors at the last stage of the preceding stitch. When you are changing color on a WS row you will need to take the old color forward and take the new one to the back, looping the old yarn around the new one so that you prevent a hole from occurring. Fasten off.

Border

Round 1: Join color C to any ch along Foundation edge with a sl st, ch 1, 1sc in same place, 1sc in every ch to corner, *[1sc, 1hdc, 1sc] in corner, work 26sc evenly along row-end edge to corner, [1sc, 1hdc, 1sc] in corner**, 1sc in each of next 26sc; rep from * to **, 1sc in every ch to end of round, change to color D when joining with sl st in first sc.

Round 2: Ch 1, 1sc in every sc and [1sc, 1hdc, 1sc] in every hdc from previous round, change to color B when joining with sl st in first sc.

Round 3: Ch 2 (counts as 1hdc), 1hdc in every sc and [1hdc, 1dc, 1hdc] in every hdc from previous round, join with sl st in 2nd ch of ch-2.

Fasten off and weave in ends.

Hourglass

See page 28

A=Nightshade
B=Cobalt
C=Blood Orange
D=Bleached

Foundation chain: Using color A, make 29 ch.

The center of the block is worked entirely from the chart.

Each square on the chart represents one stitch, but does not show any turning chain. Charts are read from bottom to top and the first row will count as a RS row and be read from right to left. The following row is a WS row and therefore read from left to right. This is illustrated by start-of-row indicators.

Change colors at the last stage of the preceding stitch. When you are changing color on a WS row you will need to take the old color forward and take the new one to the back, looping the old yarn around the new one so that you prevent a hole from occurring. Fasten off.

Border

Round 1: Join color D to any ch along Foundation edge with a sl st, ch 1, 1sc in same place, 1sc in every ch to corner, *[1sc, 1hdc, 1sc] in corner, work 26sc evenly along row-end edge to corner, [1sc, 1hdc, 1sc] in corner**, 1sc in each of next 26sc, rep from * to **, 1sc in every ch to end of round, change to color A when joining with sl st in first sc.

Round 2: Ch 2 (counts as 1hdc), 1hdc in every sc and [1hdc, 1dc, 1hdc] in every hdc from previous round, join with sl st in 2nd ch of ch-2.

Fasten off and weave in ends.

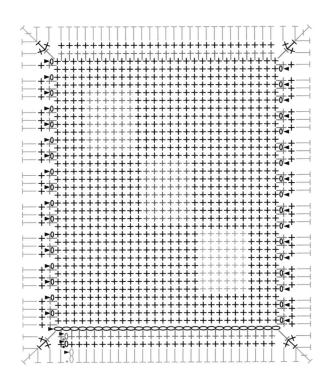

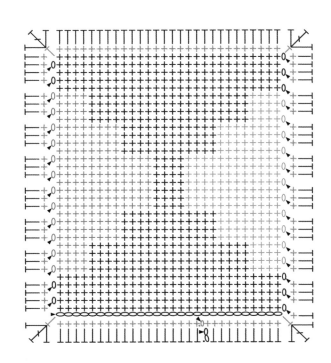

⬤⬤ Flying Carpet

See page 30

A=Oyster
B=Persimmon
C=Cobalt
D=Bleached
E=Nightshade

Foundation ring: Using color A, make a Magic Ring.

Round 1: Ch 1, 8sc into the ring, join with sl st in first sc. (8 sc)

Round 2: Ch 1, *[1sc, ch2, 1sc] in next sc, 1sc in next sc; rep from * a further 3 times, change to color B when joining with sl st in first sc. (12 sts, 4 ch-sp)

Round 3: Sl st into corner ch-sp, ch 1, [1sc, ch 2, 1sc] in same sp, *ch1, skip next st, 1sc in next st, ch 1**, skip next st, [1sc, ch 2, 1sc] in corner ch-2 sp; rep from * twice more and from * to ** once again, change to color C when joining with sl st in first st. (12 sts, 12 ch-sp)

Round 4: As Round 3, change to color D when joining with sl st in first st. (16 sts, 16 ch-sp)

Round 5: As Round 3, change to color E when joining with sl st in first st. (20 sts, 20 ch-sp)

Round 6: As Round 3, change to color A when joining with sl st in first st. (24 sts, 24 ch-sp)

Round 7: As Round 3, change to color C when joining with sl st in first st. (28 sts, 28 ch-sp)

Round 8: As Round 3, change to color B when joining with sl st in first st. (32 sts, 32 ch-sp)

Round 9: As Round 3, change to color E when joining with sl st in first st. (36 sts, 36 ch-sp)

Round 10: As Round 3, change to color D when joining with sl st in first st. (40 sts, 40 ch-sp)

Round 11: As Round 3, change to color C when joining with sl st in first st. (44 sts, 24 ch-sp)

Round 12: As Round 3, join with sl st in first st. (48 sts, 48 ch-sp).

Fasten off and weave in ends.

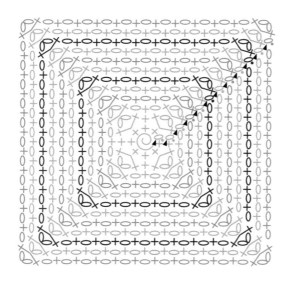

⬤⬤ Bold Block

See page 31

A=Cobalt
B=Oyster
C=Persimmon

SPECIAL STITCH

Cl (Cluster): Work 3dc sts leaving the last loop of each st on the hook each time, yrh and pull through all 4 loops on hook.

Foundation ring: Using color A, make a Magic Ring.

Round 1: Ch4 (counts as 1tr), *5dc in ring**, 1tr in ring; rep from * twice more and from * to ** once again, changing to color B when joining with sl st in 4th ch of ch-4.

Round 2: Ch5 (counts as 1dc, ch2), 1dc in same place, *[ch1, skip 1 st, Cl in next st] twice, ch1, skip next st**, [1dc, ch2, 1dc] in corner tr; rep from * twice more and from * to ** once again, join with sl st in 3rd ch of ch-5. Break color B.

Round 3: Join color A to any ch-2 corner sp, ch1, *[1sc, 1hdc, 1sc] in ch-2 sp, [1sc in next st, 1sc over ch-sp and into corresponding st from Round 1] 3 times, 1sc in next st; rep from * a further 3 times, join with sl st in first sc. Break color A.

Round 4: Join color C to any corner hdc, ch1, *[1sc, 1hdc, 1sc] in hdc, 1sc in every st to next hdc; rep from * a further 3 times, join with sl st in first sc. Break color C.

Round 5: Join color B to any corner hdc, ch5 (counts as 1dc, ch2), 1dc in same st, *[ch1, skip 1 st**, 1dc in next st] 5 times, ch1, skip 1 st**, [1dc, ch2, 1dc] in corner hdc; rep from * twice more and from * to ** once again, join with sl st in 3rd ch of ch-5. Break color B.

Round 6: Join color C to any ch-2 corner sp, ch1, *[1sc, 1hdc, 1sc] in ch-2 sp, [1sc in next st, 1sc over ch-sp and into corresponding st from Round 4] 6 times, 1sc in next st; rep from * 3 more times, join with sl st in first sc. Break color C.

Round 7: Join color A to any corner hdc, ch1, *[1sc, 1hdc, 1sc] in hdc, 1sc in every st to next hdc; rep from * a further 3 times, join with sl st in first sc.

Fasten off and weave in ends.

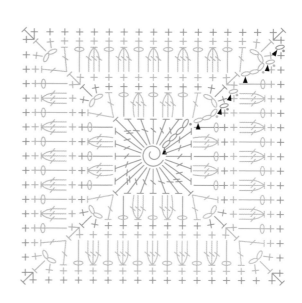

Florentine Tile

See page 28

A=Nightshade
B=Cobalt
C=Persimmon

Foundation ring: Using color A, ch 6 and join with sl st in first ch to form a ring.

Round 1: Ch 1, 16sc into ring, join with sl st in first sc. (16 sc)

Round 2: Ch 6 (counts as 1dc and ch 3), 1dc in same st, *ch 1, skip next sc, 1dc in next sc, ch 1, skip next sc**, [1dc, ch 3, 1dc] in next sc (corner made); rep from * twice more and from * to ** once again, change to color B when joining in 3rd ch of ch-6 with a sl st.

Round 3: Join color B to any ch-3 corner-sp, ch 1, 5sc in same sp, *[1sc in next sc, working behind next ch-1 sp, 1dc in next skipped st 2 rounds below] twice, 1sc in next dc**, 5sc in next ch-3 corner sp; rep from * twice more and from * to ** one again, change to color B when joining with sl st in first sc. Break color A.

Round 4: Ch 4 (counts as 1dc and ch 1), skip next st, *[1dc, ch 3, 1dc] in next st**, [ch 1, skip next st, 1dc in next st] 4 times, ch 1, skip next st; rep from * twice more and from * to ** once again, [ch 1, skip next st, 1dc in next st] 3 times, ch 1, skip last st. join with sl st in 3rd ch of ch-4. Break color B.

Round 5: Join color C to any ch-3 corner sp, ch 1, 5sc in same sp, *[1sc in next st, working behind next

ch-1 sp, 1dc in next skipped st 2 rounds below] 5 times, 1sc in next dc**, 5sc in next ch-3 corner sp; rep from * twice more and from * to ** once again, join with sl st in first sc.

Round 6: Ch 4 (counts as 1dc and ch 1), skip next st, *[1dc, ch 3, 1dc] in next st**, [ch 1, skip next sc, 1dc in next sc] 7 times, ch 1, skip next st; rep from * twice more and from * to ** once again, [ch 1, skip next sc, 1dc in next sc 6 times, ch 1, skip next st, join with sl st in 3rd ch of ch-4. Break color C.

Round 7: Join color B to any ch-3 corner sp, ch 1, 5sc in same sp, *[1sc in next st, working behind next ch-1 sp, 1dc in next skipped st 2 rounds below] 8 times, 1sc in next dc**, 5sc in next ch-3 corner sp; rep from * twice more and from * to ** one again, join with sl st in first sc.

Round 8: Join color A to 3rd sc of any 5sc corner cluster, ch 3 (counts as 1dc), 1dc in same st (half corner made), *[ch 1, skip next st, 1dc in next st] 10 times, ch 1**, skip next st, [2dc, ch 3, 2dc] in next st (corner made); rep from * twice more and from * to ** once again, skip next st, 2dc in same st as first half corner, ch 3, join with a sl st in 3rd ch of ch-3.

Fasten off and weave in ends.

Stacking Squares

See page 31

A=Sky
B=Bleached
C=Nightshade
D=Oyster
E=Persimmon

SPECIAL STITCHES

BPdc (Back Post double crochet): Yarn over hook, insert hook from front to back around post of designated stitch, yarn over hook, pull a loop through, then [yarn over hook, pull through 2 loops on the hook] twice more.

Foundation ring: Using color A, ch 4 and join with sl st in first ch to form a ring.

Round 1: Ch 3 (counts as 1dc), 2dc into ring, ch 2, [3dc into ring, ch 2] 3 times, join with sl st in 3rd ch of ch-3. Break color A. (4 groups of 3dc, 4 ch-sp)

Round 2: Join color B to any ch-3 sp, ch 3 (counts as 1dc), 1dc in same ch-sp, *BPdc around each st to corner ch-sp, [2dc**, ch 2, 2dc] in ch-2 sp; rep from * twice more and from * to ** once again, join with sl st in 3rd ch of ch-3. Break color B. (24 dc, 4 ch-sp)

Round 3: As Round 2 in color C. (44 dc, 4 ch-sp)

Round 4: As Round 2 in color D. (60 dc, 4 ch-sp)

Round 5: As Round 2 in color E. (76 dc, 4 ch-sp)

Fasten off and weave in ends.

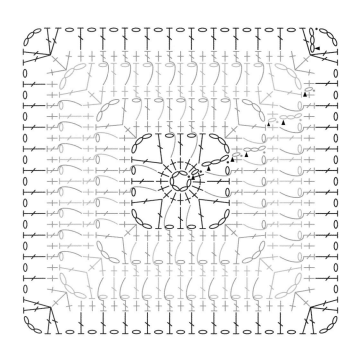

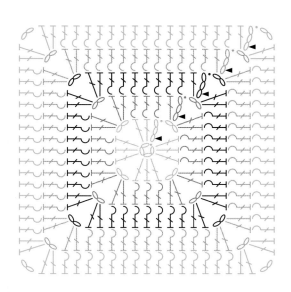

Rose of Sharon

See page 30

A=Oyster
B=Cobalt
C=Persimmon

SPECIAL STITCHES

Beg PC (Beginning popcorn): Ch3 (counts as 1dc), 4dc in same st or space, remove hook from loop, insert hook in 3rd ch of beg ch-3, pick up the dropped loop and pull a loop through.

PC (Popcorn): 4dc in same st or space, remove hook from loop, insert hook into first of 5dc just made, pick up the dropped loop and pull a loop through.

Exdc (Extended sc): Insert hook into designated st or space, yarn round hook, pull yarn through sts so that it is level with the round being worked, yarn round hook, draw through 2 loops on hook.

Extr (Extended dc): Yarn over hook, insert hook into designated st or space, yarn over hook, pull yarn through sts so that it is level with the round being worked, [yarn over hook, draw through 2 loops on hook] twice.

Foundation chain: Using color A, ch 4 and join with sl st in first ch to form a ring.

Round 1: Ch 3 (counts as 1dc), 11dc into the ring, join with sl st in 3rd ch of ch-3.

Round 2: Beg PC in first st, ch 2, [PC, ch 2] in every dc to end of round, change to color B when joining with sl st in 3rd ch of ch-3. Do not break color A.

Round 3: Sl st in first PC, ch 1, 1sc in first st, *1sc in next ch-2 sp, 1Exdc in

base of next PC, 1sc in same ch-2 sp, 1sc in next PC; rep from * to end of round, omitting last sc and joining with sl st in first sc.

Round 4: Ch 1, working blo for this round, 1sc in every st to end, changing to color A when joining with sl st in first sc.

Round 5: Beg PC in first sc, ch 3, skip next 2sc, *PC in next sc, ch 3, skip next 2sc; rep from * to end of round, changing to color B when joining with sl st in first sc. Break color A.

Round 6: Ch 1, 1sc in first st, *1sc in next ch-3 sp, 1Exdc in each of next 2sc two rounds below, 1sc in same ch-3 sp, 1sc in next PC; rep from * omitting last sc and joining with sl st in first sc. Break color B.

Round 7: Join color C between any 2 Exdc, ch 3, 2dc in same sp (half corner made), *[ch 2, skip next 3sc, 2dc between next 2Exdc] 3 times, ch 2, skip next 3sc**, [3dc, ch 3, 3dc] between next 2Exdc (corner made); rep from * twice more and from * to ** once again, 3dc in same sp as first half corner, ch 3, join with sl st in 3rd ch of ch 3.

Round 8: Ch 1, *1sc in each of next 3dc, [2sc in next ch-2 sp, 1sc in each of next 2dc] 3 times, 2sc in next ch-2 sp, 1sc in each of next 3dc, [1sc, ch 3, 1sc] in next ch-3 sp corner; rep from * a further 3 times, join with sl st in first sc.

Fasten off and weave in ends.

Tuscan Tile

See page 30

A=Persimmon
B=Nightshade
C=Cobalt

Foundation ring: Using color A, ch 4 and join with sl st in first ch to form a ring.

Round 1: Ch 5 (counts as 1tr and ch 1), [1tr, ch 1] 11 times into the ring, change to color B when joining to 4th ch of ch-5 with sl st.

Round 2: Ch 3 (counts as 1dc), [1dc, ch 3, 2dc] in same place (corner made), *[ch 1, 1dc] in each of next 2tr ch 1**, [2dc, ch 3, 2dc] in next tr, (corner made); rep from * twice more and from * to ** once again, ch 1, change to color C when joining in 3rd ch of ch-3 with sl st.

Round 3: Sl st in next ch-3 corner sp, ch 2 (counts as 1hdc), [1hdc, ch 3, 2hdc] in same sp, *1hdc in each of next 2dc, work over next ch-1 sp in Round 2 and 1tr in next ch-1 sp in Round 1, 1sc in each of next 2dc, work over next ch-1 sp in Round 2 and 1tr in next ch-1 sp in Round 1,

1hdc in each of next 2dc**, [2hdc, ch 3, 2hdc] in next ch-3 sp; rep from * twice more and from * to ** once again, change to color B when joining in 2nd ch of ch-2 with sl st.

Round 4: Sl st to next ch-3 corner sp, ch 1, *[1sc, ch 2, 1sc] in ch-2 corner sp, 1dc in each of next 12 sts; rep from * 3 times, change to color C when joining in first sc with sl st.

Round 5: Sl st in next ch-3 corner sp, ch 1, *[1sc, ch 2, 1sc] in ch-2 corner sp, 1sc in each of next 14 sts; rep from * 3 a further times, join with sl st in first sc.

Round 6: Sl st in next ch-3 corner sp, ch 3, [1dc, ch 2, 2dc] in same sp, *[ch 1, skip next sc, 1dc in each of next 2sc] 5 times, ch 1**, [2dc, ch 2, 2dc] in next ch-2 corner sp; rep from * twice more and from * to ** once again, join in 3rd ch of ch-3 with sl st.

Fasten off and weave in ends.

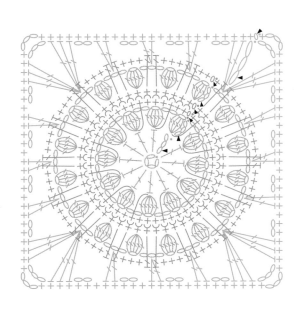

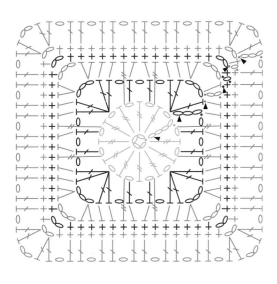

Spiky Square

See page 29

A=Persimmon
B=Bleached
C=Oyster
D=Sky

SPECIAL STITCHES

BPtr (back post treble): Yarn round hook, insert hook from back to front around the post of designated stitch, yarn round hook, pull up a loop, then [yarn round hook, pull through two loops on the hook] twice more.

Foundation ring: Using color A, ch 4 and join with sl st in first ch to form a ring.

Round 1: Ch 3 (counts as 1dc), 2dc into ring, ch 2, [3dc into ring, ch 2] 3 times, join with sl st in 3rd ch of ch-3. Break color A. (12 sts, 4ch-sp)

Round 2: Join color B to any ch-3 corner sp, ch 3 (counts as 1dc), 1dc in same sp, *1dc in next 3 dc**, [2dc, ch 2, 2dc] in ch-2 sp; rep from * twice more and from * to ** once again, [2dc, ch 2] in corner sp, join with sl st in 3rd ch of ch-3. Break color B. (28 sts, 4ch-sp)

Round 3: Join color C to any ch-3 corner sp, ch 3 (counts as 1dc), 1dc in same sp, ch 2, 2dc in same sp, *1dc in next st, ch 1, skip next st, 1dc in next st, BPtr around middle dc of 3dc from Round 1, 1dc in next st, ch 1, skip next st, 1dc in next st**, [2dc, ch 2, 2dc] in ch-2 sp; rep from * twice more

and from * to ** once again, 2dc in ch-2 sp, join with hdc in 3rd ch of ch-3. Break color C. (36 sts, 4ch-sp)

Round 4: Join color A to any ch-3 corner sp, ch 3 (counts as 1dc), 1dc in same sp, ch 2, 2dc in same sp, *1dc in next st, ch 1, skip next st, 1dc in next st, BPtr around middle 2nd dc of Round 2, 1dc in next st, ch 1, skip next st, skip next st, 1dc in next st, BPtr around middle 6th dc of Round 2, 1dc in next st, ch 1, skip next st, 1dc in next st**, [2dc, ch 2, 2dc] in ch-2 sp; rep from * twice more and from * to ** once again, 2dc in ch-2 sp, join with hdc in 3rd ch of ch-3. Break color A. (48 sts, 4ch-sp)

Round 5: Join color D to any ch-3 corner sp, ch 3 (counts as 1dc), 1dc in same sp, ch 2, 2dc in same sp *1dc in next 3 sts, BPtr around second dc from Round 3, 1dc in next 3 sts, BPtr around BPtr from Round 3, 1dc in next 3 sts, BPtr around eighth dc from Round 3, 1dc in next 3 sts**, [2dc, ch 2, 2dc] in ch-2 sp; rep from * twice more and from * to ** once again, 2dc in ch-2 sp, ch 2, join with sl st in 3rd ch of ch-3. (76 sts, 4 ch-sp)
Fasten off and weave in ends.

Dip Stitch Cross

See page 29

A=Bleached
B=Sky
C=Nightshade
D=Persimmon

SPECIAL STITCHES

Spike sc: Insert hook into stitch one round below the next stitch and pull loop through up to the level of current round, yarn round hook and pull through both loops on hook.

Foundation ring: Using color A, ch 6 and join with sl st in first ch to form a ring.

Round 1: Ch 3 (counts as 1dc), 15dc into the ring, join with sl st in 3rd ch of ch-3.

Round 2: Ch 1, 3sc in first dc, 1sc in each of next 3dc, *3sc in next dc, 1sc in each of next 3dc; rep from * twice more, change to color B when joining with sl st in first sc.

Round 3: Ch 1, *1sc in next sc, 3sc in corner sc, 1sc in each of next 4sc; rep from * a further 3 times, change to color B when joining with sl st in first sc.

Round 4: Ch 1, *1sc in each of next 2sc, 3sc in corner sc, 1sc in each of

next 5sc; rep from * a further 3 times, change to color C when joining with sl st in first sc.

Round 5: Ch 1, *Spike sc in row below next sc, 1sc in each of next 2sc, 3 Spike sc in next st 2 rows below, 1sc in next 2sc, Spike sc in row below next sc, Spike sc 2 rows below next sc, Spike sc 3 rows below next sc, Spike sc 2 rows below next sc; rep from * a further 3 times, join with sl st in first sc.

Round 6: Ch 1, 1sc in each sc around and 3sc in each corner sc, change to color D when joining with sl st in first sc.

Round 7: Ch 2 (counts as 1hdc), 1hdc in each of sc around and 3 hdc in corner sc, change to color C when joining with sl st in 2nd ch of ch-2.

Round 8: Ch 1, 1sc in each of hdc around and 3sc in corner hdc, join with sl st in first sc.
Fasten off and weave in ends.

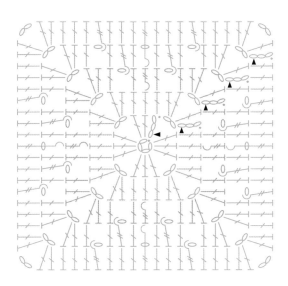

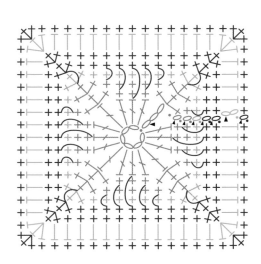

✪ ✪ *Eight-petal flower*

See page 32

A=Bleached
B=Bubbles
C=Greengage

Foundation ring: Using A, ch 8 and join with sl st in first ch to form a ring.
Round 1: Ch 1, 16sc into the ring, join with a sl st in first sc.
Round 2: Ch 8 (counts as 1dc and ch 5), [skip next sc, 1dc in next sc, ch 5] 7 times, skip last sc, join with sl st in 3rd ch of ch 8. Break color A.
Round 3: Join color B to any 5ch-sp, [1sc, 1hdc, 1dc, 2tr, ch 1, 2tr, 1dc, 1hdc, 1sc] in each 5ch-sp, join with sl st in first sc. Break color B.

Round 4: Join color C to any 1ch-sp, ch 1, 1sc in same sp, [ch 7, 1sc in next 1ch-sp, ch 9, 1sc in next 1ch-sp] 4 times, replacing last sc with sl st in first sc.
Round 5: Sl st in first 7ch-sp, ch 1, *7sc in 7ch-sp, [6sc, ch 3, 6sc] in next 9ch-sp; rep from * a further 3 times, join with sl st in first sc.
Round 6: Ch 1, 1sc in same place, 1sc in each of next 12sc, *[1sc, ch 3, 1sc] in next ch-3 sp, 1sc in each of

next 19sc; rep from * twice more, [1sc, ch 3, 1sc] in last 3ch-sp, 1sc in each of last 6sc, join with sl st to first sc.
Round 7: Ch 4 (counts as 1dc and ch 1), [skip next sc, 1dc in foll sc, ch 1] 6 times, *skip next sc, [1dc, ch 3, 1dc] in next 3ch-sp, ch 1, [skip next sc, 1dc in foll sc, ch 1] 10 times; rep from * twice more, skip next sc, [1dc, ch 3, 1dc] in next 3ch-sp, ch 1, [skip next sc, 1dc in foll sc, ch 1] 3 times, change to color A when joining with sl st in 3rd ch of ch 4.

Round 8: Ch 3 (counts as 1dc), 1dc in every dc and 1ch-sp from previous round, working [1dc, ch 3, 1dc] in every 3ch corner-sp, change to color B when joining with sl st in 3rd ch of ch 3.
Round 9: Ch 2 (counts as 1hdc), 1hdc in every dc from previous round, working 3hdc in every 3ch corner-sp, join with sl st in 3rd ch of ch-3.
Fasten off and weave in ends.

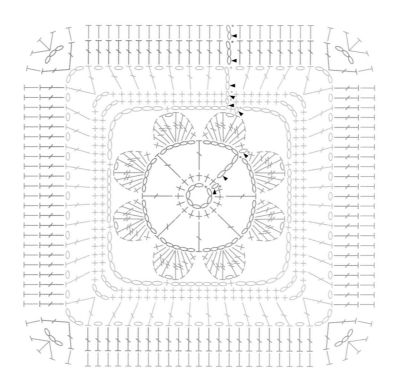

Framed Flower

See page 35

A=Bubbles
B=Bleached
C=Greengage

Foundation chain: Using color A, ch 7.

Round 1: [1dc and ch 3] 3 times in 7th ch from hook, join with sl st in 3rd ch of ch-7.

Round 2: Ch 1, 1sc in same place, *[1dc, 5tr, 1dc] in next 3ch-sp (petal made)**, 1sc in next dc; rep from * twice more and from * to ** once again, change to color B, when joining with sl st in first sc.

Round 3: Ch 1, 1sc in same place, *1dc in next dc, 2dc in each of next 2tr, 3dc in next tr, 2dc in each of next 2tr, 1dc in next dc**, 1sc in next sc; rep from * twice more and from * to **

once again, join with sl st in first sc. Break color B.

Round 4: Join color C in 4th dc of any petal, ch 1, 1sc in same place, *ch 5, skip next 5 sts, 1sc in next dc, ch 5**, 1sc in 4th dc of next petal; rep from * twice more and from * to ** once again, join with sl st in first sc.

Round 5: Sl st in next 5ch-sp, ch 3 (counts as 1dc), [3dc, ch 3, 4dc] in same 5ch-sp, *ch 1, 7dc in next 5ch-sp, ch 1**, [4dc, ch 3, 4dc] in next 5ch-sp; rep from * twice more and from * to ** once again, join with sl st in 3rd ch of ch-3. Break color C.

Round 6: Join color A in any

3ch-corner-sp, ch 2 (counts as 1hdc), [1hdc, ch 2, 2hdc in same sp, *1hdc in each of next 4dc, skip 1ch-sp, 1sc in each of next 7hdc, skip 1ch-sp, 1hdc in each of next 4dc**, [2hdc, ch 2, 2hdc] in next 3ch-corner-sp; rep from * twice more and from * to ** once again, join with sl st in 2nd ch of ch-2. Break color A.

Round 7: Join color B in any 2ch-corner-sp, ch 3 (counts as 1dc), [1dc, ch 2, 2dc] in same sp, *1dc in each hdc and sc along side of square**, [2dc, ch 2, 2dc] in next 2ch-corner-sp; rep from * twice more and from * to ** once again, change

to color C when joining with sl st in 3rd ch of ch-3. Break color B.

Round 8: Ch 3 (counts as 1dc), 1dc in every dc of previous round and work [2dc, ch 2, 2dc] in each 2ch-corner-sp to end of round, change to color B when joining with sl st in 3rd ch of ch-3. Break color C.

Round 9: Ch 3 (counts as 1dc), 1dc in every dc of previous round and work 3dc in each 2ch-corner-sp to end of round, join with sl st in 3rd ch of ch-3.

Fasten off and weave in ends.

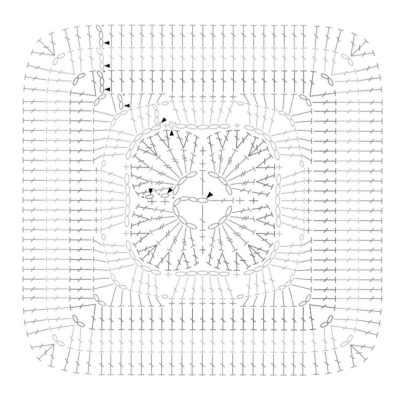

Cartwheel Flower

See page 32

A=Bleached
B=Greengage
C=Bubbles

SPECIAL STITCHES

Beg PS (Beginning Puff stitch):
Ch2, [Yarn over hook, insert hook into next stitch, draw a loop through] twice, yarn over hook and draw through all 5 loops on hook.

PS (Puff stitch): [Yarn over hook, insert hook into next stitch, draw a loop through] three times, yarn over hook and draw through all 7 loops on hook.

Foundation ring: Using color A, make a Magic Ring.

Round 1: Ch 1, 8sc into the ring, change to color B when joining with sl st in first sc. (8 sts)

Round 2: Ch 1, 2sc in same place, *2sc in next st; rep from * a further 6 times, change to color A when joining with sl st in first sc. (16 sts)

Round 3: Beg PS in same place, *ch 3, skip 1 st, PS in next st; rep from * a further 6 times, ch 3, join with sl st in top of first PS made.

Round 4: Ch 1, 1sc in same place, *3sc in next ch-3 sp, 1sc in next PS; rep from * a further 6 times, 3sc in next 3ch-sp, change to color C when joining with sl st in first sc.

Round 5: *Ch 4, [2tr in next st] twice, ch 4, sl st in next st**, sl st in next st; rep from * a further 6 times, then from * to ** once again, sl st in first ch of ch-4. Break color C.

Round 6: Join color B through the back loop of sl st between two petals from Round 5, ch 6 (counts as 1dc and ch 3), 1dc in same sp, *ch 3, 1sc in next sl st between two petals ch 3**, [1dc, ch 3, 1dc] through back loop of sl st between two petals; rep from * twice more and then from * to ** once again, join with sl st in 3rd ch of ch-6. (12 sts and 12 ch-sp)

Round 7: Ch 3 (counts as 1dc), *[3dc, 1tr, 3dc] in ch-3 corner sp, 1dc in next dc, 4dc in 3ch-sp, 1dc in next sc 4dc in 3ch-sp**, 1dc in next dc; rep from * twice more and then from * to ** once again, join with sl st in 3rd ch of ch-3.

Round 8: Ch 3 (counts as 1dc), 1dc in each dc and [1dc, 1tr, 1dc] in each corner tr to end of round, change to color A when joining with sl st in 3rd ch of ch-3.

Round 9: Ch 3 (counts as 1dc), 1dc in each dc and [1dc, 1tr, 1dc] in each corner tr to end of round, change to color C when joining with sl st in 3rd ch of ch-3.

Round 10: Ch 3 (counts as 1dc), 1dc in each dc and [1dc, 1tr, 1dc] in each corner tr to end of round, join with sl st in 3rd ch of ch-3.

Fasten off and weave in ends.

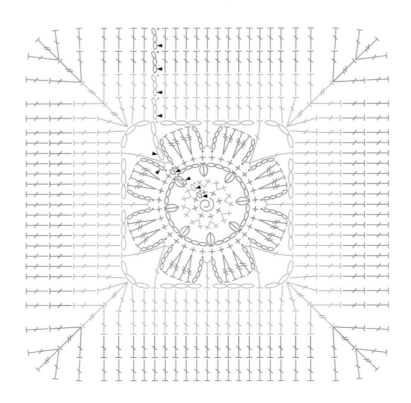

✿ ✿ Origami Flower

See page 33

A=Bleached
B=Greengage
C=Bubbles

SPECIAL STITCHES

3ch-P (3 chain picot): Sl st in st at base of 3 ch.

Foundation ring: Using color A, ch 5 and join with sl st in first ch to form a ring.

Round 1: Ch 3, 15dc into the ring, change to color B when joining with sl st in 3rd ch of ch-3.

Round 2: Sl st into space between next 2dc, 2sc in same sp, [2dc in space between next 2dc] 15 times, change to color C when joining with sl st in first sc.

Round 3: Ch 5 (counts as 1dtr), 4dtr tog in back loops of next 4sc, *ch 6, 5dtr tog over back loops of [same sc as last insertion and foll 4sc], ch7, 5dtr as before; rep from * twice more, ch 6, 5dtr tog making last insertion at base of ch-5, ch7, sl st in top of 4dtr tog. Break color C. (8 petals made)

Round 4: Join color B to any 7ch-sp. Ch 4, sl st in first of these ch 4, *5sc in same 7ch-sp, 1sc in top of petal, 7sc in ch-6 sp, 1sc in next petal, 5sc in 7ch-sp, 3ch-P: rep from * ending 4sc in 7ch-sp, sl st in first of ch-4.

Round 5: Sl st in 3ch-P, ch5 (counts as 1tr and ch2), 1tr in same ch-3P, *1tr in each of next 17dc, [1tr, ch2, 1tr] in 3ch-P, rep from * twice more, 1tr in each of next 17dc, change to yarn A when joining with sl st in 3rd ch of ch-5.

Round 6: Sl st in 2ch-sp, ch 5 (counts as 1tr and ch 2), 1dc in same 2ch-sp, *ch 1, [1dc in next dc, ch 1, skip next dc] 9 times, 1dc in next dc, ch 1**, [1dc, 2ch, 1dc] in 2ch-sp; rep from * twice more and from * to ** once again, join with sl st in 3rd ch of ch-5.

Round 7: Sl st in 2ch-sp, ch 5 (counts as 1dc and ch 2), 1dc in same 2ch-sp, *1dc in each dc and 1ch-sp, and [1dc, ch 2, 1dc] in each 2ch-sp, to end of round, change to color C when joining with sl st in 3rd ch of ch-5.

Round 8: Sl st into ch-2 sp, ch 4 (counts as 1hdc and ch 2), 1hdc in same 2ch-sp, 1hdc in each dc and [1hdc, ch 2, 1hdc] in each ch-2 corner sp, to end of round, join with sl st in 3rd ch of ch-4.

Fasten off and weave in ends.

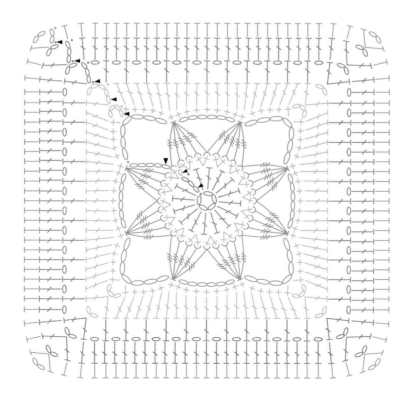

Raised Petal Flower

See page 35

A=Shell
B=Bubbles
C=Bleached
D=Greengage

Foundation ring: Using color A make a Magic Ring.

Round 1: Ch 1, 3sc into the ring, [ch 3, 3sc into ring] 3 times, ch 3, join with sl st in first sc. Break color A.

Round 2: Join color B to any 3ch-sp, ch 1, [1sc, 1hdc, 3dc, 1hdc, 1sc] in each 3ch-sp to end of round, join with sl st in first sc. Break color B.

Round 3: Join color C between any two sc, ch 1, 1sc in same place, [ch 5, 1sc between next 2sc] 3 times, ch 5, join with sl st in first sc.

Round 4: Sl st in first 5ch-sp, ch 3 (counts as 1dc), [dc2tog, ch 2, dc3tog, ch 3, dc3tog, ch 2, dc3tog] in same 5ch-sp, *ch 2, [dc3tog, ch 2, dc3tog, ch 3, dc3tog, ch 2, dc3tog]

in next 5ch-sp; rep from * twice more, join with sl st in top of first cluster. Break color C.

Round 5: Join color D to any 3ch-sp, ch 3 (counts as 1dc), [1dc, ch 2, 2dc] in same 2ch-corner-sp, *[ch 1, 2dc in next 2ch-sp] 3 times, ch 1**, [2dc, ch 2, 2dc] in 3ch-corner-sp; rep from * twice more then from * to ** once again, join with sl st in 3rd ch of ch-3.

Round 6: Sl st in next dc, sl st in 2ch-corner-sp, ch 1, [1sc, ch 1, 1sc] in same 2ch-corner-sp, 1sc in every dc and 1ch-sp, working [1sc, ch 1, 1sc] in each 2ch-corner-sp to end of round, join with sl st in first sc.

Fasten off and weave in ends.

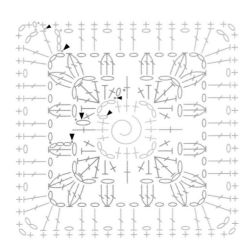

Six-petal Flower

See page 33

A=Bubbles
B=Shell
C=Bleached
D=Greengage

Foundation ring: Using color A, make a magic ring.

Round 1: Ch 2 (counts as 1hdc), 5hdc into the ring, join with sl st in 2nd ch of ch-2. (6 sts)

Round 2: Ch 2 (counts as 1hdc), 1hdc into same place, 2hdc in every st from Round 1, change to color B when joining with sl st in 2nd ch of ch-2. Break color A. (12 sts)

Round 3: Ch 1, 1sc in same place, *ch 3, skip next st**, 1sc in next st; rep from * a further 4 times, then from * to ** once again, join with sl st in first sc.

Round 4: Sl st in first 3ch-sp, *[1sc, 1hdc, 1dc, 1tr, 1dc, 1hdc, 1sc] in next 3ch-sp**, sl st in next sc; rep from * a further 4 times, then from * to ** once again, change to color C when joining with sl st in first sl st. Break color B.

Round 5: *Sl st in next sc, 1sc in hdc, 1hdc in dc, [2dc, ch 2, 2dc] in tr, 1hdc in dc, 1sc in hdc, sl st in next sc, sl st in next sl st; rep from * 5 more times, join with sl st in first sl st. Break color C.

Round 6: Join color D to any sc from Round 3, *ch 3, sl st in next sc from Round 3, [ch 4, sl st in next sc from Round 3] twice; rep from * once more, join with sl st in first sl st.

Round 7: Sl st in first 3ch-sp, ch 3 (counts as 1dc), 3dc in same 3ch-sp, [2dc, ch 2, 4dc] in next 4ch-sp, [4dc, ch 2, 2dc] in next 4ch-sp, 4dc in next 3ch-sp, [2dc, ch 2, 4dc] in next 4ch-sp, [4dc, ch 2, 2dc] in next 4ch-sp, join with sl st in 3rd ch of ch-3.

Round 8: Ch 3 (counts as 1dc), *1dc in each st to corner, [2dc, ch 2, 2dc] in next 2ch-corner-sp; rep from * 3 more times, 1dc in each st to end of round, join with sl st in 3rd ch of ch-3.

Round 9: Ch 3 (counts as 1dc), 1dc in next st, *1dc through ch-2 sp at top of petal from Round 5 and into next st from Round 8, 1dc in next 5 sts, [2dc, ch 2, 2dc] in next 2ch-corner-sp, 1dc in next st, 1dc through ch-2 sp at top of petal from Round 5 and into next st from Round 8, 1dc in next 8 sts, 1dc through ch-2 sp at top of petal from Round 5 and into next st from Round 8, 1dc in next st, [2dc, ch 2, 2dc] in next 2ch-corner-sp**, 1dc in next 6 sts; rep from * to ** once more, 1dc in next 4 sts, join with sl st in 3rd ch of ch-3.

Fasten off and weave in ends.

⭐⭐⭐ *Ruffled Flower*

See page 32

A=Shell
B=Bleached
C=Bubbles

Foundation ring: Using color A, ch 6 and join with sl st in first ch to form a ring.

Round 1: Ch 3 (counts as 1dc), 3dc into ring, ch 3, turn; 1dc in first dc, 1dc in next 2dc, 1dc in 3rd ch of ch-3, turn; * working across back of petal just made, 4dc into ring, ch 3, turn; 1dc in first dc, 1dc in next 3dc, ch 3, turn; rep from * a further 6 times, join with sl st in 3rd ch of ch-3. Break color A. (8 petals made)

Round 2: Join color B to any 3ch-sp behind one of the petals, ch 3 (counts as 1dc), [2dc, 2 ch, 3dc] in same sp, 3dc in next 3ch-sp, *[3dc, ch 2, 3dc] in next 3ch-sp, 3dc in next 3ch-sp; rep from * twice more, join with sl st in 3rd ch of ch-3. Break color B.

Round 3: Join color C to any ch-2 corner sp, ch 3 (counts as 1dc), [2dc, ch 3, 3dc] in same sp, *1dc in each of next 9dc**, [3dc, ch 3, 3dc] in next 3ch-sp; rep from * to ** once again, join with sl st in 3rd ch of ch-3. Break color C.

Round 4: Join color D to any ch-3 corner sp, ch 2 (counts as 1hdc), [2hdc, 1dc, 3hdc] in same sp, *1hdc in each of next 15dc**, [3dc, ch 3, 3dc] in same sp; rep from * twice more and from * to ** once again, join with sl st to 2nd ch of ch-2.

Fasten off and weave in ends.

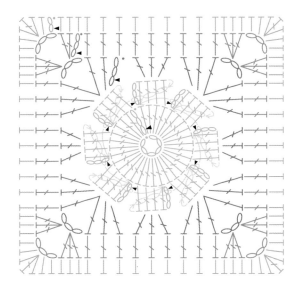

⭐⭐ *Raised Rose*

See page 32

A=Rose
B=Bleached
C=Greengage
D=Blackcurrant

Foundation ring: Using color A, ch 6 and join with sl st in first ch to form a ring.

Round 1: Ch 3 (counts as 1dc), 11dc into the ring, join with sl st in 3rd ch of ch-3.)

Round 2: Ch 2 (counts as 1hdc), 1hdc in same place, 2hdc in each of the next 11dc, join with sl st in 2nd ch of ch-2.

Round 3: Ch 1, 1sc in same place, *ch 5, skip next 2hdc, 1sc in next hdc; rep from * a further 6 times, ch 5, join with sl st in first sc. Break color A.

Round 4: Join color B in any 5ch-sp, ch 1, [1sc, 1hdc, 5dc, 1hdc, 1sc] in same 5ch-sp, [1sc, 1hdc, 5dc, 1hdc, 1sc] in each of next seven 5ch-sps, join with sl st in back loop of first sc.

Round 5: Working behind petals of previous round, [ch 5, 1BPsc round next sc] 8 times, do not join the round.

Round 6: Sl st in next 5ch-sp, [1sc, 1hdc, 7dc, 1hdc, 1sc] in same 5ch-sp, [1sc, 1hdc, 7dc, 1hdc, 1sc] in each of next seven 5ch-sps, join with sl st to back loop of first sc. Break color B.

Round 7: Join color C in 3rd dc of any 7dc group from previous round, ch 1, 1sc in same place, 1sc in each of next 2dc, *ch 5, 1sc in 3rd, 4th and 5th dc of next 7dc group, ch 8**, 1sc in 3rd, 4th and 5th dc of next 7dc group; rep from * twice more and from * to ** once again, join with sl st in first sc.

Round 8: Ch 3 (counts as 1dc), 1dc in each sc of previous round, working 5dc in each 5ch-sp and [5dc, ch 3, 5dc] in each 8ch-sp, join with sl st in 3rd ch of ch-3.

Round 9: Ch 3 (counts as 1dc), 1dc in each dc of previous round, working [2dc, ch 2, 2dc] in each ch-3 corner sp, change to color D when joining with sl st in 3rd ch of ch-3.

Round 10: Ch 1, 1sc in same place, 1sc in each dc of previous round, working 3sc in each ch-2 corner sp, join with sl st in first sc.

Fasten off and weave in ends.

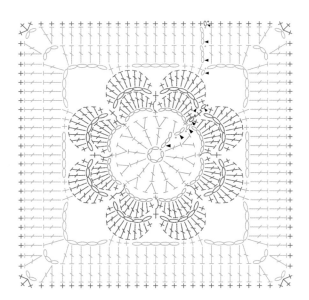

✪ ✪ Cluster Flower

See page 33

A=Shell
B=Blackcurrant
C=Dijon

SPECIAL STITCHES

dc3tog (beg cl): Work three double sts tog: [yoh, draw up a loop in next st, (yoh, pull through 2 loops on hook) 3 times] twice, yoh and draw through all 4 loops on hook.

dc4tog (cl): Work four double sts tog: [yoh, draw up a loop in next st, (yoh, pull through 2 loops on hook) 4 times] twice, yoh and draw through all 5 loops on hook.

Foundation chain: Using color A, ch 6 and join with a sl st to form a ring.
Round 1: Ch 5 (counts as 1dc and 2ch), [1dc into ring, ch 2] 7 times, join with sl st in 3rd ch of ch-5.
Round 2: Ch 3 (counts as 1dc), dc3tog in next 2ch-sp, [ch5, dc4tog in next 2ch-sp] 7 times more, ch 5, change to color B when joining with sl st in 3rd ch of ch-3.

Round 3: Ch 1, 1sc in the same place, *ch 2, work over 5ch-sp and enclose it by working 1dc in the next dc of Round 1, ch 2, 1sc in top of next cl; rep from * to end of round, omitting last sc, join with sl st in first sc.
Round 4: Sl st in next ch, ch 1, 1sc in same place, *ch 3, 1sc in next 2ch-sp; rep from * to end of round, omitting last sc, join with sl st in first sc.
Round 5: Sl st in next ch, ch 3 (counts as 1dc), [1dc, ch 2, 2dc] in same sp, *ch 2, 1sc in next ch-3 sp, [ch 3, 1sc in next ch-3 sp] twice, ch 2**, [2dc, ch 2, 2dc] in next 3ch-sp; rep from * twice and from * to ** once again, join with sl st in 3rd ch of ch-3. Break color B.
Round 6: Join color C to any ch-2 corner sp, ch 3 (counts as 1dc), [1dc, ch 2, 2dc] in same space, *ch 2 [1sc in next ch-sp, ch 3] 3 times, 1sc in next ch-sp, ch 2**, [2dc, ch 2, 2dc] in ch-2 corner sp; rep from * twice and from * to ** once more, join with sl st in 3rd ch of ch-3.
Round 7: Sl st in next ch-2 corner sp, ch 3 (counts as 1dc), [1dc, ch 2, 2dc] in the same space, *ch 2, [1sc in next ch-sp, ch 3] 4 times, 1sc in next ch-sp, ch 2**, [2dc, ch 2, 2dc] in ch-2 corner sp; rep from * twice and from * to ** once more, join with sl st in 3rd ch of ch-3.
Round 8: Sl st in next ch-2 corner sp, ch 3 (counts as 1dc), [1dc, ch 2, 2dc] in same space, *ch 2, [1sc in next ch-sp, ch 3] 5 times, 1sc in next ch-sp, ch 2**, [2dc, ch 2, 2dc] in ch-2 corner sp; rep from * twice and from * to ** once more, join with sl st in 3rd ch of ch-3.
Round 9: Sl st in next ch-2 corner sp, ch 3 (counts as 1dc), [1dc, ch 2, 2dc]

in same space, *ch 2, [1sc in next ch-sp, ch 3] 6 times, 1sc in next ch-sp, ch 2**, [2dc, ch 2, 2dc] in ch-2 corner sp; rep from * twice and from * to ** once more, join with sl st in 3rd ch of ch-3. Break color C.
Round 10: Join color A to any ch-2 corner sp, ch 2 (counts as 1hdc, [1hdc, ch2, 2hdc] in same space, *3hdc in next ch-2 sp, 3hdc in each of next 6 ch-3 sps, 3hdc in next 2 ch-sp **, [2hdc, ch 2, 2hdc] in corner 2 ch-sp space; rep from * twice more and from * to** once again, join with slst to 2nd ch of ch-2. Break color A.
Round 11: Join color B to any ch-2 corner sp, ch 3 (counts as 1dc), 4dc into same same sp, 1dc in every hdc from previous round, working 5dc into every ch-2 corner sp to end of round, join with slst to 3rd ch of ch-3.
Fasten off and weave in ends.

⭐⭐ Lacy Daisy

See page 34

A=Heather
B=Shell
C=Blackcurrant

Foundation ring: Using color A, ch 6 and join with sl st in first ch to form a ring.
Round 1: Ch 1, 12sc into the ring, change to color B when joining in back loop of first dc with sl st. Break color A. (12 sts)
Round 2: Ch 6 (counts as 1dtr and ch 1), 1dtr in back loop of same sc, ch 1, [1dtr, ch 1] twice in back loop of every sc to end of round, join with sl st in 5th ch of ch-6. Break color B.
Round 3: Join color C to any 1ch-sp, ch 5 (counts as 1dc and ch 2), 1dc in same ch-sp, *ch 1, 1hdc in next ch-sp, [ch 1, 1sc in next ch-sp] 3 times, ch 1, 1hdc in next ch-sp, ch 1**, [1dc, ch 2, 1dc] in next ch-sp; rep from * twice more and then from * to ** once again, join with sl st in 3rd ch of ch-5.
Round 4: *Sl st in next 2ch-sp, ch 5, sl st in same ch-sp, ch 4, skip [1dc, ch 1, 1hdc], sl st in next 1ch-sp, ch 4, skip [1sc, ch 1], sl st in next sc, ch 4, skip [ch 1, 1sc], sl st in next sc, ch 4, skip [1hdc, ch 1, 1dc], sl st in next 2ch-sp; rep from * a further 3 times, join with sl st in first sl st.
Round 5: Sl st in each of next 2 ch, sl st under rem 3 ch, *ch 5, sl st in same ch-sp, [ch 4, sl st in next 4ch-sp] 5 times; rep from * a further 3 times, join with sl st in first 5ch-sp.
Round 6: Sl st in each of next 2 ch, sl st under rem 3 ch, *ch 5, sl st in same ch-sp, [ch 4, sl st in next ch-sp] 6 times; rep from * a further 3 times, join with sl st in first 5ch-sp.

Round 7: Sl st in each of next 2 ch, sl st under rem 3 ch, ch 6 (counts as 1dc and ch 3), 1dc in same ch-sp, *[ch 2, 1dc in next ch-sp] 7 times, ch 3, 1dc in same ch-sp; rep from * twice more, [ch 2, 1dc in next ch-sp] 6 times, ch 2, join with sl st in 3rd ch of ch-6.
Round 8: Sl st in 3ch-sp, ch 6 (counts as 1dc and ch 3), 1dc in same ch-sp, 3dc in each 2ch-sp and [1dc, ch 3, 1dc] in each 3ch-corner-sp to end of round, join with sl st in 3rd ch of ch-6. (23dc on each side)
Round 9: Sl st in 3ch-sp, ch 2, 1sc in same ch-sp, 1sc in each sc and [1sc, ch2, 1sc] in each corner-sp to end of round, join with sl st in 2nd ch of ch-3. (25sc on each side)
Round 10: Sl st in 2ch-sp, ch 2, 1sc in same ch-sp, 1sc in each sc and [1sc, ch2, 1sc] in each corner-sp to end of round, change to color A when joining sl st to 2nd ch of ch-3. (27sc on each side)
Round 11: Sl st in 2ch-sp, ch 2, 1sc in same ch-sp, 1sc in each sc and [1sc, ch2, 1sc] in each corner-sp to end of round, change to color A when joining with sl st in 2nd ch of ch-3. (29sc on each side)
Round 12: Sl st in 2ch-sp, ch 2, 1sc in same ch-sp, 1sc in each sc and [1sc, ch2, 1sc] in each corner-sp to end of round, join with sl st in 2nd ch of ch-3. (31sc on each side)
Fasten off and weave in ends.

⭐⭐ Poppy

See page 34

A=Blackcurrant
B=Heather
C=Shell

Foundation ring: Using color A, ch 4 and join with sl st in first ch to form a ring.
Round 1: Ch 1, 8sc into the ring, join with sl st to first sc. (8sc)
Round 2: Ch 3 (counts as 1hdc and ch 1), [1hdc in front loop of next sc, ch 1] 7 times, join with sl st in 3rd ch of ch 3. Break color A.
Round 3: Join color B in back loop of any hdc, ch3 (counts as 1dc), [2dc in ch-1 sp, 1dc blo in next hdc] 7 times, 2dc in 1ch-sp, join with sl st in 3rd ch of ch-3.
Round 4: [Ch 3, 1tr in next hdc, 2dtr in next hdc, 1dtr in next hdc, 2dtr in next hdc, 1tr in next hdc, 1sc in next hdc] 4 times, working final sl st in same place as base of first ch-3. Break color B. (4 petals)
Round 5: Ch 5 (counts as 1dc and ch 2), 1dc in same dtr, *ch 5, [1dc, ch 3, 1dc] in sl st between petals, ch 5**, [1dc, ch 2, 1dc in center ctr of next petal, * rep from * twice more and from * to ** once again, join with sl st in 3rd ch of ch-5.
Round 6: Sl st in 2ch-sp, ch 5 (counts as 1dc and ch 2), 1dc in same ch-sp, * ch 5, 1sc in 5ch-sp, [3dc, ch 1, 3dc] in next 3ch-sp, 1sc in next 5ch-sp, ch 5**, [1dc, ch 2, 1dc] in next 2ch-sp; rep from * twice and from * to ** once again, join with sl st in 3rd ch of ch-5.

Round 7: Sl st in 2ch-sp, ch 5 (counts as 1dc and ch 2), 1dc in same 5ch-sp, *ch 5, 1sc in 5ch-sp, ch 5, 1sc in next 1ch-sp, ch 5, 1sc in next 5ch-sp, ch 5**, [1dc, ch 2, 1dc] in next 2ch-sp; rep from * twice more and from * to ** once again, join with sl st in 3rd ch of ch-5.
Round 8: Sl st in 2ch-sp, ch 5 (counts as 1dc and ch 2), 1dc in same ch-sp, *[ch 5, 1sc in 5ch-sp] 4 times, ch 5**, [1dc, ch 2, 1dc] in next 2ch-sp; rep from * twice more and from * to ** once again, ch 5, join with sl st in 3rd ch of ch-5.
Round 9: Sl st in 2ch-sp, ch 5 (counts as 1dc and ch 2), 1dc in same ch-sp, *4dc in next 5ch-sp, [5dc in next 5ch-sp] 3 times, 4dc in next 5ch-sp**, [1dc, ch 2, 1dc] in next 2ch-sp; rep from * twice more and from * to ** once again, change to color B when joining with sl st in 3rd ch of ch-5.
Round 10: Ch 3 (counts as 1dc), 1dc in every dc from previous round and [1dc, ch 2, 1dc] in next and each 2ch-sp to end of round, change to color A when joining with sl st in 3rd ch of ch-3.
Round 11: Ch 3 (counts as 1dc), 1dc in every dc from previous round and [1dc, ch 2, 1dc] in next and each 2ch-sp to end of round, join with sl st in 3rd ch of ch-3.
Fasten off and weave in ends.

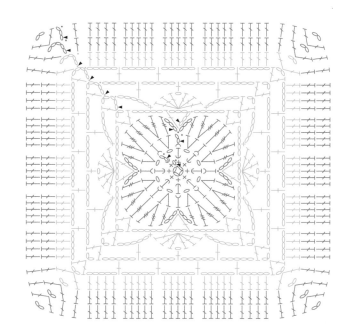

Marigold

See page 33

A=Rose
B=Bleached
C=Blackcurrant
D=Greengage

Foundation ring: Using color A, ch 6 and join with sl st in first ch to form a ring.

Round 1: Ch 5 (counts as 1dc and 2ch), [1dc into ring, ch 2] 7 times, join with sl st in 3rd ch of ch-5.

Round 2: Sl st in next 2ch-sp, ch 1, [1sc, 1hdc, 1dc, 1hdc, 1sc] in same sp (petal made), [1sc, 1hdc, 1dc, 1hdc, 1sc] in each rem 2ch-sp to end of round, join with sl st in first sc. Break color A.

Round 3: Working behind the petals of the previous round, join color B between two petals, ch 3, [sl st in back loop of first sc of next petal, ch 3] 7 times, join with sl st in first of ch-3.

Round 4: Sl st in next 3ch-sp, ch 1, [1sc, 2hdc, 1dc, 2hdc, 1sc] in same sp, [1sc, 2hdc, 1dc, 2hdc, 1sc] in each rem 3ch-sp to end of round, join with sl st in first sc. Break color B.

Round 5: Working behind the petals of the previous round, join color C between two petals, ch 4, [sl st in back loop of first sc of next petal, ch 4] 7 times, join with sl st in first ch of ch-4.

Round 6: Sl st in next 4ch-sp, ch 1, [1sc, 2hdc, 3dc, 2hdc, 1sc] in same sp, [1sc, 2hdc, 3dc, 2hdc, 1sc] in each rem 4ch-sp to end of round, join with sl st in first sc. Break color C.

Round 7: Working behind the petals of the previous round, join color D between two petals, ch 5, [sl st in back loop of first sc of next petal, ch 5] 7 times, join with sl st in first of ch-5.

Round 8: Sl st in next 5ch-sp, ch 3 (counts as 1dc), 5dc in same sp, *[3dc, ch 2, 3dc] in next 5ch-sp, (corner made)**, 6dc in next 5ch-sp; rep from * twice more and from * to ** once again, join with sl st in first dc.

Round 9: Ch 3 (counts as 1dc), 1dc in each dc of previous round, working [2dc, ch 2, 2dc] in each 2ch-corner-sp, join with sl st in 3rd ch of ch-3.

Round 10: Sl st in next dc, ch 5 (counts as 1dc and ch 2), skip 2dc, 1dc in next dc, ch 2, skip 2dc, 1dc in next dc, skip 3dc, *[3dc, ch 2, 3dc] in next 2ch-corner-sp, skip 3dc**, [1dc in next dc, ch 2, skip 2dc] 3 times, 1dc in next dc; rep from * twice more and from * to ** once again, 1dc in next dc, ch 2, skip 2dc, join with sl st in 3rd ch of ch-5.

Round 11: Ch 5 (counts as 1dc and ch 2), [1dc in next dc, ch 2] twice, 1dc in next dc, *[3dc, ch 2, 3dc] in next 2ch-corner-sp, 1dc in next dc**, ch 2, skip 2dc, [1dc in next dc, ch 2] 4 times, 1dc in next dc; rep from * twice and from * to ** once again, ch 2, 1dc in next dc, ch 2, join with sl st in 3rd ch of ch-5.

Round 12: Ch 5 (counts as 1dc and ch 2), [1dc in next dc, ch 2] 3 times, 1dc in next dc, *[3dc, ch 2, 3dc] in next 2ch-corner-sp, 1dc in next dc, ch 2, skip 2dc**, [1dc in next dc, ch 2] 6 times, skip 2dc, 1dc in next dc; rep from * twice and from * to ** once again, [1dc in next dc, ch 2] twice, join with sl st in 3rd ch of ch-5.

Round 13: Ch 5 (counts as 1dc and ch 2), [1dc in next dc, ch 2] 4 times, skip 2dc, 1dc in next dc, *[3dc, ch 2, 3dc] in next 2ch-corner-sp, 1dc in next dc, ch 2, skip 2dc**, [1dc in next dc, ch 2] 8 times, skip 2dc, 1dc in next dc; rep from * twice more and from * to ** once again, [1dc in next dc, ch 2] 3 times, join with sl st in 3rd ch of ch-5.

Round 14: Ch 1, 1sc in same place, 1sc in each dc of previous round, working 2sc in each 2ch-sp along sides of square and 3sc in each 2ch-corner-sp, join with sl st to first sc. **Fasten off and weave in ends.**

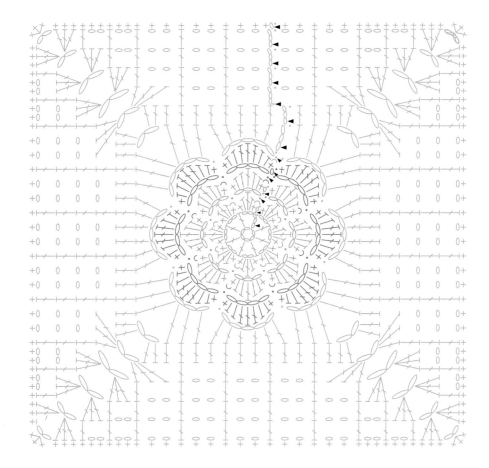

Flame Flower

See page 32

A=Bleached
B=Rose
C=Greengage
D=Blackcurrant

Foundation ring: Using color A, ch 4 and join with sl st in first ch to form a ring.

Round 1: Ch 4 (counts as 1dc and ch 1), [1dc into ring, ch 1] 7 times, join with sl st in 3rd ch of ch-4. (8 sts, 8 ch-sp)

Round 2: Ch 1 and sc in same sp, *sl st in next 1ch-sp, ch 9, sl st in same 1ch-sp**, 1sc in next dc; rep from * a further 6 times then from * to ** once again, join with sl st in first sc. (8 sts, 8 ch-sp)

Round 3: Ch 1, *(5sc, ch 2, 5sc) in ch-9 sp**, sl st in next sc; rep from * 6 more times and from * to ** once again, change to color B when joining with sl st to first sl st. (80 sts, 16 sl sts, 8 ch-sp.) Break color A.

Round 4: Ch 1, *1sc in first sc of petal, 1hdc in next 2 sts, 1dc in next 2sc, (2dc, ch 2, 2dc) in 2ch-sp, 1dc in next 2 sts, 1hdc in next 2sts, 1sc in next st**, FPsc around dc from Round 1; rep from * 6 more times and from * to ** once again, change to color C

when joining with sl st to first sc of petal. Break color B. (120 sts, 8 ch-sp)

Round 5: Join color C with a BP sl st around dc from Round 1, ch3, skip 1tr, *BPsl st around dc from Round 1, ch 3, skip 1dc; rep from * 3 more times, join with sl st in first sl st made. (4 BPsl sts, 4ch-sp)

Round 6: Sl st in 3ch-sp, ch 3 (counts as 1dc), 2dc, ch 2, 3dc in same ch-sp, ch 1, *(3dc, ch 2, 3dc) in next 3ch-sp, ch 1; rep from * twice more, join with sl st in 3rd ch of ch-3. (24 sts, 8 ch-sp)

Round 7: Sl st to next 2ch-sp, ch 3 (counts as 1dc), 2dc, ch 2, 3dc in same 1ch-sp, ch 1, *3dc in 1ch-sp, ch 1**, (3dc, ch 2, 3dc) in next 2ch-sp, ch 1; rep from * twice more and from * to ** once again join with sl st in 3rd ch of ch-3. (36 sts, 12ch-sp)

Round 8: Sl st to next 2ch-sp, ch 3 (counts as 1dc), 2dc, ch 2, 3dc in same ch-sp, ch 1, *[3dc in 1ch-sp, ch 1] twice**, [3dc, ch 2, 3dc] in next 2ch-sp, ch 1; rep from * twice more and then

from * to ** once again join with sl st in 3rd ch of ch-3. (48 sts, 16ch-sp)

Round 9: Sl st to next 2ch-sp, ch 3 (counts as 1dc), 2dc, ch 2, 3dc in same ch-sp, ch 1, *[3dc in 1ch-sp, ch 1] 3 times**, [3dc, ch 2, 3dc] in next 2ch-sp, ch 1; rep from * twice more and then from * to ** once again, join with sl st in 3rd ch of ch-3. (60 sts, 20ch-sp)

Round 10: Ch 1, 1sc in same sp, 1sc in each of next 2 sts, *(1sc, 1hdc, 1sc) in 2ch-sp, 1sc in each of next 5 sts and ch-sp, 1sc through 2ch-sp of Round 4 petal and in next st, 1sc in next 7 sts and ch-sp, 1sc through 2ch-sp of Round 4 petal and in next st**, 1sc in each of next 5 sts and ch-sp to 2ch-corner-sp; rep from * twice more and from * to ** once again, sc to end of round, join with sl st in first sc made. (88 sts)

Round 11: Sl st to next 2ch-sp, ch 3 (counts as 1dc), [2dc, ch 3, 3dc] in same sp, *[ch 1, skip next st, 1dc in

each of next 3 sts] 5 times, ch 1, skip next st**, [3dc, ch 3, 3dc] in next ch-2 corner sp; rep from * twice more and from * to ** once again, join with sl st in 3rd ch of ch-3.

Round 12: Sl st to next 3ch-sp, ch 3 (counts as 1dc), [2dc, ch 3, 3dc] in same sp, *[ch 1, 3dc in next 1ch-sp] 6 times, ch 1**, [3dc, ch 3, 3dc] in next 3ch-corner-sp; rep from * twice more and from * to ** once again, join with sl st in 3rd ch of ch-3.

Round 13: Sl st to next 3ch-sp, ch 3 (counts as 1dc), [2dc, ch 3, 3dc] in same sp, *[ch 1, 3dc in next 1ch-sp] 7 times, ch 1**, [3dc, ch 3, 3dc] in next 3ch-corner-sp; rep from * twice more and from * to ** once again, change to color D when joining with sl st in 3rd ch of ch-3.

Round 14: Ch 1, 1sc in every dc and ch-sp, from previous round, working 3sc in every 3ch-corner-sp, join with sl st in first sc.

Fasten off and weave in ends.

American Beauty

See page 35

A=Rose
B=Shell
C=Dark Forest

Foundation ring: Using color A, ch 12 and join with sl st to form a ring.
Round 1: Ch 1, 18sc into the ring, join with a sl st in first sc. (18 sc)
Round 2: Ch 1, 1sc in same place, [ch 3, skip 2sc, 1sc into next sc] 5 times, ch 3, skip 2sc, join with sl st in first sc. (6 ch-3 loops)
Round 3: Ch 1, [1sc, ch 3, 5dc, ch 3, 1sc] in each of next 6 ch-3 loops, join with sl st in first sc. (6 petals)
Round 4: Ch 1, 1sc in same place, [ch 5 behind petal of previous round, 1sc between 2sc] 5 times, ch 5 behind

petal of previous round, join with sl st in first sc. (6 ch-5 loops)
Round 5: Ch 1, [1sc, ch 3, 7dc, ch 3, 1sc] in each of next 6 ch-5 loops, join with sl st in first sc. (6 petals)
Round 6: Ch 1, 1sc in same place, [ch 7 behind petal of previous round, 1sc between 2sc] 5 times, ch 7 behind petal of previous round, join with sl st in first sc. (6 ch-7 loops)
Round 7: Ch 1, [1sc, ch 3, 9dc, ch 3, 1sc] in each of next 6 ch-7 loops, join with sl st in first sc. (6 petals). Break color A.

Round 8: Join color B between any 2sc, ch 1, [1sc between 2sc, ch 8 behind petal of previous round] 6 times, join with sl st in first sc. (6 ch-8 loops)
Round 9: Sl st in next ch-8 loop, ch 3 (counts as 1dc), [7dc, ch 2, 3dc] in same loop, *10dc in next ch-8 loop, [3dc, ch 2, 8dc] in next ch-8 loop**, [8dc, ch 2, 3dc] in next ch-8 loop; rep from * to ** once more, join with sl st in 3rd ch of ch-3. (16dc along each side of square)
Round 10: Ch 3 (counts as 1dc), 1dc

in each dc of previous round, working [3dc, ch 2, 3dc] in each 2ch-corner-sp, change to color C when joining with sl st in 3rd ch of ch 3.
Rounds 11–13: Ch 3 (counts as 1dc), 1dc in each dc of previous round, working [2dc, ch 2, 2dc] in each 2ch-corner-sp, join with sl st in 3rd ch of ch 3.
Round 14: Ch 1, 1sc in each dc of previous round, working 3sc in each 2ch-corner-sp, join with sl st in first sc.
Fasten off and weave in ends.

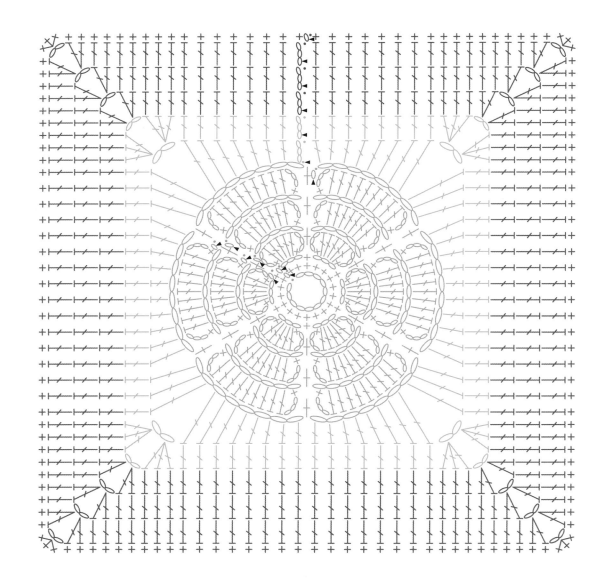

⭐⭐⭐ *Chrysanthemum*

See page 34

A=Blackcurrant
B=Bleached
B=Rose

Central flower
Using A, ch 6, sl st in 3rd ch from hook, ch 2, skip 2ch, 1sc in first ch, do not turn, [ch 5, sl st in 3rd ch from hook, ch 2, skip 2 ch, 1sc in side edge of sc, do not turn] 8 times, [ch 7, sl st in 3rd ch from hook, ch 4, skip 4 ch, 1sc in side edge of sc, do not turn] 9 times, [ch 9, sl st in 3rd ch from hook, ch 6, skip 6 ch, 1sc in side edge of sc, do not turn] 9 times, do not turn. Count along side edge, sl st in 8th sc. Fasten off color A.

Block
Round 1: Turn central flower over and join color B to back loop of any sc in the ring just made, ch 2, 2dc in back loop of each of next 7 sts, 1dc in base of ch 3, sl st in 3rd ch of of ch-3. (16 dc)

Round 2: Ch 3, 2dc in each dc, 1dc in base of ch 3, sl st in 3rd ch of ch-3. (32 dc)

Round 3: Ch 3, [1dc in next dc, 2dc in next dc] 15 times, 1dc in last dc, 1dc in base of ch 3, sl st in 3rd ch of ch-3. (48 dc)

Round 4: Ch 3, [1dc in next dc, 2dc in next dc] 15 times, 1dc in last dc, 1dc in base of ch 3, sl st in 3rd ch of ch-3. Break color B. (64 dc)

Round 5: Join color C to any dc, ch 3, dc3tog in same place as base of ch-3, [ch 4, skip 3dc, dc4tog in next dc] 15 times, ch 4, skip 3dc, sl st in first dc3tog. Break color C. (80 sts)

Round 6: Join color B in any 4ch-sp, ch 6 (counts as 1tr and ch 2), [2tr, 1dc] in same 4ch-sp, *[2dc, 3hdc] in next 4ch-sp, 5hdc in next 4ch-sp, [3hdc, 2dc] in next 4ch-sp, [1dc, 2tr, ch 2, 2tr, 1dc] in next 4ch-sp; rep from * a further 3 times ending last rep with [1dc, 1tr] in first ch-sp, sl st in 4th ch of ch-6. (21 sts on each side)

Round 7: Sl st in 2ch-sp, ch 5 (counts as 1dc and ch 2), 2dc in same 2ch-sp, *1dc in each of next 21 sts, [2dc, ch 2, 2dc] in 2ch-sp; rep from * a further 3 times ending last rep with 1dc in first 2ch-sp, sl st in 3rd ch of ch-5. (25 sts on each side)

Round 8: Sl st into 2ch-sp, ch 5 (counts as 1dc and ch 2), 2dc in same 2ch-sp, *1dc in each of next 25 sts, [2dc, ch 2, 2dc] in 2ch-sp; rep from * a further 3 times, ending last rep with 1dc in first ch-sp, sl st in 3rd ch of ch-5. (29 sts on each side)

Round 9: Sl st into 2ch-sp, ch 5 (counts as 1dc and ch 2), 2dc in same 2ch-sp, *1dc in each of next 29 sts, [2dc, ch 2, 2dc] in 2ch-sp; rep from * a further 3 times, ending last rep with 1dc in first ch-sp, sl st in 3rd ch of ch-5. (33 sts on each side)

Fasten off and weave in ends.

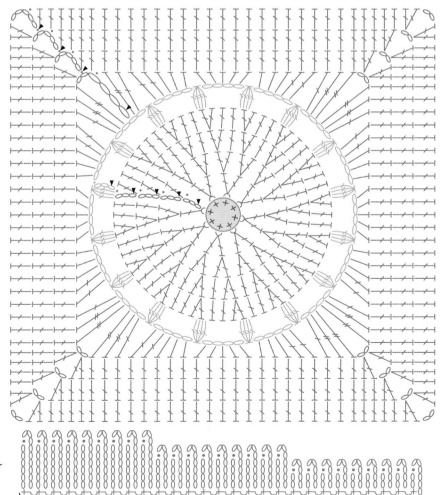

Central flower

See page 33

★★★ *Primrose Square*

A=Shell
B=Bleached
C=Greengage

SPECIAL STITCHES

1gp (2 linked sts together): Yarn round hook twice, insert hook into designated st, [yarn round hook, pull 2 loops through] twice, yarn round hook, insert hook in lowest link of st just made, yarn round hook, pull through link, yarn round hook, pull through 2 loops, yarn round hook, pull through 3 loops on hook.

5chP (5-ch picot): Ch5, slst to first of ch-5.

7chP (7-ch picot): Ch7, slst to first of ch-7.

First primrose

Using color A make a Magic Ring.

Round 1: Sl st into ring, ch 1, 4sc into ring, join with sl st to first ch. Break color A. (5 sts)

Round 2: Join color B to to any sc, ch 3, 1dc in first of these ch 3, ch 1, 1gp in same sc, *ch 3, [1gp, ch 1, 1gp] in next sc; rep from * a further 3 times,

ch 3, join with sl st in first dc of the round. Break color B.

Round 3: Join color C to any 3ch-sp, ch 1, 2sc in same ch-sp, *sc2tog over [same 3ch-sp and next 1ch-sp], 5chP, sc2tog over [same ch-1 sp and next 3ch-sp], 4sc in same 3ch-sp**; rep from * once more, sc2tog as set, 7chP, sc2tog as set, 4sc in same 3ch-sp; rep from * to ** twice more ending 1sc in first ch-sp, join with sl st in first ch of round.

Fasten off.

Second primrose

Work as first primrose, joining to first primrose on last round by linking the second 5chP and the 7chP to corresponding picots.

Third primrose

Work as first primrose, linking to second primrose as before.

Fourth primrose

Work as first primrose without fastening off color C, joining to first,

second and third primroses on last round by linking the second 5chP, the 7chP and the next 5chP forming a square. Do not fasten off. Rejoin color C to last sl st of Round 3 of first primrose.

Round 4: Ch 5 (counts as 1dc and ch 2), *1dc in next sc, ch 3, sl st in 5chP, ch 3, [1tr, ch 3, 1tr] in st linking two 5chP, ch 3, sl st in next ch 5P, ch 3**, 1dc in 2nd ch of 4sc, ch 2; rep from * twice more then from * to ** once again join with sl st in 3rd ch of ch-5.

Round 5: Sl st in next 2ch-sp, ch 5 (counts as 1dc and ch 2), 2dc in same ch-sp, *4dc in each of next two 3ch-sp, 3dc in next 3ch-sp (between tr), 4dc in each of next two 3ch-sp**, [2dc, ch 2, 2dc] in 2ch-corner-sp; rep from * twice more then from * to ** once again, 1dc in first corner ch-sp, join with sl st in 3rd ch of ch-5. (23 dc on each side.)

Round 6: Sl st in next 2ch-sp, ch 5 (counts as 1dc and ch 2), 1dc in same ch-sp, *1dc in each of next 23dc**, [1dc, ch 2, 1dc] in 2ch-corner-sp; rep from * twice more then from * to ** once again, join with sl st in 3rd ch of ch-3.

Round 7: Sl st in next 2ch-sp, ch 5 (counts as 1dc and ch 2), 1dc in same ch-sp, *1dc in each of next 25dc**, [1dc, ch 2, 1dc] in 2ch-corner-sp; rep from * twice more then from * to ** once again, join with sl st in 3rd ch of ch-3. (25 dc on each side.)

Round 8: Sl st in next 2ch-sp, ch 1, [1sc, ch 2, 1sc] in same ch-sp, *1sc in each dc around and work [1sc, ch 2, 1sc] in 2ch-corner-sp, join with sl st in 3rd ch of ch-3. (29 dc on each side)

Fasten off and weave in ends.

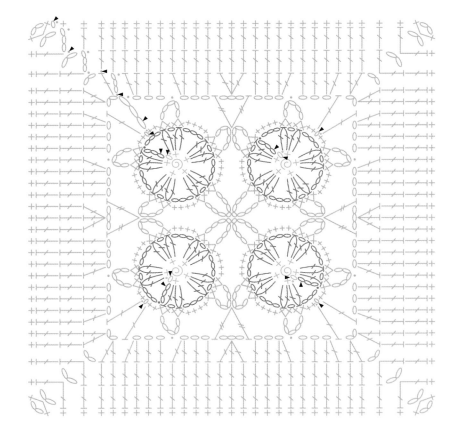

⭐⭐ Waterlily
See page 35

A=Shell
B=Bleached
C=Greengage

Foundation ring: Using color A, ch 8 and join with sl st in first ch to form a ring.

Round 1: Ch 6 (counts as 1dc and ch 3), [1dc into the ring, ch 3] 7 times, join with sl st in 3rd ch of ch-3. Break color A. (8 spaced dc)

Round 2: Join color B to any ch-3 sp, ch 1, [1sc, ch 2, 3dc, ch 2, 1sc] in same sp, *[1sc, ch 2, 3dc, ch 2, 1sc] in next ch-3 sp; rep from * 7 times, do not join. (8 petals)

Note: Rounds 3–6 are worked in a continuous spiral. You might find it helpful to use a stitch marker to keep track of the start of the round.

Round 3: Ch 5 working behind petal, skip 1 petal, 1sc in top of next sc of Round 1, [ch 5, working behind petal, skip 1 petal, 1sc in top of next sc of round 1] 7 times, do not join. (8 ch-5 loops)

Round 4: *[1sc, ch 2, 5dc, ch 2, 1sc] in next ch-5 loop; rep from * to end of round, do not join. (8 petals)

Round 5: Ch 7 working behind petal, skip1 petal, 1sc in top of next sc of round 3, [ch 7, working behind petal, skip1 petal, 1sc in top of next sc of round 3] 7 times, do not join. (8 ch-7 loops)

Round 6: *[1sc, ch 2, 7dc, ch 2, 1sc] in next ch-7 loop; rep from * to end of round, do not join. Break color B. (8 petals)

Round 7: Working behind petals, join color C to any sc on Round 5, ch 3 (counts as 1dc), 2dc in same sc, ch 3, *[3dc, ch 3, 3dc] in next sc of Round 5 to make corner, ch 3**, 3dc in next sc, ch 3; rep from * twice more and from * to ** once again, join with sl st in 3rd ch of ch-3.

Round 8: Ch 3 (counts as 1dc), 1dc in every dc and 3dc in each 3ch-sp of previous round, working [2dc, ch 3, 2dc] in each ch-3 corner sp, join with sl st in 3rd ch of ch-3.

Round 9: Ch 3 (counts as 1dc), 1dc in every dc of previous round, working [2dc, ch 3, 2dc] in each ch-3 corner sp, with sl st in 3rd ch of ch-3.

Round 10: Ch 1, 1sc in every dc of previous round, working [2sc, ch 1, 2sc] in each 3ch-corner-sp, changing to color B when joining with sl st in first sc.

Round 11: Ch 1, 1sc in every sc of previous round, working [1sc, ch 1, 1sc] in each 1ch-corner-sp, join with sl st in first sc.

Round 12: Ch 1, 1sc in every sc of previous round, working [1sc, ch 1, 1sc] in each 1ch-corner-sp, changing to color A when joining with sl st in first sc.

Rounds 13–14: Ch 1, 1sc in every sc of previous round, working [1sc, ch 1, 1sc] in each 1ch-corner-sp, join with sl st in first sc.

Fasten off and weave in ends.

⭐⭐ Filet Flower
See page 34

A=Rose

SPECIAL STITCHES

Dc2tog (work two double sts tog): [Yoh draw up a loop in next st, (yoh, pull through 2 loops on hook) twice] twice, yoh and draw through all 3 loops on hook.

Foundation ring: Using color A, ch 6 and join with sl st in first ch to form a ring.

Round 1: Ch 1, 12sc into the ring, join with a sl st in first sc.

Round 2: Ch 3 (counts as 1dc), 4dc in same place, [ch 3, skip 2sc, 5dc in next sc] 3 times, ch 3, join with sl st in 3rd ch of ch-3.

Round 3: Ch 3 (counts as 1dc), 1dc in next dc, 5dc in next dc, 1dc in each of next 2dc, *ch 3, skip 3ch, 1dc in each of next 2dc, 5dc in next dc, 1dc in each of next 2dc; rep from * twice more, ch 3, skip 3ch, join with sl st in 3rd ch of ch-3.

Round 4: Ch 3 (counts as 1dc), 1dc in each of next 3dc, 5dc in next dc, 1dc in each of next 4dc, *ch 3, skip 3ch, 1dc in each of next 4dc, 5dc in next dc, 1dc in each of next 4dc; rep from * twice more, ch 3, skip 3ch, join with sl st in 3rd ch of ch-3.

Round 5: Ch 2, 1dc in each of next 4dc, *dc2tog over next 2dc, ch 7, dc2tog over [same dc as last insertion and next dc], 1dc in each of next 3dc, dc2tog over next 2dc, ch 5, skip 3ch**, dc2tog over next 2dc, 1dc in each of

next 3dc; rep from * twice more and then from * to ** once again, join with sl st in first dc.

Round 6: Ch 2, 1dc in each of next 2dc, *dc2tog over next 2 sts, ch 3, skip 2ch, 1dc in next ch, ch 3, skip 1ch, 1dc in next ch, ch 3, skip next 2ch, 1dc in next ch, ch 3, dc2tog over next 2sts, 1dc in next dc, dc2tog over next 2 sts, ch 3, skip 2ch, 1dc in next ch, ch 3, skip 2ch**, dc2tog over next 2 sts, 1dc in next dc; rep from * twice more and from * to ** once again, join with sl st in first dc.

Round 7: Ch 4 (counts as 1dc and ch 1), skip first 2dc, 1dc in dc2tog, ch 1, skip 1ch, 1dc in next ch, *ch 5, skip 3ch, 1dc in next dc, ch 1, skip 1ch, 1dc in next ch, ch 1, skip 1ch, 1dc in next dc2tog, ch 1, skip 1dc, 1dc in next dc2tog, ch 1, skip 1ch, 1dc in next ch, skip 1 ch, 1dc in next dc, ch 1, skip 1ch**, 1dc in next dc2tog, ch 1, skip 1dc, 1dc in next dc2tog, ch 1, skip 1ch, 1dc in next ch, skip 1 ch, 1dc in next dc; rep from * twice more and from * to ** once again, join with sl st in 3rd ch of ch-4.

Round 8: Ch 2 (counts as 1hdc), 1hdc in every dc and 1ch-sp and [2hdc, ch 3, 2hdc] in every 5ch-corner sp to end of round, join with sl st in 2nd ch of ch-2.

Fasten off and weave in ends.

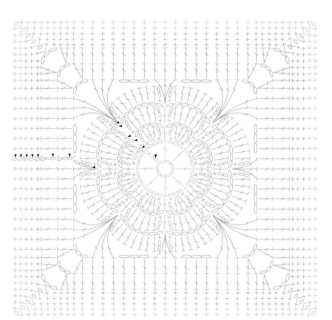

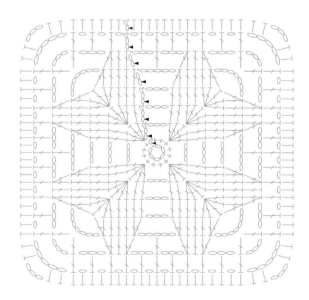

Rosetta

See page 35

A=Shell
B=Rose
C=Dark Forest

SPECIAL STITCHES

Dtr (double treble crochet): Take yarn over the hook 3 times before inserting in designated st or space, yoh and pull through st or space, [yoh and pull through 2 loops on hook] 4 times.

Sc2tog (single crochet 2 sts together): Insert hook through next st, yoh and pull through st, skip 2 sts, insert hook through next st, yoh and pull through st, yoh and pull through all 3 loops on hook.

Spike hdc (spiked half dc): Yoh and insert hook in skipped sc from previous round, pull loop through so that it is level with current round, yoh and pull through all 3 loops on hook.

Foundation ring: Using color A, work 8 ch and join with sl st to form a ring.

Round 1: Ch 1, 12sc in ring, join with a sl st to first sc. (12 sc)

Round 2: Ch 5 (counts as 1dc and ch 2), [1dc, ch 2] in every sc, join with sl st to 3rd ch of beg ch-5. (12 ch-2 sps)

Round 3: Ch 1, 1sc in same st, *3sc in next ch-2 sp**, 1sc in next dc; rep from * a further 10 times and from * to ** once more, change to color D when joining with a sl st to first sc. (48 sts)

Round 4: Join color B, ch 5 (counts as dtr), 1dtr in each of next 3sc, *ch 6, 1dtr in each of next 4sc; rep from * a further 10 times, ch 6, join with a sl st to 5th ch of beg ch-5.

Round 5: Ch 1, sc2tog across first 4dtr, *8sc in next ch-6 sp**, sc2tog across next 4dtr; rep from * a further 10 times and from * to ** once more, join with a sl st to first sc2tog. Fasten off color B.

Round 6: Join color C to any sc2tog from previous round, ch 4 (counts as 1tr), 1tr in same place (half corner made), [ch 2, skip next 3sc, 1sc in each of next 2sc, ch 2, skip next 3sc, 1dc in next sc2tog] twice, ch 2, skip next 3sc, 1sc in each of next 2sc, ch 2, skip next 3sc**, [2tr, ch 3, 2tr in next sc2tog] (corner made); rep from * twice more and from * to ** once again, 2tr in first sc2tog of round, ch 3, join with sl st to 4th ch of beg ch-4.

Round 7: Ch 1, 1sc in same place, 1sc in every st, 2sc in every ch-2 sp, [2sc, ch 3, 1sc] in every ch-3 corner sp to end of round, changing to color A when joining with sl st to first sc.

Round 8: Join color C, ch 1, 1sc in same place, 1sc in every st, [1sc, ch 1, 1sc] in every ch-3 corner sp to end of round, join with sl st to first sc.

Round 9: Ch 1, 1sc in same place, ch 1, skip next sc, work [1sc in next st, ch 1, skip next sc to next corner sp] and [2sc, ch 1, 2sc] in every ch-1 corner sp to end of round, changing to color B when joining with sl st to first sc.

Round 10: Ch 2 (counts as 1hdc), skip next sc, *[spike hdc in next skipped sc of previous round, ch 1**, skip 1sc] to corner sp, [1sc, ch 1, 1sc] in ch-1 corner sp, ch 1, skip next sc; rep from * twice more times and then from * to ** once again, join with sl st to 2nd ch of beg ch-2.

Fasten off and weave in ends.

✦ ✦ *Poinsettia*

See page 34

A=Rose

SPECIAL STITCHES

dc2tog (work two double sts tog):
[Yoh draw up a loop in next st, (yoh, pull through 2 loops on hook) twice] twice, yoh and draw through all 3 loops on hook.

dc5tog (work five double sts tog):
[Yoh draw up a loop in next st, (yoh, pull through 2 loops on hook) twice] 5 times, yoh and draw through all 6 loops on hook.

Foundation chain: Using color A, ch 6 and join with sl st in first ch to form a ring.

Round 1: Ch 3 (counts as 1dc), 15dc into the ring, join with sl st to 3rd of ch-3.

Round 2: Ch 4 (counts as 1dc and ch 1), *5dc in next dc, ch 1**, 1dc in next dc, ch 1; rep from * a further 6 times and from * to ** once more, join with sl st in 3rd ch of ch-4.

Round 3: Ch 4 (counts as 1dc and ch 1), 1dc in same place, *ch 1, 2dc in each of next 5dc, ch 1**, [1dc, ch 1, 1dc] in next dc, ch 1; rep from * a further 6 times and from * to ** once more, join with sl st in 3rd ch of ch-4.

Round 4: Ch 3 (counts as 1dc), 1dc in same place, ch 1, 2dc in next dc, ch 1, *[dc2tog over next 2 sts] 5 times, ch 1**, [2dc in next dc, ch 1] twice; rep from * 6 more times and from * to ** once more, join with sl st in 3rd of ch-3.

Round 5: Ch 4 (counts as 1dc and ch 1), [1dc, ch 1] in each of next 3dc, *dc5tog over next 5 sts, ch 1**, [1dc, ch 1] in each of next 4dc; rep from * a further 6 times and from * to ** once more, join with sl st in 3rd ch of ch-4.

Round 6: Ch 4 (counts as 1dc and ch 1), *1dc in next dc, ch 1, [2tr, ch 3, 2tr] in next 1ch-sp, [ch 1, 1dc] in each of

next 2dc, ch 1, 1hdc in next dc5tog, [ch 1, 1sc] in each of next 4dc, ch 1, 1hdc in next dc5tog, ch 1**, 1dc in next dc, ch 1; rep from * twice more and from * to ** once again, join with sl st in 3rd ch of ch-4.

Round 7: Ch 3 (counts as 1dc), 1dc in every st and 1ch-sp around, working [2dc, ch2, 2dc] in each 3-ch corner sp, join with sl st in 3rd ch of ch-3.

Round 8: Ch 2 (counts as 1hdc), 1hdc in every st around, working 3dc in every ch-2 corner sp, join with sl st in 2nd ch of ch-2.

Fasten off and weave in ends.

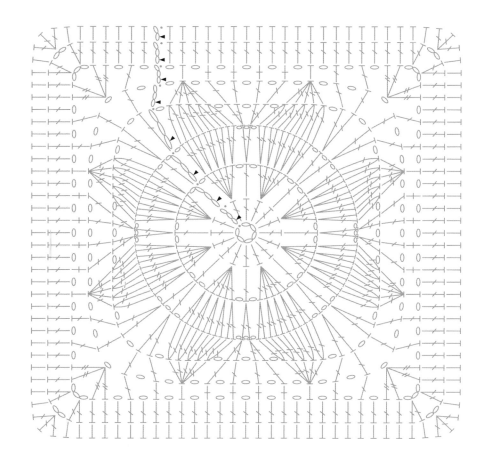

★ ★ Mitered Increase

See page 37

A=Rose
B=Ecru
C=Ultramarine
D=Oyster

Foundation chain: Using color A, make 6ch.

Row 1: 1dc in 4th ch from hook, 1dc in each of next 2 ch, turn.

Row 2: Ch 3 (counts as 1dc), 1dc in each of next 2dc, 4dc in loop made between tch and first dc of previous row, turn.

Row 3: Ch 3 (counts as 1dc), 1dc in each of next 2dc, [2dc, ch 2, 2dc] in next dc, 1dc in each of next 2dc, 1dc in 3rd ch of tch, turn.

Row 4: Ch 3 (counts as 1dc), 1dc in each of next 4dc, [2dc, ch 2, 2dc] in 2ch-sp, 1dc in each of next 4dc, change to color B when working 1dc in 3rd ch of tch, turn.

Row 5: Ch 3 (counts as 1dc), 1dc in each of next 6dc, [2dc, ch 2, 2dc] in 2ch-sp, 1dc in each of next 6dc, 1dc in 3rd ch of tch, turn.

Row 6: Ch 3 (counts as 1dc), 1dc in each of next 8dc, [2dc, ch 2, 2dc] in 2ch-sp, 1dc in each of next 8dc, change to color C when working 1dc in 3rd of tch, turn.

Row 7: Ch 3 (counts as 1dc), 1dc in each of next 10dc, [2dc, ch 2, 2dc] in 2ch-sp, 1dc in each of next 10dc, change to color D when working 1dc in 3rd ch of tch, turn.

Row 8: Ch 3 (counts as 1dc), 1dc in each of next 12dc, [2dc, ch 2, 2dc] in 2ch-sp, 1dc in each of next 12dc, 1dc in 3rd ch of tch, turn.

Row 9: Ch 3 (counts as 1dc), 1dc in each of next 14dc, [2dc, ch 2, 2dc] in 2ch-sp, 1dc in each of next 14dc, 1dc in 3rd ch of tch, turn.

Row 10: Ch 3 (counts as 1dc), 1dc in each of next 16dc, [2dc, ch 2, 2dc] in 2ch-sp, 1dc in each of next 16dc, change to color A when working 1dc in 3rd ch of tch, turn.

Row 11: Ch 3 (counts as 1dc), 1dc in each of next 18dc, [2dc, ch 2, 2dc] in 2ch-sp, 1dc in each of next 18dc, 1dc in 3rd ch of tch, turn.

Row 12: Ch 3 (counts as 1dc), 1dc in each of next 20dc, [2dc, ch 2, 2dc] in 2ch-sp, 1dc in each of next 20dc, 1dc in 3rd ch of tch, turn.

Row 13: Ch 3 (counts as 1dc), 1dc in each of next 22dc, [2dc, ch 2, 2dc] in 2ch-sp, 1dc in each of next 22dc, change to color B when working 1dc in 3rd ch of tch, turn.

Row 14: Ch 3 (counts as 1dc), 1dc in each of next 24dc, [2dc, ch 2, 2dc] in 2ch-sp, 1dc in each of next 24dc, change to color C when working 1dc in 3rd ch of tch, turn.

Row 15: Ch 3 (counts as 1dc), 1dc in each of next 26dc, [2dc, ch 2, 2dc] in 2ch-sp, 1dc in each of next 26dc, 1dc in 3rd ch of tch, do not turn.

Border

Round 1: Ch 1, 1sc in same place, [2sc in every row end to last row end, [3sc in top ch of corner st] twice, 1sc in every dc to corner, 3sc in ch-2 corner sp, 1sc in every dc to last dc, 3sc in last dc, join with sl st to first sc.

Fasten off and weave in ends.

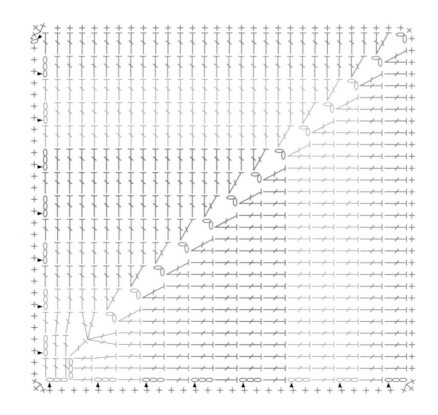

★★ Mitered Decrease

See page 37

A=Oyster
B=Ultramarine
C=Ecru
D=Rose
E=Bleached

SPECIAL STITCHES

Sc3tog: Decrease 2 sts by working the next 3 sts together.

Foundation chain: Using color A, work 58 ch.

Foundation row (WS): 1sc in 2nd ch from hook, 1sc in every ch to end of row, turn. (57 sc)

Row 1 (RS): Ch 1, 1sc in next 27sc, sc3tog, 1sc in each of rem 27sc, turn. (55 sc)

Row 2: Ch 1, 1sc in next 26sc, sc3tog, 1sc in each of rem 26sc, turn. Break color A. (53 sc)

Row 3: Join color B, ch 1, 1sc in next 25sc, sc3tog, 1sc in each of rem 25sc, turn. (51 sc)

Row 4: Ch 1, 1sc in next 24sc, sc3tog, 1sc in each of rem 24sc, turn. (49 sc)

Continue in pattern as set, working sc3tog over 3 center sts on every row. At the same time change colors in the following sequence.

2 more rows in B.
4 rows in C.
3 rows in D.
2 rows in E.
4 rows in A.
2 rows in B.

1 row in C.
2 rows in D.
1 row in E.
1 row in B.

Next row: Sc3tog. Fasten off.

Border

Join color D to end of Foundation row with sl st.

Row 1 (RS): Ch 1, 1sc in same place, 1sc in next 26 row ends, 3sc in corner, 1sc in following 27 row ends, turn. (57 sc)

Row 2: Ch 1, 1sc in next 28sc, 3sc in center st of 3sc corner, 1sc in rem 27sc, turn. (59 sc)

Row 3: Ch 1, 1sc in next 29sc, 3sc in center st of 3sc corner, 1sc in rem 28sc, turn. (61 sc)

Row 4: Join color A, ch 2 (counts as 1hdc), 1hdc in next 30sc, 3hdc in center st of 3sc corner, hdc in rem 28sc, turn. Break color A. (63 hdc)

Row 5: Join color B, ch3 (counts as 1dc), 1dc in next 30sc, 3dc in center st of 3hdc corner, 1dc in rem 29sc, turn. (65 dc)

Fasten off and weave in ends.

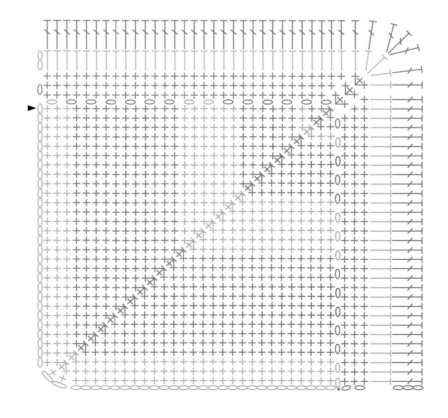

Log Cabin Granny

See page 39

A=Greengage
B=Bleached
C=Sky
D=Blackcurrant
E=Oyster
F=Persimmon
G=Burnt Orange

Foundation ring: Using color A, ch 6 and join with sl st in first ch to form a ring.

Section 1: Ch 3, (counts as 1dc throughout), 2dc into ring, ch 3, *3dc into ring, ch 3; rep from * twice more, join with sl st in 3rd ch of ch-3. Break color A.

Section 2: Join color B to any ch-3 corner sp, ch 3 (counts as 1dc), 2dc in same sp, 3dc in next ch-3 corner sp, ch 3, turn, 3dc between 2 clusters from previous row, 1dc in 3rd ch of ch-3. Fasten off.

Section 3: Join color C to ch-3 sp from previous section, ch 3, 2dc in same sp, 3dc in each sp between two clusters to end of row, ch 3, 3dc in each sp between two clusters to end of row, 1dc in 3rd ch of ch-3. Fasten off.

Section 4: As Section 3 in color D.
Section 5: As Section 3 in color E.
Section 6: As Section 3 in color F.
Section 7: As Section 3 in color G.
Section 8: As Section 3 in color A.
Section 9: As Section 3 in color B.
Section 10: As Section 3 in color C.
Section 11: As Section 3 in color D.
Section 12: As Section 3 in color E.
Section 13: As Section 3 in color F.
Section 14: As Section 3 in color G.
Section 15: As Section 3 in color A.
Section 16: As Section 3 in color B.
Section 17: As Section 3 in color C.
Fasten off and weave in ends.

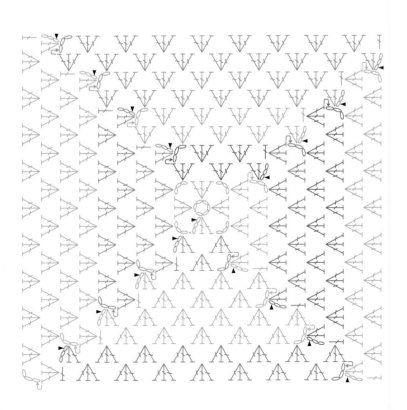

Vertical Woven Block

See page 37

A=Rose
B=Blackcurrant
C=Oyster

Foundation chain: Using color A, ch 33.

Row 1: 1dc in 4th ch from hook, 1dc in next ch, *ch 1, skip next ch, 1dc in each of next 3dc; rep from * to end of row, turn.

Row 2: Ch 3, skip first dc, 1dc in each of next 2dc, *ch 1, skip 1ch, 1dc in each of next 3dc; rep from * to end of row, 1dc in 3rd of tch, turn. Rep Row 2 a further 12 times. Do not fasten off.

Border

Round 1: Ch 1, 1sc in same place, 1sc in same row-end post, *2sc in each of next 12 row-end posts, [2sc, 1hdc, 2sc] in last row-end post**, 1sc in each foundation ch to corner, [2sc, 1hdc, 2sc] in next row-end post; rep from * to **, 1sc in each dc to end of round, [1hdc, 2sc] in first row-end post, join with sl st in first sc.

Round 2: Ch 2, 1hdc in each sc and 1dc in each dc from previous round, join with sl st in 2nd ch of ch-2. Fasten off and weave in ends.

Weaving

*Cut three strands of color B approx. 9in (23cm) long and weave over and under the bars created by the ch-sps**.

Cut three strands of color C approx. 9in (23cm) long and weave under and over the bars created by the ch-sps. Rep from * twice more and from * to ** once again.

Gently stretch the block in both directions to ensure that the weaving is not too tight before weaving in the ends.

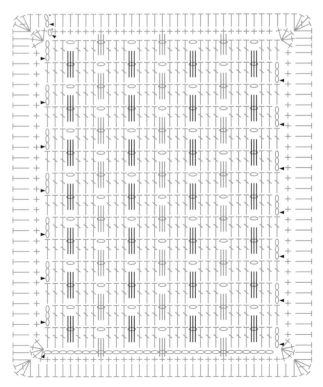

Corner Log Cabin

See page 39

A=Greengage
B=Bleached
C=Sky
D=Blackcurrant
E=Oyster
F=Persimmon

Section 1

Using color A, ch 11.

Row 1: 1dc in 4th ch from hook, 1dc in every ch to end of row, turn.

Row 2: Ch 2, skip first dc, 1dc in sp between first and second dc, *skip next dc, 1dc in foll sp; rep from * to last dc, skip last dc, 1dc in ch-sp, turn.

Rows 3–6: As Row 2, ending color A at end of Row 6 and joining color B.

Rows 7–12: As Row 2, ending color B at end of Row 12 and joining color C.

Section 2

Row 1: Ch 3, 1dc in each of next 11 row-ends, 2dc in last row-end, turn.

Row 2: Ch 2, skip first dc, 1dc in sp between first and second dc, skip next dc, 1dc in next sp, skip next dc, *2dc in next sp, skip next dc, 1dc in next sp, skip next dc; rep from * to end, 1dc in ch-sp, turn.

Row 3: Ch 2, skip first dc, 1dc in sp between first and second dc, *skip next dc, 1dc in next sp; rep from * to last dc, skip last dc, 1dc in ch-sp, turn.

Rows 4–6: As Row 3, ending color C at end of Row 6 and joining color D.

Section 3

Row 1: Ch 3, 1dc in same row-end sp as ch 3, 1dc in each of next 5 row-ends, skip next dc, 1dc in every sp between dc to end of row, 1dc in ch-sp, turn.

Row 2: Ch 2, skip first dc, 1dc in sp between first and second dc, skip next dc, [1dc in next sp, skip next dc] 6 times, [2dc in next sp, skip next dc, 1dc in next sp, skip next dc] 3 times, 1dc in ch-sp, turn.

Row 3: Ch 2, skip first dc, 1dc in sp between first and second dc, *skip next dc, 1dc in next sp; rep from * to last dc, skip last dc, 1dc in ch-sp, turn.

Rows 4–6: As Row 3, ending color D at end of Row 6 and joining color E.

Section 4

Row 1: Ch 3, 1dc in same row-end sp as ch 3, 1dc in each of next 5 row-ends, skip next dc, 1dc in every sp between dc to end of row, 1dc in ch-sp, turn.

Row 2: Ch 2, skip first dc, 1dc in sp between first and second dc, skip next dc, [1dc in next sp, skip next dc] 16 times, [2dc in next sp, skip next dc, 1dc in next sp, skip next dc] 3 times, 1dc in ch-sp, turn.

Row 3: Ch 2, skip first dc, 1dc in sp between first and second dc, *skip next dc, 1dc in next sp; rep from * to last dc, skip last dc, 1dc in ch-sp, turn.

Rows 4–6: As Row 3.

Fasten off.

Border

Round 1: Join color F to any dc from Section 4 with a sl st, ch 2, 1hdc in every dc to last dc, 3hdc in last dc, [1hdc in next row-end sp, 2hdc in next row-end sp] 3 times, 1hdc in each of next 16dc, 3hdc in next dc, [1hdc in next row-end sp, 2hdc in next row-end sp] 9 times, 3hdc in first foundation ch, 1hdc in each of next 8 foundation ch, [2hdc in next row-end sp, 1hdc in next row-end sp] 6 times, 3hdc in next dc, 1hdc in every rem dc to end of round, join with sl st in 2nd ch of ch-2.

Fasten off and weave in ends.

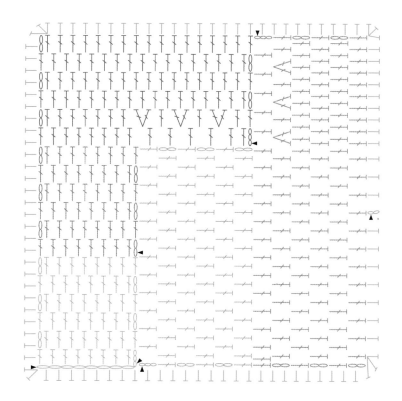

Log Cabin

See page 39

A=Greengage
B=Bleached
C=Sky
D=Blackcurrant

E=Oyster
F=Persimmon
G=Dark Forest

Center
Using color A, make 11ch.
Row 1: (RS): 1sc in 2nd ch from hook, 1sc in every ch to end of row, turn. (10 sts)
Row 2: Ch 1 (does not count as st throughout), 1sc in every sc to end of row, turn.
Rows 3–10: As Row 2. Fasten off.

Section 1
With RS facing, join color B with a sl st to first sc at top right of center block.
Row 1: Ch 1, 1sc in same place as sl st, 1sc in each of next 8sc, 3sc in next sc, 1sc in each of next 9 row-ends, turn.
Row 2: Ch 1, 1sc in each of next 10sc, 3sc in next sc, 1sc in each of last 10sc, turn.
Row 3: Ch 1, 1sc in each of next 11sc, 3sc in next sc, 1sc in each of last 11sc, turn.
Row 4: Ch 1, 1sc in each of next 12sc, 3sc in next sc, 1sc in each of last 12sc. Fasten off.

Section 2
With RS facing and first section at lower right, join color C with a sl st to first row end.
Row 1: Ch 1, 1sc in same place as sl st, 1sc in each of next 3 row-ends, 1sc in each of next 9ch, 3sc in next ch, 1sc in each of next 13 row-ends, turn.
Row 2: Ch 1, 1sc in each of next 14sc, 3sc in next sc, 1sc in each of last 14sc, turn.
Row 3: Ch 1, 1sc in each of next 15sc, 3sc in next sc, 1sc in each of last 15sc, turn.
Row 4: Ch 1, 1sc in each of next 16sc, 3sc in next sc, 1sc in each of last 16sc. Fasten off.

Section 3
With RS facing and second section at lower right, join color D with a sl st to first row end.
Row 1: Ch 1, 1sc in same place as sl st, 1sc in each of next 3 row-ends, 1sc in each of next 13sc, 3sc in next ch, 1sc in each of last 13sc, turn.
Row 2: Ch 1, 1sc in each of next 18sc, 3sc in next sc, 1sc in each of last 18sc, turn.
Row 3: Ch 1, 1sc in each of next 19sc, 3sc in next sc, 1sc in each of last 19sc, turn.
Row 4: Ch 1, 1sc in each of next 20sc, 3sc in next sc, 1sc in each of last 20sc. Fasten off.

Section 4
With RS facing and third section at lower right, join color E with a sl st to first row end.
Row 1: Ch 1, 1sc in same place as sl st, 1sc in each of next 3 row-ends, 1sc in each of next 17sc, 3sc in next ch, 1sc in each of last 17sc, turn.
Row 2: Ch 1, 1sc in each of next 22sc, 3sc in next sc, 1sc in each of last 22sc, turn.
Row 3: Ch 1, 1sc in each of next 23sc, 3sc in next sc, 1sc in each of last 23sc, turn.
Row 4: Ch 1, 1sc in each of next 24sc, 3sc in next sc, 1sc in each of last 24sc. Fasten off.

Section 5
With RS facing and fourth section at lower right, join color F with a sl st to first row end.
Row 1: Ch 1, 1sc in same place as sl st, 1sc in each of next 3 row-ends, 1sc in each of next 21sc, 3sc in next ch, 1sc in each of last 21sc, turn.

Row 2: Ch 1, 1sc in each of next 26sc, 3sc in next sc, 1sc in each of last 26sc, turn.
Row 3: Ch 1, 1sc in each of next 27sc, 3sc in next sc, 1sc in each of last 27sc, turn.
Row 4: Ch 1, 1sc in each of next 28sc, 3sc in next sc, 1sc in each of last 28sc. Fasten off.

Section 6
With RS facing and fifth section at lower right, join color G with a sl st to first row end.
Row 1: Ch 1, 1sc in same place as sl st, 1sc in each of next 3 row-ends, 1sc in each of next 25sc, 3sc in next ch, 1sc in each of last 25sc, turn.
Row 2: Ch 1, 1sc in each of next 30sc, 3sc in next sc, 1sc in each of last 30sc, turn.
Row 3: Ch 1, 1sc in each of next 31sc, 3sc in next sc, 1sc in each of last 31sc, turn.
Row 4: Ch 1, 1sc in each of next 32sc, 3sc in next sc, 1sc in each of last 32sc. Fasten off.

Section 7
With RS facing and sixth section at lower right, join color C with a sl st to first row end.
Row 1: Ch 1, 1sc in same place as sl st, 1sc in each of next 3 row-ends, 1sc in each of next 29sc, 3sc in next ch, 1sc in each of last 29 sc, turn.
Row 2: Ch 1, 1sc in each of next 34sc, 3sc in next sc, 1sc in each of last 34sc, turn.
Row 3: Ch 1, 1sc in each of next 35sc, 3sc in next sc, 1sc in each of last 35sc, turn.
Row 4: Ch 1, 1sc in each of next 36sc, 3sc in next sc, 1sc in each of last 36sc.

Fasten off and weave in ends.

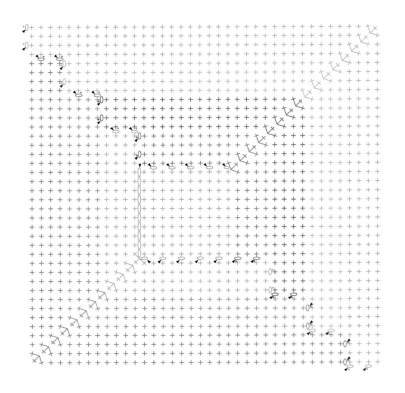

⭐⭐ *Beaded Single Crochet*

See page 38

A=Sky
261 size 6 glass beads

SPECIAL STITCHES

Bsc (beaded single crochet): Insert hook as directed, yoh, pull loop through, slide bead up yarn close to work, yoh (catching yarn beyond bead), pull through both loops on hook.

Foundation chain: Start by threading beads onto color A. Make 34 ch.
Row 1 (WS): 1sc in 2nd ch from hook, 1sc in every ch to end of row, turn. (33 sts)
Row 2: Ch 1, skip first st, [1sc in every st to end of row, 1sc in tch, turn.

Row 3: Ch 1, skip first st, 1sc in each of next 2sc, *1Bsc in next sc, 1sc in next sc; rep from * to end, 1sc in tch, turn.
Row 4: As Row 2.
Row 5: Ch 1, 1sc in each of next 3sc, *1Bsc in next sc, 1sc in next sc; rep from * to last 2 sts, 1sc in each of last 2 sts, turn.

Rep Rows 2–5 a further 8 times then Row 2 once more.

Fasten off and weave in ends.

⭐⭐ *Sequined Single Crochet*

See page 38

A=Sky
261 7mm flat sequins

SPECIAL STITCHES

SQsc (sequined single crochet): Insert hook as directed, yoh, pull loop through, slide sequin up yarn close to work, yoh (catching yarn beyond sequin), pull through both loops on hook.

Foundation chain: Start by threading sequins onto color A. Make 34 ch.
Row 1 (WS): 1sc in 2nd ch from hook, 1sc in every ch to end of row, turn. (33 sts)
Row 2: Ch 1, skip first st, [1sc in every st to end of row, 1sc in tch, turn.

Row 3: Ch 1, skip first st, 1sc in each of next 2sc, *1SQsc in next sc, 1sc in next sc; rep from * to end, 1sc in tch, turn.
Row 4: As Row 2.
Row 5: Ch 1, 1sc in each of next 3sc, *1SQsc in next sc, 1sc in next sc; rep from * to last 2 sts, 1sc in each of last 2 sts, turn.

Rep Rows 2–5 a further 8 times then Row 2 once more.

Fasten off and weave in ends.

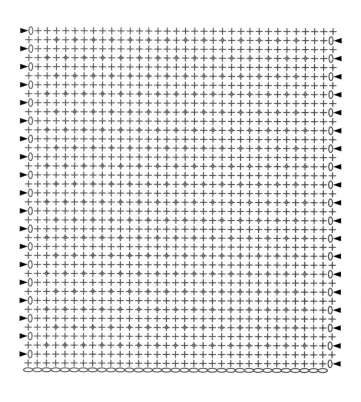

Loop Stitch Columns

See page 38

 ## Chain Loops Flower

See page 38

A=Sky

A=Persimmon
B=Ecru

SPECIAL STITCHES

Loop st: Use the left hand to control the size of the loop, insert hook into designated stitch, pick up both threads of the loop and pull through, yarn over hook, draw through all loops on the hook.

Foundation chain: Using color A, make 34 ch.
Row 1 (RS): 1dc in 4th ch from hook, 1dc in every ch to end of row, turn. (31 sts and ch-3)

Row 2: Ch 1, 1sc in each of first 2dc, *1 Loop st in each of next 4dc**, 1sc in each of next 4dc; rep from * ending last repeat at **, 1sc in last dc, 1sc in 3rd ch of ch-3, turn.
Row 3: Ch3 (counts as 1dc), skip first dc, 1dc in every st to end of the row, turn.
Rep Rows 2–3 a further 10 times.
Fasten off and weave in ends.

Foundation ring: Using color A, make a Magic Ring.
Round 1: Ch 1, 12sc into ring, change to color B when joining with sl st in first sc. (12 sc)
Round 2: Ch 13, *sl st in next sc, ch 13; rep from * a further 10 times, join with sl st in first ch. Break color B.
Round 3: Join color A in any 13ch-sp, ch 1, 1sc in same sp, ch 4, *1sc in next 13ch-sp, ch 4; rep from * to end of round, change to color B when joining with sl st in first sc.
Round 4: Sl st in next 4ch-sp, ch3, [1dc, ch4, dc2tog] in same sp, *[ch4, 1sc in next 4ch-sp] twice, ch 4**, [dc2tog, ch4, dc2tog] in next 4ch-sp; rep from * twice more, then from * to ** once again, change to color A when joining with sl st in 3rd ch of ch-3.
Round 5: Ch 1, 1sc in same place,

*[2sc, ch2, 2sc] in next 4ch-sp, 1sc in next st, [3sc in next 4ch-sp, 1sc in next sc] twice, 3sc in next 4ch-sp, 1sc in next cluster; rep from * to end of round, omitting last sc and change to color B when joining with sl st in first sc.
Round 6: Ch 3 (counts as 1dc), 1dc in every st from previous round and 3dc in every 2ch-corner-sp, change to color A when joining with sl st in 3rd ch of ch3.
Round 7: Ch 3 (counts as 1dc), 1dc in every st from previous round and 3dc in center dc of each 3dc corner-sp, change to color B when joining with sl st in 3rd ch of ch3.
Round 8: Ch 3 (counts as 1dc), 1dc in every st from previous round and 3dc in center dc of each 3dc corner-sp, join with sl st in 3rd ch of ch3.
Fasten off and weave in ends.

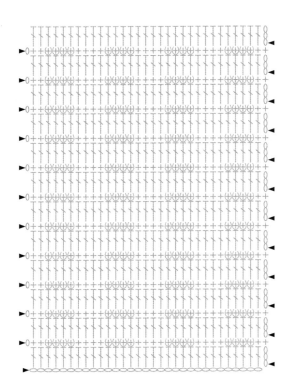

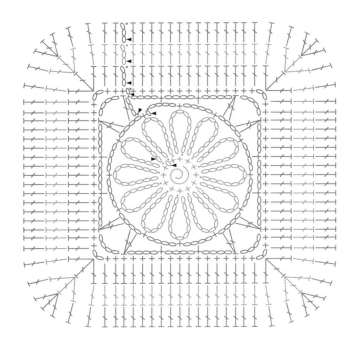

⭐ Horizontal Woven Block

See page 37

A=Rose
B=Blackcurrant
C=Oyster

Foundation chain: Using color A, ch 33.

Row 1: 1dc in 4th ch from hook, 1dc in next ch, *ch 1, skip next ch, 1dc in each of next 3dc; rep from * to end of row, turn.

Row 2: Ch 3, skip first dc, 1dc in each of next 2dc, *ch 1, skip 1ch, 1dc in each of next 3dc; rep from * to end of row, 1dc in 3rd of tch, turn.

Rep Row 2 a further 12 times. Do not fasten off.

Border

Round 1: Ch 1, 1sc in same place, 1sc in same row-end post, *2sc in each of next 12 row-end posts, [2sc, 1hdc, 2sc] in last row-end post**, 1sc in each foundation ch to corner, [2sc, 1hdc, 2sc] in next row-end post; rep from * to **, 1sc in each dc to end of round, [1hdc, 2sc] in first row-end post, join with sl st in first sc.

Round 2: Ch 2, 1hdc in each sc and 1dc in each dc from previous round, join with sl st in 2nd ch of ch-2. Fasten off.

Weaving

* Cut three strands of color B approx. 9in (23cm) long and starting at the bottom right hand corner, weave over and under the 3dc clusters by working in and out of the ch-sps**.

Cut three strands of color C approx. 9in (23cm) long and weave under and over the 3dc clusters by working in and out of the ch-sps.

Rep from * twice more and from * to ** once again.

Gently stretch the block in both directions to ensure that the weaving is not too tight before weaving in the ends.

⭐⭐ Harlequin

See page 38

A=Shell
B=Lavender
C=Bleached
D=Blackcurrant

Foundation chain: Using color A, ch 6 and join with sl st in first ch to form a ring.

Round 1: Ch 1, 12sc into the ring, join with a sl st in first sc.

Round 2: [Sl st in next sc, ch 4, 1dc in each of next 2sc, ch 4] 4 times, join with sl st in first sl st. Fasten off. (4 blocks made)

Round 3: Join color B to 1st ch of last ch-4 of previous round *ch 4, 1dc in each of next 2 ch, sl st in top of next ch-4 of previous round, ch 4, 1dc in each of next 2dc, ch 4, sl st in top of next ch-4 of previous round; rep from * a further 3 times. Fasten off.

Round 4: Join color C to 1st ch of last ch-4 of previous round, *ch 4, 1dc in each of next 2 ch, sl st to top of next ch-4 of previous round, ch 4, 1dc in each of next 2dc, sl st to top of next ch-4 of previous round, ch4; rep from * to end of round. Fasten off.

Round 5: Join color A to to 1st ch of last ch-4 of previous round *ch 4, 1dc in each of next 2 ch, sl st to top of next ch-4 of previous round, [ch 4, 1dc in each of next 2dc, sl st to top of next ch-4 of previous round, ch4] twice, ch 4, 1dc in each of next 2dc, ch 4, sl st to top of next ch-4 of previous round; rep from * to end of round. Fasten off.

Round 6: Join color A to to 1st ch of last ch-4 of previous round, *ch 4, 1dc in each of next 2 ch, sl st to top of next ch-4 of previous round, [ch 4, 1dc in each of next 2dc, sl st to top of next ch-4 of previous round, ch4] 3 times, ch 4, 1dc in each of next 2dc, ch 4, sl st to top of next ch-4 of previous round; rep from * to end of round. Fasten off.

Round 7: Join color A to to 1st ch of last ch-4 of previous round, *ch 4, 1dc in each of next 2 ch, sl st to top of next ch-4 of previous round, [ch 4, 1dc in each of next 2dc, sl st to top of next ch-4 of previous round, ch4] 4 times, ch 4, 1dc in each of next 2dc, ch 4, sl st to top of next ch-4 of previous round; rep from * to end of round. Fasten off.

Round 8: Join color D to to 1st ch of last ch-4 of previous round, ch1, *1sc in first ch, 1hdc in next ch, 1dc in next ch, 1tr in next ch, [1sc in top of next ch-4, 1hdc in next tr, (1dc, 1tr in next tr)] 5 times, [1sc, 1hdc] in top of next ch-4, [1dc, ch 2, 1dc] in next dc, [1hdc, 1sc] in next tr; rep from * a further 3 times, join with sl st in first sc.

Fasten off and weave in ends.

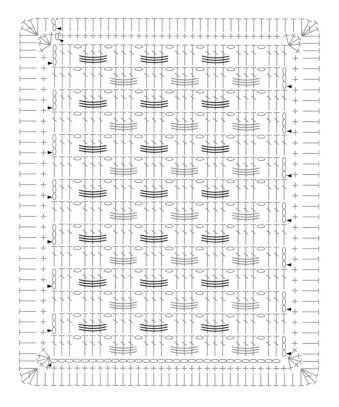

Two-sided Granny

See page 37

A=Shell
B=Lavender

Foundation ring: Using color A, make a Magic Ring.

Round 1: Using color A, ch 3 (counts as 1dc throughout), 2dc into the ring, ch 2, 3dc into the ring, ch 1, using color B, ch 1, 3dc into the ring, ch 2, 3dc into the ring, ch 1, join with a hdc in 3rd ch of ch-3, turn.

Round 2: Using B, ch 3, 2dc in same sp, ch 1, [3dc, ch 2, 3dc] in next sp, ch 1, 3dc in next ch-3 sp, ch 1; using A, ch 1, 3dc in same sp, ch 1, [3dc, ch 2, 3dc] in next sp, ch 1, 3dc in next sp, ch 1, join with a hdc in 3rd ch of ch-3, turn.

Round 3: Using A, ch 3, 2dc in same sp, ch 1, 3dc in next ch-1 sp, ch 1, (3dc, ch 3, 3dc) in next sp, ch 1, 3dc in next ch-1 sp, ch 1, 3dc in next ch sp, ch 2; using B, ch 1, 3dc in same sp, ch 1, 3dc in next ch-1 sp, ch 1, [3dc, ch 2, 3dc] in next sp, ch 1, 3dc in next sp, ch 1, join with a hdc in 3rd ch of ch-3, turn.

Round 4: Using B, ch 3, 2dc in same sp, [ch 1, 3dc in next sp] twice, ch 1, [3dc, ch 3, 3dc] in next sp, [ch 1, 3dc in next sp] 3 times, ch 2; using A, ch 1, 3dc in same sp, [ch 1, 3dc in next sp] twice, ch 1, [3dc, ch 3, 3dc] in next sp, [ch 1, 3dc in next sp] 3 times, ch 1, join with a hdc in 3rd ch of ch-3, turn.

Round 5: Using A, ch 3 (counts as 1dc), 2dc in same sp, ch 1, 3dc in next ch-1 sp, ch 1, [3dc, ch 3, 3dc] in next sp, ch 1, 3dc in next ch-1 sp, ch 1, 3dc in next ch sp, ch 2; using B, ch 1, 3dc in same sp, ch 1, 3dc in next ch-1 sp, ch 1, [3dc, ch 2, 3dc] in next sp, ch 1, 3dc in next sp, ch 1, join with a hdc in 3rd ch of ch-3, turn.

Round 6: Using B, ch 3, 2dc in same sp, [ch 1, 3dc in next sp] 3 times, ch 1, [3dc, ch 3, 3dc] in next sp, [ch 1, 3dc in next sp] 4 times, ch 2; using A, ch 1, 3dc in same sp, [ch 1, 3dc in next sp] 3 times, ch 1, [3dc, ch 3, 3dc] in next sp, [ch 1, 3dc in next sp] 4 times, ch 1, join with a hdc in 3rd ch of ch-3, turn.

Round 7: Using A, ch 3, 2dc in same sp, [ch 1, 3dc in next sp] 4 times, ch 1, [3dc, ch 3, 3dc] in next sp, [ch 1, 3dc in next sp] 5 times, ch 2; using B ch 1, 3dc in same sp, [ch 1, 3dc in next sp] 4 times, ch 1, [3dc, ch 3, 3dc] in next sp, [ch 1, 3dc in next sp] 5 times, ch 1, join with a hdc in 3rd ch of ch-3, turn.

Round 8: Using B, ch 3, 2dc in same sp, [ch 1, 3dc in next sp] 5 times, ch 1, [3dc, ch 3, 3dc] in next sp, [ch 1, 3dc in next sp] 6 times, ch 2; using A ch 1, 3dc in same sp, [ch 1, 3dc in next sp] 5 times, ch 1, [3dc, ch 3, 3dc] in next sp, [ch 1, 3dc in next sp] 6 times, ch 1, join with a hdc in 3rd ch of ch-3, turn.

Round 9: Using A, ch 3, 2dc in same sp, [ch 1, 3dc in next sp] 6 times, ch 1, [3dc, ch 3, 3dc] in next sp, [ch 1, 3dc in next sp] 7 times, ch 2; using B ch 1, 3dc in same sp, [ch 1, 3dc in next sp] 6 times, ch 1, [3dc, ch 3, 3dc] in next sp, [ch 1, 3dc in next sp] 7 times, ch 1, join with a hdc in 3rd ch of ch-3.

Fasten off and weave in ends.

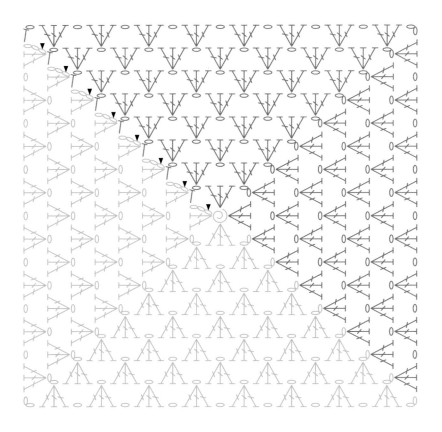

Shell Border

See page 36

A=Ecru
B=Greengage

SPECIAL STITCHES

V-st: [1dc, ch 1, 1dc] in next st.
Open shell: [ch 1, (2dc, ch1, 2dc)].

Center block

Foundation ring: Using color A, ch 4 and join with sl st in first ch to form a ring.

Round 1: Ch 3 (counts as 1dc), 11dc in the ring, join with sl st in 3rd ch of ch-3.

Round 2: Ch 3 (counts as 1dc), *[2dc, 1tr] in next dc, [1tr, 2dc] in next dc**, 1dc in next dc; rep from * twice more and from * to ** once again, join with sl st in 3rd ch of ch-3.

Round 3: Ch 3 (counts as 1dc), 1dc in each of next 2dc, *[2dc, 1tr] in next tr, [1tr, 2dc] in next tr**, 1dc in each of next 5dc; rep from * twice more and from * to ** once again, 1dc in each of next 2dc, join with sl st in 3rd ch of ch-3.

Round 4: Ch 3 (counts as 1dc), 1dc in each of next 4dc, *[2dc, 1tr] in next tr, [1tr, 2dc] in next tr**, 1dc in each of next 9dc; rep from * twice more and from * to ** once again, 1dc in each of next 4dc, join with sl st in 3rd ch of ch-3. Fasten off.

Border

Join color B 4 sts to the left of the corner st.

Round 1: Ch 4 (counts as 1dc and ch 1), 1dc in same st, *ch 2, skip 3 sts, 1dc in next st, ch 2, skip 3 sts, V-st in next st, ch 2, skip 3 sts, [1dc, (ch1, 1dc) 4 times] in middle tr, ch 2, skip 3 sts**, V-st in next st; rep from * twice more and from * to ** once again, join with sl st in 3rd ch of ch-4.

Round 2: Sl st in next 1ch-sp, ch 4 (counts as 1dc and ch 1), 1dc in same sp, ch 2, *[1dc in next dc, ch 2, V-st in ch-sp of next V-st, ch 2, 1dc in next dc, ch 2, skip next dc, [V-st in next ch-sp, ch1] twice, ch 1, skip 1dc**, [1dc in next dc, ch 2, V-st in ch-sp of next V-st, ch 2] twice; rep from * twice more and from * to ** once again, 1dc in next dc, ch 2, join with sl st in 3rd ch of ch-4.

Round 3: Sl st in next 1ch-sp, ch 3 (counts as 1dc), 1dc, ch 1, 2dc in same sp, ch 1, skip 1dc, 1dc in next dc, *[open shell in ch-sp of V-st, ch 1, skip 1dc, 1dc in next dc] twice, ch 1, skip 1ch-sp, open shell in ch-sp of V-st, ch 3, skip 1ch-sp, open shell in ch-sp of V-st, ch 1, skip 1dc, 1dc in next dc**, ch 1, open shell in ch-sp of next V-st; rep from * twice more and from * to ** once again, join with sl st in 3rd ch of ch-3.

Round 4: Ch 1, 1sc in last dc, skip joining st and 2dc, [5dc in ch-sp of next open shell, 1sc in next dc] twice, 5dc in ch-sp of next open shell, *1sc in corner ch-1 sp , [5dc in ch-sp of next open shell, 1sc in next dc] three times, 5dc in ch-sp of next open shell; rep from * twice more, 5dc in ch-sp of next open shell, join with sl st in first sc.

Fasten off and weave in ends.

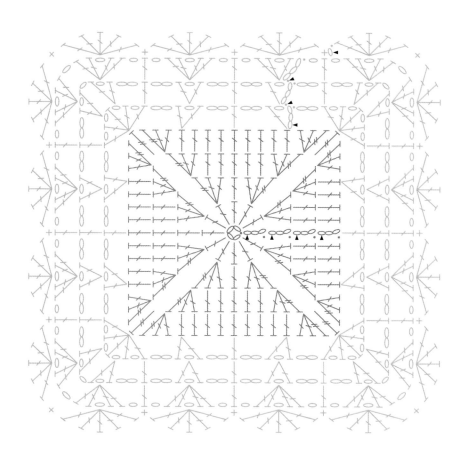

Shell and Bar Border

See page 36

A=Ecru
B=Greengage

Center block
Foundation ring: Using color A, ch 4 and join with sl st in first ch to form a ring.

Round 1: Ch 3 (counts as 1dc throughout), 11dc into the ring, join with sl st in 3rd ch of ch-3.

Round 2: Ch 3, *[2dc, 1tr] in next dc, [1tr, 2dc] in next dc**, 1dc in next dc; rep from * twice more and from * to ** once again, join with sl st in 3rd ch of ch-3.

Round 3: Ch 3, 1dc in each of next 2dc, *[2dc, 1tr] in next tr, [1tr, 2dc] in next tr **, 1dc in each of next 5dc; rep from * twice more and from * to ** once again, 1dc in each of next 2dc, join with sl st in 3rd ch of ch-3.

Round 4: Ch 3, 1dc in each of next 4dc, *[2dc, 1tr] in next tr, [1tr, 2dc] in next tr **, 1dc in each of next 9dc; rep from * twice more and from * to ** once again, 1dc in each of next 4dc, join with sl st in 3rd ch of ch-3.

Round 5: Ch 3, 1dc in each of next 6dc, *[2dc, 1tr] in next tr, 1tr in sp before next st, [1tr, 2dc] in next tr**, 1dc in each of next 13dc; rep from * twice more and from * to ** once

again, 1dc in each of next 6dc, join with sl st in 3rd ch of ch-3. Fasten off.

Border
Join color B, 2 sts to the left of the corner st.

Round 1: Ch 3 (counts as 1dc), *1dc in each of next 2 sts, ch 5, skip 5 sts, 1dc in next st, ch 5, skip 5 sts, 1dc in each of next 3 sts, ch 3, skip 1 st, 1dc in corner st, ch 3, skip 1dc, 1dc in next st; rep from * to end of round, omitting last dc, join with sl st in 3rd ch of ch-3.

Round 2: Ch 3 (counts as 1dc), *1dc in each of next 2dc, ch 3, [1dc, ch 2, 1dc] in next dc, ch 3, 1dc in each of next 3dc, ch 3, [1dc, ch 3, 1dc] in next dc, ch 3, 1dc in next dc; rep from * to end of round, omitting last dc, join with sl st in 3rd ch of ch-3.

Round 3: Ch 3 (counts as 1dc), *1dc in each of next 2dc, ch 2, skip 1dc, 7dc in next ch-2 sp, ch 2, skip 1dc, 1dc in each of next 3dc, ch 2, 9dc in 3-ch corner sp, ch 2, skip 1dc, 1dc in next dc; rep from * to end of round, omitting last dc, join with sl st in 3rd ch of ch-3.

Fasten off and weave in ends.

Picot Border

See page 36

A=Ecru
B=Greengage

SPECIAL STITCHES
Picot-3: Ch 3, sl st in 3rd ch from hook.

Picot-5: Ch 5, sl st in 5th ch from hook.

Center block
Foundation ring: Using color A, ch 4 and join with sl st in first ch to form a ring.

Round 1: Ch 3 (counts as 1dc), 11dc in the ring, join with sl st in 3rd ch of ch-3.

Round 2: Ch 3 (counts as 1dc), *[2dc, 1tr] in next dc, [1tr, 2dc] in next dc**, 1dc in next dc; rep from * twice more and from * to ** once again, join with sl st in 3rd ch of ch-3.

Round 3: Ch 3 (counts as 1dc), 1dc in each of next 2dc, *[2dc, 1tr] in next tr, [1tr, 2dc] in next tr**, 1dc in each of next 5dc; rep from * twice more and from * to ** once again, 1dc in each of next 2dc, join with sl st in 3rd ch of ch-3.

Round 4: Ch 3 (counts as 1dc), 1dc in each of next 4dc, *[2dc, 1tr] in next tr, [1tr, 2dc] in next tr**, 1dc in each of next 9dc; rep from * twice more and from * to ** once again, 1dc in each of next 4dc, join with sl st in 3rd ch of ch-3.

Round 5: Ch 3 (counts as 1dc), 1dc in each of next 6dc, *[2dc, 1tr] in next tr, 1tr in space before next st, [1tr, 2dc] in next tr**, 1dc in each of next 13dc; rep from * twice more and from * to ** once again, 1dc in each of next 6dc, join with sl st in 3rd ch of ch-3. Fasten off.

Border
Join color B, 4 sts to the left of the corner st.

Round 1: Ch 1, 1sc in same place, ch 5, skip 3 sts, [1sc in next st, ch 5, skip 3 sts] 3 times, *[1sc, ch 3, 1sc] in corner st, ch 5**, skip 3 sts, [1sc in next st, ch 5, skip 3 sts] 4 times; rep from * twice more and from * to ** once again, changing to color A when joining with sl st to first sc. Break color B.

Round 2: Ch 1, 1sc in same place, ch 5, *1sc in next sc, ch 5; rep from * to end of round, join with sl st in first sc.

Round 3: Sl st in 5ch-sp, ch 3 (counts as 1dc), [3dc, Picot-3, Picot-5, Picot-3, 4dc] in same sp, *[2sc, ch 3, 2sc] in next ch-sp**, [4dc, Picot-3, Picot-5, Picot-3, 4dc] in next ch-sp; rep from * twice more and from * to ** once again, join with sl st in 3rd ch of ch-3.

Fasten off and weave in ends.

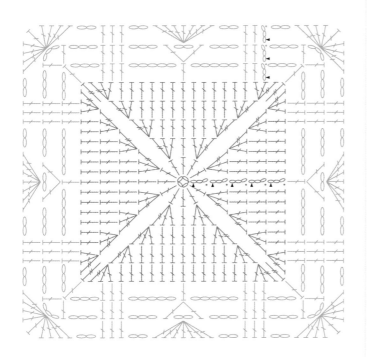

⭐⭐ *Fan Border*

See page 36

A=Ecru
B=Greengage
C=Winsor

SPECIAL STITCHES

V-st: (1dc, ch 1, 1dc) in next st.
Shell: 9dc in next st.

Center block

Foundation ring: Using color A, ch 4 and join with sl st in first ch to form a ring.

Round 1: Ch 3 (counts as 1dc throughout), 11dc into the ring, join with sl st in 3rd ch of ch-3.

Round 2: Ch 3, *[2dc, 1tr] in next dc, [1tr, 2dc] in next dc**, 1dc in next dc; rep from * twice more and from * to ** once again, join with sl st in 3rd ch of ch-3.

Round 3: Ch 3, 1dc in each of next 2dc, *[2dc, 1tr] in next dc, [1tr, 2dc] in next dc**, 1dc in each of next 5dc; rep from * twice more and from * to ** once again, 1dc in each of next 2dc, join with sl st in 3rd ch of ch-3.

Round 4: Ch 3, 1dc in each of next 4dc, *[2dc, 1tr] in next dc, 1tr in sp before next st, [1tr, 2dc] in next dc**, 1dc in each of next 9dc; rep from * twice more and from * to ** once again, 1dc in each of next 4dc,

join with sl st in 3rd ch of ch-3. Fasten off.

Border

Join color B in second st to left of corner st.

Round 1: Ch 1, 1sc in same place, *[skip 3 sts, shell in next st, skip 3 sts, 1sc in next st] twice, skip 1 st, 7dc in corner tr, skip 1st, 1sc in next st; rep from * to end of round, omitting last sc, change to color C when joining with sl st in first sc. Break color B.

Round 2: Ch 4 (counts as 1dc and ch-1), 1dc in same st, *[ch 2, skip 4dc, 1sc in next dc (fifth dc of shell), skip 4dc, ch 2, V-st in next sc] twice, ch 2, skip 3dc, [1sc, ch 1, 1sc] in corner dc, ch 2, V-st in next sc; rep from * to end of round, omitting last V-st, join with sl st in 3rd ch of ch-4.

Round 3: Sl st into next ch-1 sp, ch 3 (counts as 1dc), 8dc in same sp, 1sc in next sc, *[shell in ch-sp of next V-st, 1sc in next sc twice, 7dc in corner ch-sp, 1sc in next sc; rep from * to end of round, join with sl st in 3rd ch of ch-3.

Fasten off and weave in ends.

⭐⭐ *Arched Border*

See page 36

A=Ecru
B=Dawn Gray
C=Winsor

SPECIAL STITCHES

Partial dc: Yarn over hook, insert hook into stitch or space indicated and pull a loop through, yarn over hook and pull through two loops on the hook.

Center block

Foundation ring: Using color A, ch 4 and join with sl st in first ch to form a ring.

Round 1: Ch 3 (counts as 1dc throughout), 11dc into the ring, join with sl st in 3rd ch of ch-3.

Round 2: Ch 3, *[2dc, 1tr] in next dc, [1tr, 2dc] in next dc**, 1dc in next dc; rep from * twice more and from * to ** once again, join with sl st in 3rd ch of ch-3.

Round 3: Ch 3, 1dc in each of next 2dc, *[2dc, 1tr] in next tr, [1tr, 2dc] in next tr**, 1dc in each of next 5dc; rep from * twice more and from * to ** once again, 1dc in each of next 2dc, join with sl st in 3rd ch of ch-3.

Round 4: Ch 3, 1dc in each of next 4dc, *[2dc, 1tr] in next tr, [1tr, 2dc] in next tr**, 1dc in each of next 9dc; rep from * twice more and from * to ** once again, 1dc in each of next 4dc, join with sl st in 3rd ch of ch-3.

Border

Join color B in eighth st to left of corner st.

Round 1: Ch 5 (counts as 1tr and ch-1), 1dc in same place, ch 7, skip 7 sts, *[1dc, ch 1, 1dc, ch 7, 1dc, ch 1, 1dc] in corner tr, ch 7, skip 7 sts**,

[1dc, ch1, 1tr, ch1, 1dc] in next st ch 7, skip 7 sts; rep from * twice more and then from * to ** once again, 1dc in st at base of ch-5, join with sl st in 4th ch of ch-5.

Round 2: Ch 1, 1sc in same place, [4dc, ch 1, 4dc] in next 7ch-sp, *[1sc in 1ch-sp, [4dc, ch 1, 4dc] in corner sp, 1sc in next ch-sp, [4dc, ch 1, 4dc] in next 7ch-sp**, 1sc in next tr, [4dc, ch 1, 4dc] in next 7ch-sp; rep from * twice more and from * to ** once again, join with sl st in first sc. Break color B.

Round 3: Join color C to last ch-sp, ch 1, 1sc in same sp, ch 7, 1sc in next ch-sp, ch 7, *[1sc, ch 1, 1sc] in corner ch-1 sp, ch 7**, [1sc in next ch-sp, ch7] twice; rep from * twice more and from * to ** once again, join with sl st in first sc.

Round 4: Sl st in next ch-sp, ch 2 (counts as Partial dc), [4dc, ch 3, 4dc] in same sp, Partial dc in same sp, Partial dc in next sp, yoh and pull through all 3 loops on hook, [(4dc, ch 3, 4dc) in same ch- sp], *1sc in corner-sp, [5dc, ch 3, 4dc] in next sp**, [Partial dc in same sp, Partial dc in next sp, yoh and pull through all 3 loops on hook, [4dc, ch 3, 4dc] in same ch- sp] twice; rep from * twice more then from * to ** once again, Partial dc in last ch-sp, insert hook in top of ch-2 and pull up a loop, yoh and pull through all 3 loops.

Fasten off and weave in ends.

★★ *Cluster Border*

See page 39

A=Ecru
B=Dawn Gray
C=Winsor

SPECIAL STITCHES

Tr2tog (work two treble sts tog):
[(Yoh) twice draw up a loop in next st, (yoh, pull through 2 loops on hook) twice] twice, yoh and draw through all 3 loops on hook.

Tr3tog (work three treble sts tog):
[(Yoh) twice draw up a loop in next st, (yoh, pull through 2 loops on hook) 3 times] twice, yoh and draw through all 4 loops on hook.

Center block

Foundation ring: Using color A, ch 4 and join with sl st in first ch to form a ring.

Round 1: Ch 3 (counts as 1dc), 11dc in the ring, join with sl st in 3rd ch of ch-3.

Round 2: Ch 3 (counts as 1dc), *[2dc, 1tr] in next dc, [1tr, 2dc] in next dc**, 1dc in next dc; rep from * twice more and from * to ** once again, join with sl st in 3rd ch of ch-3.

Round 3: Ch 3 (counts as 1dc), 1dc in each of next 2dc, *[2dc, 1tr] in next tr, [1tr, 2dc] in next tr**, 1dc in each of next 5dc; rep from * twice more and from * to ** once again, 1dc in each of next 2dc, join with sl st in 3rd ch of ch-3.

Round 4: Ch 3 (counts as 1dc), 1dc in each of next 4dc, *[2dc, 1tr] in next tr, [1tr, 2dc] in next tr**, 1dc in each of next 9dc; rep from * twice more and from * to ** once again, 1dc in each of next 4dc, join with sl st in 3rd ch of ch-3.

Round 5: Ch 3 (counts as 1dc), 1dc in each of next 6dc, *[2dc, 1tr] in next tr, 1tr in space before next st, [1tr, 2dc] in next tr**, 1dc in each of next 13dc; rep from * twice more and from * to ** once again, 1dc in each of next 6dc, join with sl st in 3rd ch of ch-3. Fasten off.

Border

Join color B, 1 st to the left of the corner st.

Round 1: Ch 1, 1sc in same place, *[ch 4, skip 2 sts, tr3tog in next st, ch 4, skip 2 sts, 1sc in next st] 3 times, ch 4, tr3tog in corner st, ch 4, 1sc in next st; rep from * to end of round, omitting last sc, join with sl st in first sc.

Round 2: Ch 1, 1sc in same place, *ch 4, 1sc in top of cluster, ch 4, 1sc in next sc; rep from * to end of round, omitting last sc, change to color C when joining with sl st to first sc. Break color B.

Round 3: Ch 4, tr2tog in same place, *ch 4, 1sc in next sc, ch 4, tr3tog in next sc; rep from * to end of round, omitting last tr3tog, join with sl st in 4th ch of ch-4.

Round 4: Ch 1, 1sc in same place, *ch 4, 1sc in next sc, ch 4, 1sc in top of cluster; rep from * to end of round, omitting last sc, join with sl st in first sc.
Fasten off and weave in ends.

Cross-stitched Border

See page 39

A=Ecru
B=Winsor
C=Dawn Gray
D=Greengage

SPECIAL STITCHES

Dc5tog (work five double sts tog):
[Yoh draw up a loop in next st, (yoh, pull through 2 loops on hook) 5 times] twice, yoh and draw through all 6 loops on hook.

Crossed dc: skip 1 st, 1dc in next st; working behind previous st, 1dc in the skipped st.

Center block

Foundation ring: Using color A, ch 4 and join with sl st in first ch to form a ring.

Round 1: Ch 3 (counts as 1dc), 11dc in the ring, join with sl st in 3rd ch of ch-3.

Round 2: Ch 3 (counts as 1dc), *[2dc, 1tr] in next dc, [1tr, 2dc] in next dc**, 1dc in next dc; rep from * twice more and from * to ** once again, join with sl st in 3rd ch of ch-3.

Round 3: Ch 3 (counts as 1dc), 1dc in each of next 2dc, *[2dc, 1tr] in next tr, [1tr, 2dc] in next tr**, 1dc in each of next 5dc; rep from * twice more and from * to ** once again, 1dc in each of next 2dc, join with sl st in 3rd ch of ch-3.

Round 4: Ch 3 (counts as 1dc), 1dc in each of next 4dc, *[2dc, 1tr] in next tr, [1tr, 2dc] in next tr**, 1dc in each of next 9dc; rep from * twice more and from * to ** once again, 1dc in each of next 4dc, join with sl st in 3rd ch of ch-3.

Round 5: Ch 3 (counts as 1dc), 1dc in each of next 6dc, *[2dc, 1tr] in next tr, 1tr in space before next st, [1tr, 2dc] in next tr**, 1dc in each of next 13dc; rep from * twice more and from * to ** once

again, 1dc in each of next 6dc, join with sl st in 3rd ch of ch-3. Fasten off.

Border

Join color B in third st to the left of corner st.

Round 1: Ch 3 (counts as 1dc), 1dc in st to the right of the last st, *[work Crossed dc in next 2 sts] to corner (working first dc of final Crossed dc pair in corner tr), ch 3, work Crossed dc pair in next st and corner st; rep from * to end of round, join with sl st in first Crossed dc. Break color B.

Round 2: Join color C to sp between a Crossed dc pair, *ch 1, skip 1 Crossed dc pair, [1sc in space between Crossed dc pairs, ch 1, skip 1 Crossed dc pair] to corner sp**, [1sc, ch 1, 1sc, ch 1, 1sc] in corner sp; rep from * twice more and from * to **

once more, change to color D when joining with sl st in first sc. Break color C.

Round 3: Ch 3 (counts as 1dc), *dc5tog in next ch-sp, [1dc in next sc, dc5tog in next ch-sp]** to corner sc, 3dc in corner sc, dc5tog in next ch-sp; rep from * a further 3 times and from * to ** once again, change to color B when joining with sl st in 3rd ch of ch-3. Break color D.

Round 4: Ch 1, 1sc in same place, *[ch 1, skip 1 st, 1sc in next dc] to corner st, ch 1, [1sc, ch 1] twice in corner dc, 1sc in next dc; rep from * to end of round, ending last rep [ch 1, skip 1 st, 1sc in next dc] twice, skip 1 st, join with 1sc to last sc.

Fasten off and weave in ends.

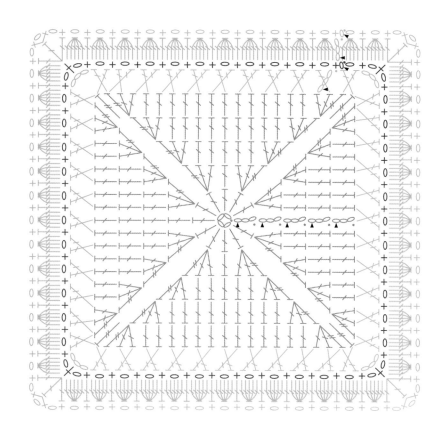

The projects

The blocks in this book can be used to decorate a whole host of different items. These inspirational projects demonstrate just a few ideas including homewares, toys, and stationery.

YOU WILL NEED

- 2 × 4oz (100g) balls of linen/ cotton mix worsted weight yarn in red
- 2 × 4oz (100g) balls of linen/ cotton mix worsted weight yarn in blue
- 1 × 4oz (100g) ball of linen/ cotton mix worsted weight yarn in white
- 1 × 4oz (100g) ball of linen/ cotton mix worsted weight yarn in gray
- 24in (60cm) square cushion pad
- Backing fabric measuring 25in (62cm) square (¾in/ 2cm seam allowance)
- E4 (3.5mm) crochet hook

Floor Cushion

A boldly patterned cushion is a great way to brighten an interior. I have combined a simple geometric pattern with hard-wearing yarn to make this useful accessory.

WORKING THE CROCHET
Gauge: After blocking, one square will measure 7 × 7in (18 × 18cm)
Finished size: 24 × 24in (60 × 60cm)
Work: 4 × Spiky Square (see page 107), where A=Blue, B=White, C=Gray, and D=Red (BSS)
Work: 4 × Spiky Square, where A=Red, B=White, C=Gray, and D=Blue (RSS)

BASIC SINGLE CROCHET SQUARE
Ch 29.
Row 1: 1sc in 2nd ch from hook, 1sc in every ch to end of row, turn.
Row 2: Ch 1, 1sc in every sc to end of row, turn.
Rep Row 2 until work is square. Fasten off.
Join contrast yarn to any ch along Foundation edge.
Round 1: Ch 3 (counts as 1dc), 1dc in every ch and row end, working 3dc in each corner to end of round, join with a sl st to 3rd of ch-3. Fasten off.
Work 4 x single crochet squares in blue with gray border. (BDC)
Work 4 x single crochet squares in red with gray border. (RDC)

FINISHING
Weave in any loose ends and block according to ball band instructions. Arrange blocks in the following sequence:
Row 1: RDC, RSS, BDC, BSS
Row 2: RSS, BDC, BSS, RDC
Row 3: BDC, BSS, RDC, RSS
Row 4: BSS, RDC, RSS, BDC
Join all seams using slip stitch.
Stitch backing fabric to the crocheted panel along three sides.
Insert cushion pad and close with a slipstitch.

YOU WILL NEED

- 1 × 2oz (50g) ball fingering-weight cotton yarn in color of choice
- C/2 (2.5mm) crochet hook
- Clean glass jar approx 3¼in (8cm) in diameter and 10in (26cm) tall

Vase Cover

Use your crochet skills to turn throwaway items, such as glass jars, into something useful or decorative. The lacy panels would look attractive with the light from a candle shining through. Alternatively, fill with water and add a bunch of flowers.

WORKING THE CROCHET
Make: 2 × Old Vienna (see page 62)
Gauge: After blocking, one square will measure 5 × 5in (13 × 13cm)
Finished size: According to jar size

FINISHING
Weave in any loose ends and block according to ball band instructions. Slip stitch side seams together. Using C/2 (2.5mm) hook, join yarn to bottom edge and work four rounds of single crochet, decreasing stitches where necessary to ensure a snug fit. Fasten off. Using C/2 (2.5mm) hook, join yarn to top edge and work four rounds of double crochet, decreasing stitches where necessary to ensure a snug fit. Continue to work in rounds of single crochet without further decreases so that the top of the jar is covered—this will be typically 6–8 rounds. Fasten off.

YOU WILL NEED

- 1 × 2oz (50g) ball fingering-weight cotton in mulberry
- 1 × 2oz (50g) ball fingering-weight cotton in white
- 1 × 2oz (50g) ball fingering-weight cotton in pale pink
- 1 × 1oz (25g) ball fingering-weight metallic yarn in hot pink
- D/3 (3mm) crochet hook
- Journal measuring 6 × 9in (15 × 22cm)

Journal Cover

A journal is a very personal item. A cover made from small blocks will make this item unique for your own use or it could add an extra special touch for the journal's recipient.

WORKING THE CROCHET

Gauge: After blocking, one square will measure 3 × 3in (7 × 7cm)
Finished size: 6 × 9in (15 × 22cm)
Work: 15 × Raised Petal (see page 112), where A=Hot Pink, B=Mulberry, C=White, and D=Pale Pink

FINISHING

Weave in any loose ends and block according to ball band instructions. Arrange blocks in the three rows of five squares and join together with slip stitch.
Join color D to any dc.
Round 1: Ch 1, 1sc in every sc and 3sc in every corner sc to end of round, join with sl st to first sc. Fasten off.
Join color B to center sc at top right-hand corner edge.
Row 1: Ch 1, 1sc in every sc to center sc at top left-hand corner. Fasten off.
Join color B to center sc at bottom left-hand corner edge.
Row 2: Ch 1, 1sc in every sc to center sc at bottom right-hand corner. Fasten off.

FLAPS

Join color D to bottom right-hand corner.
Row 1: Ch 1, 1sc in every sc to end of row, turn.
Rep last row, 8 more times. Fasten off.
Join color D to top left-hand corner.
Row 2: Ch 1, 1sc in every sc to end of row, turn.
Rep last row, 8 more times. Fasten off.
Fold flaps over and stitch to top and bottom edges of main fabric; insert journal.

YOU WILL NEED

- 1 × 2oz (50g) ball of soft light worsted weight cotton yarn in 3 colors
- E/4 (3.5mm) crochet hook
- 6in (15cm) square foam cube

Baby Block

A soft toy for a new baby is always welcome. I have used two blocks that feature bobbles so that the toy is interesting, yet still soft to touch. The bobbles will also help a young child develop a sense of pattern and early counting skills.

WORKING THE CROCHET
Make: 1 × Candy Stripe Bobbles (see page 50), where A=Brown, B=Orange, and C=Cream
Make: 1 × Candy Stripe Bobbles, where A=Orange, B=Cream, and C=Brown
Make: 1 × Candy Stripe Bobbles, where A=Cream, B=Brown, and C=Orange
Make: 3 × Alternating Bobbles (see page 50)—one in each color.
Gauge: After blocking, one square will measure 6 × 6in (15cm x 15cm)
Finished size: 6 × 6 × 6in (15 × 15 × 15cm)

FINISHING
Weave in any loose ends and block according to ball band instructions. Arrange blocks so that all Candy Stripe Bobbles form one strip. Use slip stitch to join first Alternating Bobble block to top edge of center block. Join second and third Alternating blocks and then join with a slip stitch to bottom edge of center Candy Stripe Bobble block. Join side seams so that you start to form a cube, but insert foam before joining last four seams around the base.

YOU WILL NEED

- 6 × 2oz (50g) balls worsted-weight yarn cotton in slate blue
- 6 × 2oz (50g) balls worsted-weight cotton yarn in chalky gray
- H/8 (5mm) crochet hook

Lap Blanket

A small blanket is always handy and can be used at home, in the car, or on the beach. The design is made up of alternating crosses. One is made from chain spaces and the other by working clusters on the diagonal.

WORKING THE CROCHET

Gauge: After blocking, one square will measure 9 × 9in (23 × 23cm)

Finished size: Approx. 27 × 45in (69 × 115cm)

Make: 7 × Lacy Cross (see page 86) and 8 × Wisteria (see page 95)

FINISHING

Weave in any loose ends and block according to ball band instructions.

Arrange blocks in the following sequence. Rows 1, 3, and 5: 75, 71, 75. Rows 2 and 4: 71, 75, 71.

Join all seams using slip stitch.

Crochet Refresher Course

For readers who are new to crochet (and those who could use a review), this section provides instruction on the stitches used in this book.

HOLDING THE HOOK AND YARN

1 Holding the hook as if it were a pen is the most widely used method. Center the tips of your right thumb and forefinger over the flat section of the hook.

2 An alternative way to hold the hook is to grasp the flat section of the hook between your right thumb and forefinger as if you were holding a knife.

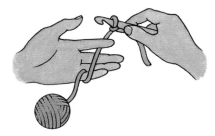

3 To control the supply and keep an even gauge on the yarn, hold the short end of the yarn in place with your right thumb. Take the yarn coming from the ball loosely around the little finger of your left hand and loop it over the left forefinger. Use the middle finger on the same hand to help hold the work. If you are left-handed, hold the hook in the left hand and the yarn in the right.

MAKING A SLIP KNOT

1 Loop the yarn as shown, insert the hook into the loop, catch the yarn with the hook, and pull it through to make a loop over the hook.

2 Gently pull the yarn to tighten the loop around the hook and complete the slip knot.

WORKING A SLIP STITCH (SL ST)

The main uses of slip stitches are for joining rounds but also for making seams and carrying the hook and yarn from one place to another. Insert the hook from front to back into the required stitch. Wrap the yarn over the hook (yarn over) and draw it through both the work and the loop on the hook. One loop remains on the hook and one slip stitch has been worked.

WORKING A FOUNDATION CHAIN (CH)

The foundation chain is the equivalent of casting on in knitting and it's important to make sure that you have made the required number of chains for the pattern you are going to work. Count each V-shaped loop on the front of the chain as one chain stitch, except for the loop on the hook, which is not counted. You may find it easier to turn the chain over and count the stitches on the back of the chain. When working the first row of stitches (usually called the foundation row) into the chain, insert the hook under one thread or two, depending on your preference.

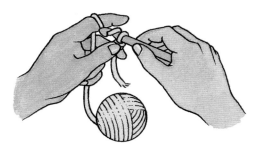

1 Holding the hook with the slip knot in your right hand and the yarn in your left, wrap the yarn over the hook. Draw the yarn through to make a new loop and complete the first chain stitch.

2 Repeat this step, drawing a new loop of yarn through the loop already on the hook until the chain is the required length. Move the thumb and second finger that are grasping the chain upward after every few stitches to keep the gauge even. When working into the chain, insert the hook under one thread (for a looser edge) or two (for a firmer edge), depending on your preference.

WORKING A SINGLE CROCHET (SC)

1 Begin with a foundation chain (see left) and insert the hook from front to back into the second chain from the hook. Wrap the yarn over the hook (yarn over) and draw it through the first loop, leaving two loops on the hook.

2 To complete the stitch, yarn over and draw it through both loops on the hook, leaving one loop on the hook. Continue in this way, working one single crochet into each chain.

3 At the end of the row, turn and work one chain for the turning chain (remember that this chain does not count as a stitch). Insert the hook into the first single crochet at the beginning of the row. Work a single crochet into each stitch of the previous row, being careful to work the final stitch into the last stitch of the row, but not into the turning chain.

WORKING A HALF DOUBLE CROCHET (HDC)

1 Begin with a foundation chain (see page 147), wrap the yarn over the hook (yarn over), and insert the hook into the third chain from the hook.

2 Draw the yarn through the chain, leaving three loops on the hook. Yarn over and draw through all three loops on the hook, leaving one loop on the hook. One half double crochet complete.

3 Continue to work one half double crochet into each chain. At the end of the row, work two chains to turn. Skip the first stitch and work a half double crochet into each stitch on the previous row. At the end of the row, work the last stitch into the top of the turning chain.

WORKING A DOUBLE CROCHET (DC)

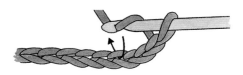

1 Begin with a foundation chain (see page 147), wrap the yarn over the hook, and insert the hook into the fourth chain from the hook.

2 Draw the yarn through the chain, leaving three loops on the hook. Yarn over again and draw the yarn through the first two loops on the hook, leaving two loops on the hook.

3 Yarn over and draw the yarn through the two loops on the hook leaving one loop on the hook. One double crochet complete. Continue along the row, working one double crochet stitch into each chain. At the end of the row, work three chains to turn. Skip the first stitch and work a double crochet into each stitch made on the previous row. At the end of the row, work the last stitch into the top of the turning chain.

WORKING A TREBLE CROCHET (TR)

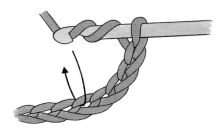

1 Begin with a foundation chain (see page 147), wrap the yarn over the hook twice (yarn over twice), and insert the hook into the fifth chain from the hook.

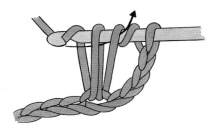

2 Draw the yarn through the chain, leaving four loops on the hook. Yarn over again and draw the yarn through the first two loops on the hook, leaving three loops on the hook.

3 Yarn over again and draw through the first two loops on the hook leaving two loops on the hook.

4 Yarn over again and draw through the two remaining loops, leaving one loop on the hook. Treble crochet is now complete.

5 Continue along the row, working one treble crochet stitch into each chain. At the end of the row, work four chains to turn. Skip the first stitch and work a treble crochet into each stitch made on the previous row. At the end of the row, work the last stitch into the top of the turning chain.

LONG TREBLES

A double treble or treble treble (or an even longer stitch) may be made in a similar way to a treble, above. At step 1, wrap the yarn three, four, or more times around the hook. Work step 2, then repeat step 3 as many times as necessary, until two loops remain on the hook. Work step 5 to complete the long treble. For any long treble, the number of turning chains required at the beginning of a row is two more than the number of times the yarn is wrapped around the hook.

POPCORN (PC)

A popcorn is formed when several complete double crochet stitches (or longer stitches) are worked in the same place, and the top of the first stitch is joined to the last to make a "cup" shape. A four-double crochet popcorn is shown here.

1 Work four doubles (or the number required) in the same place.

2 Slip the last loop off the hook. Reinsert the hook in the top of the first double of the group, as shown, and catch the empty loop. (On a wrong-side row, reinsert the hook from the back, to push the popcorn to the right side of the work.)

PUFF

A puff is normally a group of three or more half double crochet stitches joined at both top and bottom (a three-half-double puff [Hdc3tog] is demonstrated below).

1 *Wrap the yarn over the hook, insert the hook where required, draw through a loop, repeat from * two (or more) times in the same place. You now have seven loops (or more) on the hook. Wrap the yarn over the hook again, and pull through all the loops on the hook.

2 Often, one chain is worked in order to close the puff.

SPIKE STITCHES

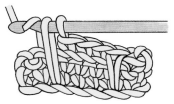

Many pattern variations may be made by inserting the hook one or more rows below the previous row. The insertion may be directly below the next stitch, or one or more stitches to the right or left. Insert the hook as directed, wrap the yarn over the hook, and pull the loop through the work, lengthening the loop to the height of the working row. Complete the stitch as instructed. (Single crochet spike shown here.)

WORKING INTO THE FRONT AND BACK OF THE STITCHES

Unless pattern details instruct you otherwise, it's usual to work crochet stitches under both loops of the stitches made on the previous row.

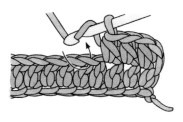

Working into the front When instructions tell you to work into the front of the stitches, insert the hook only under the front loops of stitches on the previous row.

Working into the back Likewise, to work into the back of the stitches, insert the hook only under the back loops of stitches on the previous row.

CHANGING COLOR

Often when you are working a pattern, you will need to change yarn color.

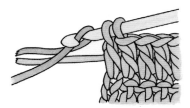

1 To make a neat join between colors, leave the last stitch of the old color incomplete so there are two loops on the hook and wrap the new color around the hook.

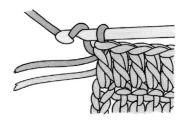

2 Draw the new color through to complete the stitch and continue working in the new color. The illustrations show a color change in a row of double crochet stitches—the method is the same for single crochet and other stitches.

BLOCKING

A trim that is crocheted separately and then sewn into place lacks a base to anchor it, and may tend to curl or spiral. (This is particularly true of edgings that are crocheted lengthwise.) You can correct this by blocking: soak the edging in cold water, press it flat and straight, and set it on a towel until it is completely dry. You will then be able to handle, sew, or glue it more easily.

Working in Rounds

Some features are worked in rounds, which means that they are worked outward from a central ring called a foundation ring.

MAKING A FOUNDATION RING

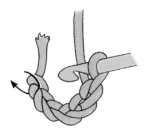

1 Work a short length of foundation chain (see page 147) as specified in the pattern. Join the chains into a ring by working a slip stitch into the first stitch of the foundation chain.

WORKING INTO THE RING

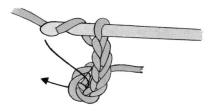

1 Work the number of turning chains specified in the pattern—three chains are shown here (counting as a double crochet stitch). Inserting the hook into the space at the center of the ring each time, work the number of stitches specified in the pattern into the ring. Count the stitches at the end of the round to check you have worked the correct number.

2 Join the first and last stitches of the round together by working a slip stitch into the top of the turning chain.

MAKING A MAGIC RING

A Magic Ring can be used in place of a Foundation Ring for crocheting in the round. The benefit of this method is that after pulling the yarn tail to draw the stitches together there is no hole at the center of your work.

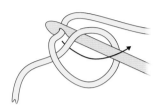

1 Wind the yarn around your finger once, leaving the yarn tail on the left and the working yarn on the right.

2 Insert your hook under the strands of the ring and draw through a loop of the working yarn.

3 Now work the number of starting chains required in the pattern.

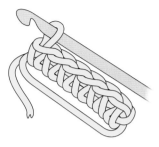

4 Continue in the same manner as for working into a Foundation Ring.

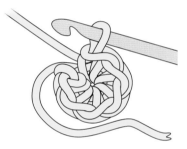

5 When the first round is complete, pull tightly on the yarn tail to close the Magic Ring.

Symbols & Abbreviations

These are the abbreviations and symbols used in the charts and patterns in this book. Charts represent how a stitch pattern is constructed, and may not bear much resemblance to the appearance of the finished stitch. Always read the written instructions as well as the chart.

BASIC STITCHES, ABBREVIATIONS & SYMBOLS

American crochet terms are used throughout this book, abbreviated as shown. For detailed methods of working, see pages 146–153.

Stitch	Abbreviation	Symbol
chain	ch	o
slip stitch	sl st	•
single crochet	sc	+ † ╪
extended single crochet	exsc	╪
half double	hdc	╥ ╥
double	dc	╪ ╪
treble	tr	╪ ╪ ╪ ╳
double treble	dtr	╪ ╪
quintuple treble	quintr	╪

ADDITIONAL SYMBOLS

These are used on some charts to clarify the meaning.

Stitch	Abbreviation	Symbol
direction of working	-	← ↰
stitch worked in front loop only	-	± ╤
stitch worked in back loop only	-	± ╤
beaded single crochet	Bsc	◆
beaded double	Bdc	╪
sequined single crochet	Sqsc	⊕
sequined double	Sqdc	╪
work in back loop (left); work in front loop (right)	-	◡

SPECIAL STITCHES

In addition, various patterns use special stitch constructions and, where these occur in this book, the abbreviation is indicated in the Special Stitches instructions for that pattern. Always refer to Special Stitches instructions where they occur.

Stitch	Abbreviation	Symbol
front raised single crochet	**Frsc**	
back raised single crochet	**Brsc**	
front raised double (left); back raised double (right)	**Frdc, Brdc**	
front raised treble	**Frtr**	
front raised double treble	**Frdtr**	
spiked single crochet	**Ssc**	
group	**Gp**	
extended half double	**EXhdc**	
magic ring	-	

Stitch	Abbreviation	Symbol
spike cluster	**Scl**	
pineapple	**Ps**	
raised pineapple	**Rps**	
puff stitch	-	
popcorn	**PC**	
bullion stitch	**Bs**	
loop stitch	-	
surface crochet	-	
joining bar	-	

ARRANGEMENT OF SYMBOLS

Description	Abbreviation	Explanation
symbols joined at top		A group of symbols may be joined at the top, indicating that these stitches should be worked together as a cluster.
symbols joined at base		Symbols joined at the base should all be worked into the same stitch below.
symbols joined at top and bottom		Sometimes a group of stitches is joined at both top and bottom, making a puff, bobble, or popcorn, as page 150.
symbols on a curve		Sometimes symbols are drawn along a curve, depending on the construction of the stitch pattern.
distorted symbols		Some symbols may be lengthened, curved, or spiked to indicate where the hook is inserted below, as for spike stitches, page 151.

COMMON ABBREVIATIONS

Term	Abbreviation	Term	Abbreviation
stitch(es)	st(s)	yarn over	yo
chain space	ch sp	right side	RS
turning chain	tch	wrong side	WS
together	tog	yarn over hook	yoh

AMERICAN/BRITISH EQUIVALENT TERMS

Some British terms differ from the American system, as shown below: patterns you may encounter that are published using British terminology can be very confusing unless you understand the difference.

American	British	British abbreviation	Symbol
single crochet	double crochet	dc	
extended single crochet	extended double crochet	exdc	
half double	half treble	htr	
double	treble	tr	
treble	double treble	dtr	
double treble	triple treble	ttr	
quintuple treble	sextuple treble	sextr	

Index

Credits

Quarto are grateful to Rowan Yarns who supplied all the yarns used in this book and a special thanks must go to David MacLeod and Vicky Sedgewick.

The author wishes to thank Amanda Golland and Jools Yeo for their enthusiasm and beautiful crochet work.

All photographs and illustrations are the copyright of Quarto Publishing plc. While every effort has been made to credit contributors, Quarto would like to apologize should there have been any omissions or errors—and would be pleased to make the appropriate correction for future editions of the book.

To my husband Paul, who supports me in knit, crochet, love and life.